T0247790

The Rivalry Peril

The Rivalry Peril

How Great-Power Competition Threatens
Peace and Weakens Democracy

VAN JACKSON

AND

MICHAEL BRENES

Yale UNIVERSITY PRESS

New Haven and London

Published with assistance from the Kingsley Trust Association
Publication Fund established by the Scroll and Key Society of
Yale College, and from the Mary Cady Tew Memorial Fund.

Yale University Press books may be purchased in quantity for
educational, business, or promotional use. For information, please
e-mail sales.press@yale.edu (U.S. office) or sales@yaleup.co.uk
(U.K. office).

Set in Minion type by Integrated Publishing Solutions.
Printed in the United States of America.

ISBN 978-0-300-27289-5 (hardcover : alk. paper)
Library of Congress Control Number: 2024938875

A catalogue record for this book is available from the British
Library.

This paper meets the requirements of ANSI/NISO z39.48-1992
(Permanence of Paper).

10 9 8 7 6 5 4 3 2 1

Contents

The Rivalry Peril

Introduction

In 2017, mere days before the White House fired him, Steve Bannon, the one-time strategist and campaign manager for Donald Trump, placed an unsolicited call to *The American Prospect,* a progressive magazine. He was looking to connect with its editor, Robert Kuttner, to discuss U.S.-China relations.

Bannon thought Kuttner was an ideal interlocutor—the two like-minded on U.S. policy toward China. "It's a great honor to finally track you down. I've followed your writing for years and I think you and I are in the same boat when it comes to China," Bannon cheerily announced when Kuttner got on the line. Kuttner had just written a column arguing that China profited from the diplomatic impasse between the United States and North Korea and that China's economic interests sabotaged the possibility of peace on the Korean peninsula. Bannon concurred. The United States "is at economic war with China," said Bannon. "One of us [the United States or China] is going to be hegemon in 25 or 30 years," Bannon argued; "we have to be maniacally focused on that."[1]

Bannon's call came days after white nationalists rioted in Charlottesville, Virginia, where a neo-Nazi rammed his car into a crowd, killing Heather Heyer and injuring thirty-five others.

Media pundits at the time painted Bannon as irresponsible and deranged—a marginal figure from the far right whose policy proposals on China, like those of many advisers in the Trump administration, relied on and fueled xenophobia. Tina Nguyen, a reporter for *Vanity Fair,* called Bannon the Trump administration's "resident 'alt-right' ideologue" whose "bizarre" comments during an interview were proof that he was "champing for a trade war with China."[2] Of course, contra what Bannon insisted in his call to Kuttner, Washington was not yet in an "economic war" with China. And it was just as likely that in the 2040s neither China nor the United States would be the global hegemon. Bannon betrayed a distorted sense of reality.

But his preoccupation with China, and his sinister view of the country and its government, soon crept across Congress, the presidency, and large swaths of the electorate. Two years later, both Republicans and Democrats warned that China posed "possibly the largest threat to U.S. democratic values in history," even a threat to "Western civilization."[3] "In a country that's so divided . . . the thing that pulls it together is China," mused Bannon in 2019.[4] And by the time Joe Biden came to office in 2021, Americans were living in Bannon's world. His dark, racialized prognostications became something approximating common sense, an assumed reality. Biden did not just embrace Trump's aggressive stance toward China; in most respects, he took it further.

Democrats and Republicans now characterize China as America's preeminent adversary, "the threat that will define this century."[5] With little contention and much less public debate, the United States has committed itself to a full-throated rivalry with China, relying on the hyperbolized rhetoric first used by the likes of Steve Bannon.

How did this happen?

Since the waning days of the Obama administration, U.S.

policymakers had zeroed in on threats from "great powers" and "strategic competition," phrases with a nineteenth-century vintage that referred obliquely to China and, sometimes, to Russia. America's foreign policy establishment hoped to end the War on Terror without reflecting on what had gone wrong with American foreign policy since 2001. China, and Washington's larger "pivot to Asia," became the answer, the place to direct U.S. resources in the absence of obvious traditional threats and without acknowledging that the wars in Iraq and Afghanistan had been abject failures. Many U.S. officials thought that "outcompeting" China did not require hostility—at first. In announcing the Asian pivot in 2011, Secretary of State Hillary Clinton argued that "fair competition" or "healthy economic competition" should determine the U.S.-China relationship, that both countries "have much more to gain from cooperation than from conflict."[6]

Circumstances changed by the end of Obama's presidency. China increasingly looked capable of being an expansionist power under the leadership of President Xi Jinping: its gross domestic product grew at an average of 7.25 percent during Obama's second term, and Xi had spread China's newfound economic influence into parts of Asia, the Pacific, and Africa. China's "Belt and Road Initiative" reached into sixty countries and accounted for 40 percent of global domestic product by 2017.

Then came the so-called China shock. The parts of America most decimated by deindustrialization—a process made by American politicians and from which China's economy benefited—became strongholds of both Trump support and anti-China animus.[7] Trump, predictably enough, seized on Americans' anxieties over China's power and launched a trade war in 2018. He lavished new funds on the Pentagon to increase military readiness, normalized hostility and racialized rhetoric toward China, and instituted higher tariffs on Chinese-made products ranging from textiles to heating and cooling systems to salt.

Building on the momentum of anti-China politics during the Covid-19 pandemic and the presidential election of 2020, the Republican Senatorial Campaign Committee issued messaging guidance that "Coronavirus was a Chinese hit-and-run followed by a cover-up that cost thousands of lives," that Democrats are "soft on China," and that Republicans should "push for sanctions on China for its role in spreading the pandemic."[8] Trump made anti-China dog whistles an explicit part of his re-election campaign in 2020, calling the Covid-19 pandemic "kung flu" and the "China virus."[9] Trump also described his opponent, Joe Biden, as "Beijing Biden," tried to implicate Biden's son in a scandal involving Chinese corruption and nuclear espionage, and publicly accused the Communist Party of China (CCP) of trying to help Biden win.[10] A broad right-wing network of campaign surrogates alleged that and more in talk shows, podcasts, and propagandist documentaries with titles like *Riding the Dragon: The Bidens' Chinese Secrets*.[11] By 2022, some Democrats too embraced the politics of China-bashing, using their campaigns for political office to caricature their opponents as "weak" on China and to blame the People's Republic of China (PRC) for the economic distress expressed by growing numbers of Americans.[12]

Although Democrats universally excoriated Trump's trade war at the time, within two years Trump-like policies had become the foundation for the Democratic Party's vision for the U.S. political economy. Biden kept Trump's tariffs in place and added more, dramatically expanded two-way restrictions on Sino-U.S. investments, and refused to engage in bilateral talks over trade disputes.[13] Decoupling in technologies relevant to defense and the balance of military power was Washington's new means to pursue long-standing ends—global primacy.

By 2021, the specter of China had become all-consuming, and the institutions of the national security state retooled for "great-power competition." The Pentagon publicly designated China as the U.S. military's "pacing threat," making the ability to out-modernize and out-arm China's military in scenarios on China's border the justification for an annual defense budget that eclipsed the Biden administration's $860 billion.[14] At the Federal Bureau of Investigation (FBI), a counter-espionage mission targeting the "great powers" displaced counter-terrorism as the agency's new purpose.[15] The director of Biden's Central Intelligence Agency (CIA) boasted of "more than doubling the percentage of our overall budget focused on China over just the last two years."[16] The Treasury and the Department of Commerce framed Sino-U.S. economic ties in the language of national security—breaking with a generation of rhetoric touting globalization and unfettered markets—both to squeeze China out of U.S. supply chains and to hobble China's power and influence.[17] And the State Department allocated the lion's share of its clout to encourage the rest of the world to align *with* the United States *against* China.

U.S. foreign policy once again had a singular purpose: to obstruct China's growing power while maximizing its own. A familiar language of dichotomies emerged from this moment: democracy against autocracy, free versus unfree. Suddenly, Washington found the "communist" label in the title of China's reactionary party-state—the Communist Party of China—far more menacing than it had been only a few years earlier. Pundits invariably cheered and feared the coming of a "New Cold War," which was codified in both the publication of the National Security Strategy (NSS) of 2022 and the new House Select

Committee on Strategic Competition between the United States
and the Chinese Communist Party, chaired by Mike Gallagher,
a Republican from Wisconsin.

But this obsessive focus on China as a threat substitutes
bombastic rhetoric and wild-eyed prescriptions in place of careful analysis. It allows proponents of great-power competition
to elide the recent failures of U.S. foreign policy without reflecting how rivalry with China promises to reproduce them.
At the very least, the proponents of great-power competition
do not recognize how their bellicosity and their extremist positions on China feed Chinese nationalism and anti-American
policies elsewhere. Instead, the U.S. government and much of
the Beltway pundit class have come to see geopolitical competition as not just the future of American foreign policy but
nothing short of democracy's salvation.

This is a dark path for America and the world. The basis
for rivalry with China derives from a misreading not only of
the country but also of the past, leading to a misguided vision
for the United States and its global role. Accordingly, we make
two interrelated arguments in this book.

First, U.S. policymakers are responding to China—and
the fear of great-power war—by drawing on a selective history
of the Cold War and U.S. foreign policy. They imagine the Cold
War to have been a zero-sum struggle that culminated in an
unequivocal victory for the United States and its allies in 1991,
yielding a peaceful, more democratic world. This oversanguine
image disregards the absurdly large-scale violence inherent to
the Cold War—the global destruction wrought when the United
States deployed its economic and military might in the decades
after World War II.

Second, this blinkered reading of Cold War history—and
how it shaped our current era—underestimates the costs and
risks that geopolitical rivalry poses to economic prosperity, the

quality of democracy in the United States and abroad, and, ultimately, global stability. Washington's response to the China challenge makes U.S. foreign policy a surplus source of partisan division and domestic insecurity; great-power rivalry promotes fracture and crisis, not national cohesion.

Great-power rivalries throughout history, and especially during the Cold War, have entailed mass brutality, sacrifice, and perils borne disproportionately by ordinary citizens rather than governing elites. This assertion will doubtless be hard to swallow for anyone who endorses U.S. policy in the Cold War or sees opposition to China as the ticket to political progress and American renewal. But we believe governments everywhere—not least the United States—must reexamine the relative merits of long-term confrontation as the basis of world politics to ensure a saner, more democratically accountable foreign policy.

To be clear, we do not summarily reject zero-sum policies, nor do we deny that some democratic political developments can occur within a competitive geopolitical framework. Indeed, the Cold War yielded real benefits for some Americans. But the unrealistic view of the Cold War now shaping U.S. foreign policy—or the hyperbolic claim that China today is more threatening than the Soviet Union then—is unbalanced. To the extent that U.S.-Soviet competition generated positive outcomes for American democracy, they came at a great cost in the United States and the Global South. The historical memories of policymakers do not account for all that it took to wage the Cold War. Rivalry has as much to do with maladies in the body politic as it does with "war games" on sprawling maps. Politicians, bureaucrats, and hangers-on of all sorts amplify great-power competition to secure personal advancement, stymie democratic change, concentrate political power, and pillory opponents and dissidents for short-term gain. China rivalry

is a policy framework that favors demagogues and jingoes in domestic politics even as it perverts U.S. grand strategic thinking.

The public, as well as future policymakers, must understand that rivalry makes international relations and domestic
politics more combustible, more dangerous. Rivalry narrows
the relevance of diplomacy; it militarizes foreign policy options;
it sacrifices liberty by mobilizing societies against external
enemies at the expense of political and economic equality at
home and abroad. And it encourages tunnel vision rather than
long-term foresight.

The same damaging political forces unleashed during the
Cold War are with us today. The zeal to outcompete China—
and to do so by drawing explicitly from Cold War metaphors
and rationales—is actively hindering struggles for equality,
heightening rather than ameliorating military dangers, and empowering reactionary political trends in Washington and across
the globe.

We recognize that we are swimming upstream, against
the current mood in Washington, D.C. But that is precisely why
our argument is needed. It repudiates much of the popularist
literature that attempts to steel its readers' nerves for a "New
Cold War" and the myriad harms it inevitably requires. Im-
bued with a mix of uncritical American exceptionalism, fear,
and a romantic sense of past glories, many modern scribes of
great-power competition can only reach conclusions that justify militarism—a plague on democracy wherein "the military
aspect of politics [is] a state's overriding concern . . . [and] preparations for war [gain] the upper hand over considerations of
'the steady art of statecraft.'"[18] Hal Brands, for instance, has argued that the insanity and injustice of an arms race is an art
form to be cultivated; that "one war is not enough" if primacy
is our aim; that Cold Wars are inevitable because history is
tragic; and that a Cold War could be *good* for American de-

mocracy.[19] Writing with Michael Beckley, Brands also made the case that China—not the United States—was past its peak and therefore a growing danger that should be met with, among other things, filling the Taiwan Strait with sea-based mines (an action that would violate international law and be a casus belli, a trigger for war).[20] Robert Kaplan, who was prophesying about military conflict with China as early as 2005, insisted in 2019 that "the new Cold War is permanent . . . because the differences between the United States and China are stark and fundamental."[21] Rush Doshi—a political appointee in the Biden White House—helped popularize the idea that China seeks to displace America and achieve global hegemony, even though the community of China experts is divided about the correctness of his analysis.[22] And Elbridge Colby—who served as a political appointee in the Trump administration and as an adviser to Ron DeSantis's presidential campaign—made a mission of ringing alarm bells about preparing for a war with China that was inevitable, he argued, unless Washington optimized for war now regardless of the sacrifices it required.[23]

These Beltway voices range from center left to far right. Yet they converge toward common advice for America's governing elites—China's hegemonic ambitions and military power represent the threat of our time, and, if democracy has any chance at all, it resides in a project that stops at nothing to secure American preeminence in military, economic, and political life.

Nonsense. With these commentators and authors, concerns for American democracy fall by the wayside of their analysis; competition is our fate and therefore the future for freedom-loving democracies. Their collective misfire is part of the problem to which we are responding. Seeing China as the preeminent global threat to democracy—and competition as the means to resolving that threat—not only misdiagnoses the problems China represents; it also fails to deal with the context that gave rise to China as a supposed menace and directs attention and resources away from other issues that more immediately threaten the globe: the climate crisis, global pandemics, poverty, racial injustice, and sovereign indebtedness, to name a few.

The inability to ameliorate these problems feeds reactionary far-right movements around the world. It forces the United States to cozy up to despotic regimes that hypothetically challenge China's power in the short term but concretely obstruct human rights and democratic movements in the long term. It pushes China to further disengage from diplomacy and bilateral agreements. "Strategic competition" makes the Pentagon and the defense budget the arbiter of what is fiscally and socially possible in the United States—what can and cannot be sacrificed to ensure America's national security. Historically, increases in defense spending have tended to come at the cost of domestic welfare, racial justice, and (paradoxically) national infrastructure investment. *That* lesson is playing out again in debates over military spending in our time.

The paradigm of great-power competition is already functioning in a manner that denies others political rights, ignores growing economic precarity, and supports despotism, racism, and militarism, at home and abroad. But it is not too late to pull back from the brink.

Great-power competition is a choice made by policymakers. To reverse course, Americans must have an honest reckoning with our country's role in Cold War history. We can then evaluate how a zero-sum confrontation with other great powers is, at best, a violent, unpromising way to fix what ails American democracy. Through policy options beyond competition alone, the United States can pursue a more nuanced foreign policy that responds to current crises, none of which are

improved by pouring endless resources into the national security state or empowering ethnonationalists the world over.

Our intervention proceeds by first offering a brief critical
account of the history of great-power rivalry: the blood and
treasure spilled; the risks taken without consent; the policies
not pursued.

Chapter 1 interprets the history of great-power competition in a global context since the eighteenth century to show
how such contests made the world less democratic and less
equitable, especially during the Cold War. It would derail our
argument to dwell too intensively on pre–Cold War history,
but we need to say enough to situate the large gap between the
image policymakers have of the Cold War and the real effects
the imagined "long peace" had on the American people and
the world. Doing so will shed light on how the Cold War reinforced racial and gender hierarchies at home, increased economic insecurity, stymied democratic pluralism, and helped
radicalize right-wing forces in American political life—all in
addition to spurring nuclear crises, proxy wars, and aid to Third
World despots.

We expand this historical analysis in Chapter 2, where
we cover the history of the post–Cold War "unipolar moment."
America's quest for primacy after 1991—its abandonment of
the "peace dividend" and a more restrained foreign policy—
led to overreach and blowback that negatively shaped China's
behavior. Although the United States wanted a cooperative relationship with China during the presidencies of Bill Clinton
and George W. Bush, the failures of the War on Terror after September 11, 2001, engendered China's skepticism that its own
stability would be assured in a context of U.S. primacy. This uncertainty, coupled with the financial crisis of 2008, led China
to shore up its regional and global influence in both economic
and military terms. China's policy shift convinced American

policymakers that cooperation with China was no longer possible and that the world had entered a new era of great-power rivalry.

We then evaluate the rivalry peril today, showing how it engenders a darker, more dangerous political situation in the United States and globally.

Chapter 3 describes the corrosive effects of geopolitical competition on political democracy at home, detailing how the "China threat" has become a political wedge that divides society and empowers extreme reactionary voices opposed to democracy. The challenge posed by China does not bring us together. By approaching China as if it represented a Cold War challenge, great-power competition has fueled measurable increases in anti-Asian violence, channeled civil liberties–denying surveillance and investigations against Chinese Americans, and heightened paranoia about fifth columns and enemies within.

Chapter 4 focuses on the threat rivalry poses to economic prosperity in America. It draws links between Sino-U.S. competition and an increasingly oligarchic political economy that renders most workers economically insecure. Strategic competition impels national investments in advanced technologies that shape industrial policy, but such investments redistribute society's wealth upward, subsidizing large firms and higher wages for a small technocratic elite with advanced degrees and an advantaged position in the economy. These economic policies offer nothing for the working majority.

Chapter 5 defines how we see the state and future of China. At the root of the China problematic are inequalities sustained by China's statist regime of capital accumulation in the world economy. It is powered by a complex of export dependence, labor exploitation, and ethnonationalism, features that do not exist in a vacuum but rather are intimately tied to U.S. choices.

Sino-U.S. competition strengthens ethnonationalism in China and the United States.

This chapter also explains how great-power competition makes the world less peaceful. Rivalry erodes ameliorative or peaceful effects that come from economic interdependence, diplomacy, and multilateral cooperation. At the same time, it strengthens oligarchy and corruption in the Global South by compelling the United States to not only countenance but sometimes actively support foreign despotism—provided it has a prospect of inhibiting Chinese power or influence.

Finally, Chapter 6 answers the question "If not rivalry, then what?" It outlines elements of a pragmatic grand strategy that builds toward peace and democracy rather than jingoism and war. It presents a positive alternative to great-power competition that addresses the deeper political and economic dysfunctions in U.S. statecraft and world politics. The root conditions of global insecurity must be addressed if peace and democracy are to have a real chance in this world. Accordingly, we highlight the ingredients needed for a better statecraft—on China, climate adaptation, racial equality, economic policy, and human rights.

We hope that policymakers and the public will better appreciate how great-power competition destabilizes world politics; empowers reactionary forces in the United States and abroad; leads to more (not less) racial conflict; and, despite hopes to the contrary, becomes the justification that right-wing reactionaries use to oppose investing in greater equality and democracy at home.

The future of global freedom *is* at stake. But geopolitical rivalry imperils it.

1

The Cold War and the Origins of "Great-Power Competition"

W hen we think about the United States today, an appropriate analogy to the Cold War would be one that focuses on the violence, hierarchy, and exclusion that superpower competition unleashed: one where the Cold War limited democracy in the Global South, risked the annihilation of the entire planet, and killed nearly fourteen million people. A different Cold War analogy—an extended struggle against totalitarianism that produced an unqualified U.S. victory and invigorated U.S. social reform—is both misplaced and imprecise.

Yet this latter analogy to the Cold War prevails in Washington, reinforcing policymakers' confidence to lead the "free world" in what they see as a modern-day reprisal of a once-successful great-power conflict. Policymakers believe the United States can manage the international order and derail China's ambitions without bringing the world into war because they believe they did it before. As Antony Blinken said in June 2023, America can ultimately "stabilize our relations" with the People's Republic of China through steady leadership and communication to "ensure that competition does not veer into conflict." The United States can be "responsibly managing the relationship" with China while perpetuating confrontation in the short and long terms.[1]

This is dangerous thinking. Such optimism is ultimately a blind faith that the present will reflect an illusory past. In making historical analogies to the Cold War and its relevance to great-power competition, policymakers, perhaps unintentionally, distort history to serve the ends of policy. They ignore how the Cold War created global disorder, exploited and killed millions in the Global South, and brought the world to the brink of nuclear destruction in the name of democracy and freedom. Great-power competition, even during the Cold War, was not peaceful and did not leave a peaceful legacy.

A more holistic and representative accounting of the Cold War is the first step to rethinking great-power rivalry with China. The dominant depiction of the Cold War in Washington, D.C., and popular culture is misleading. Recognizing this will correct presumptions about how the United States can conduct its foreign policy to win a great-power competition without significant harm to the American Republic. If we understand the history of the Cold War in more balanced terms, it is impossible to think that a great-power conflict in the twenty-first century will be productive for the United States and the world.

Great-Power Rivalry Before the Cold War

Great-power competition is not new to the twenty-first century; it is endemic to world history, though infrequently described as such prior to the later nineteenth century. Wars between European great powers profoundly shaped the modern era: they reorganized states, territories, and global markets into and beyond the twentieth century. England, France, and Spain spent much of the seventeenth century fighting over colonies, prestige, and the supremacy of Catholicism or Protestantism. By the eighteenth century, the Spanish empire's influence waned, leaving Great Britain and France to war over access to colonies and markets in Asia and Africa for more than half of the century. Both the American and French revolutions became proxy conflicts for great-power dominance—whether Britain or France would control both the colonies and the European metropole— by the end of the 1700s.

Enduring war wreaked havoc on the international system until the Enlightenment engendered new frameworks for cooperation. The Treaty of Utrecht in 1713 solidified a balance of power between the major European empires after the War of Spanish Succession; it created the basis for stability among the leading European nations. The Treaty of Utrecht prevented further conflict between Spain and France over the Spanish throne and ensured that the British empire would preserve its dependence on slave labor and commercial interests in Spain and France. After continental war broke out in the wake of the French Revolution and the Napoleonic Wars, the Congress of Vienna in 1815 aimed to restore the imperial order. The Congress of Vienna expanded the British and Russian empires and solidified alliances between Germany and Austria-Hungary. Like the Treaty of Utrecht, the Congress of Vienna sought stability, not peace. International diplomacy maintained a world controlled by empires; it constrained nationalism and movements for independence as a condition of the uneasy stability it arranged among great powers.

Although it had conservative, if not reactionary, origins, the Congress of Vienna allowed great-power balancing to inhibit conflict for almost half a century. Imperial wars were waged in the nineteenth century—among them the Franco-Prussian

War of 1871, the Crimean War in 1853, the Opium Wars of 1839 and 1856—but wars for independence, for nationhood, proliferated too. Simón Bolívar spurred independence movements against the Spanish in South America, and former slaves in Haiti, led by Toussaint L'Ouverture, overthrew French rule. Independence movements also fed an "age of revolution" in both political and scientific terms. The decrease in great-power wars, combined with technological progress and the ideals of the Enlightenment, engendered new ideas of nationalism and equality.[2]

The revolutions of 1848 were born from this era. Great-power stability after the Napoleonic Wars ultimately prioritized the economic and military interests of European leaders over the needs of their citizens. As a result, the Congress of Vienna failed "to keep domestic peace," in the words of the historian Stella Ghervas.[3] A new wave of democratic uprisings not seen since the American and French revolutions swept over the continent. The nineteenth-century version of "liberal world order" failed to fulfill democratic expectations. Economic inequality and social dislocation rampaged Europe in the wake of the Industrial Revolution, while ideas of socialism, communitarianism, and feminism challenged the status quo. The combination became combustive, and social upheavals from France to Norway to Australia were the result. The revolutions of 1848 challenged monarchical rule and economic stratification among the wealthy and the working class.[4] After the 1848 revolutions were quelled, France and Britain expanded their reach over African and Asian colonies, suppressing nationalist movements in countries including Vietnam and Kenya in the name of European democracy.

This conservative order collapsed again after the outbreak of World War I (or the Great War, as it was then known) in 1914. The assassination of Archduke Franz Ferdinand provided the pretext for Germany to launch a war on two fronts (France and

Russia), bringing England and Italy into the war with Austria-Hungary, which allied with Germany. Modern warfare—chemical weapons, machine guns, aerial attacks—created death tolls in the millions, and World War I descended into a stalemate by 1915. German capitulation to the Entente powers occurred only after the United States entered the conflict in 1917. The Paris Peace Conference then led to the ratification of the Treaty of Versailles in 1919. The American president, Woodrow Wilson, an essential figure at the conference, believed the Great War would be the "war to end all wars," and he pursued a lasting peace instead of stability. The negotiations at Paris, Wilson hoped, would depart from precedent; they would create a peace accord under the auspices of his "Fourteen Points": free trade, self-determination, and open diplomatic treaties.

Wilson fell short of his aims. The Treaty of Versailles rectified the errors of the Congress of Vienna but created new problems. The treaty failed to address the growing nationalism in Europe and Asia and the demand to end colonialism in nations in the Global South. This nationalism fueled independence movements in countries such as Vietnam and India; by the 1930s, the liberation movement in Vietnam materialized in a Marxist-Leninist government led by Ho Chi Minh. And instead of a "peace without victory," the Treaty of Versailles left Germany ostracized from the international community and mired in a precarious fiscal position. In 1924 the Dawes Plan sanctioned German payments (provided from U.S. loans) to pay British and French war debts, whereupon those two countries used those payments to pay debts to the United States, leading to a financial house of cards that collapsed following the stock market crash of 1929. Then the Great Depression created 25 percent unemployment, brought the financial system to its knees, and killed the precarious and transactional nature of the postwar peace, leading to World War II.

World War II, in turn, surpassed the atrocities of the Great War and birthed a new "new world order." The German Third Reich and Adolf Hitler's genocidal campaign against Jewish citizens, combined with Japanese imperialism and Italian fascism, left millions dead and the future of Europe and Asia in doubt. The Allied victory over that fascist threat relied on the mass bombing of civilians (including the atomic bomb), killing millions more. The aftermath of World War II created fear and overcorrection: policymakers emerged determined not to let the world descend into mass death again but believing that—since force was what vanquished fascists—force was the currency of stability. With Europe and Japan shattered, the United States took the helm on reconstructing and propping up the "free world," even though on the Pacific front the war had been a fight between empires for the reconquest of imperial control.[5] The horrors of World War II provoked fears of new expansionist threats akin to Hitler's and raised questions about how to head them off, to thwart evil. Franklin D. Roosevelt's vision to thwart imperialist dictators sought international cooperation on diplomacy and trade—a world that looked like Wilson's—undergirded by American power.

The barbarities of World War II—genocide, atomic weapons, the blanket destruction of cities, mass torture and execution—were unprecedented, but policymakers feared they could happen again. Hitler personified an evil empire—the potential for a new order premised on genocide and conquest. The United States knew it had beaten back an existential threat like no other. With Britain and France reeling from the war's destruction and no major democratic power left able to stabilize global affairs, the United States felt obligated to rescue the world from darkness. The providential mission of the United States as a "beacon of freedom" fortuitously aligned with its possession of unprecedented economic and military power. The United States can use its power for good—for the benefit of the world, rather than its own interests. As a moral nation, the United States would depart from the great powers of the eighteenth and the nineteenth centuries. It would not—could not—be a British or French empire. American primacy would create an empire by invitation—nations would be seeking U.S. protection rather than avoiding subjugation.

Here lie the origins of the U.S. approach to China in the twenty-first century. When Americans hear talk about great-power competition with China today, they think of it in moralistic terms, in binaries of good versus evil. China is the aggressor, the communist nation that seeks territorial dominance. They picture the United States standing strong against the forces of evil.

This mindset derives from a skewed history of America's status as a great power after World War II. It went like this: By virtue, and accident, the United States became the sole democratic hegemon after World War II. It had no aspirations for dominance, no goal of being an empire. But the fate of the world called, and the United States answered to preserve democracy and freedom. This empirically incomplete moral vision, of the United States rescuing the world through its military and economic power, remains intact today. It fuels hawkishness and extremism, perpetuating the idea that great-power competition is both necessary and good.

The aftermath of World War II, even more than the war itself, also created a set of experiences that were seen as lessons, understandings that shaped the postwar period and that resonate in a new age of great-power competition. Many of these lessons were also warnings: plan for unexpected military attack, deter dictators from reaching their imperial ambitions, and ensure a strong economy supported by a strong national defense. These lessons birthed a series of analogies that carried over into the postwar years: appeasement, Munich, Pearl Harbor. These terms operated as synecdoches—totemic representations—for how the United States should approach foreign policymaking in a postwar environment. Do not capitulate to dictators; do not seek cooperation with foreign foes; project resolve above all else. These axioms resonated in a Cold War culture where being "soft on communism" ensured political doom.[6]

The United States constructed its Cold War foreign policy around these lessons of history. A new "liberal world order" took shape to counter fears of a World War III and to codify American military and economic primacy. In 1945, the United States spearheaded institutions that aimed to integrate the global community with America's unrivaled military and economic power. The World Bank and the Global Agreement on Tariffs and Trade (GATT) connected American markets to the world, eliminating the protectionist measures that characterized international relations in the 1930s. GATT encouraged exports from Japan, South Korea, and China (after 1972); it promoted free trade at a time when the United States possessed 60 percent of the capital stock in advanced countries.[7] While the World Bank and GATT aspired to liberalize economic relations, the creation of the United Nations offered a liberal internationalist vision that hoped to stave off conflict by relying on deliberation and consensus to prevent future global wars. But its power proved ineffective in the face of U.S. opposition: decision-making at the U.N. depended upon a Security Council in which the great powers held veto power over substantive issues, and the United States, being the leading superpower, directed its priorities. Issues that fell under the U.N.'s purview, such as international control of atomic weapons, were stymied by U.S. interests to preserve atomic control in the United States and Britain, excluding the Soviets.

The emergence of the "liberal world order" thereby

coincided with U.S. policymakers' preoccupation with the threat the Soviet Union posed to global stability. In the months after World War II ended in September 1945, the Soviet premier Joseph Stalin failed to comply with agreements he had made with the United States and Great Britain in February 1945 at the Yalta Conference regarding the independence of Eastern European states, particularly Poland. Instead of encouraging free elections, Stalin installed Soviet-friendly regimes in Eastern Europe by fiat or coup. Stalin's behavior bewildered American policymakers. Why did Stalin renege on his agreements? What motivated the Soviets' postwar behavior? Officials in the U.S. government wanted clear answers.

George F. Kennan provided them with his "long telegram." A Russophile and longtime foreign service officer, Kennan wrote to the State Department in February 1946 that Soviet Russia sought to heighten tensions between "capitalist powers" and expand its influence further into Europe and the Middle East. The Soviet Union posed a clear threat to the West. To prevent Soviet aggression, the United States must contain the spread of communism with its diplomatic and economic might and wait for the dissolution of the Soviet Union, which would come in due time. As Kennan wrote months later in his *Foreign Affairs* article "The Sources of Soviet Conduct," the United States must adopt a strategy of a "long-term, patient but firm and vigilant containment of Russian expansive tendencies" and be willing to "promote tendencies which must eventually find their outlet in either the breakup or the gradual mellowing of Soviet power."[8]

Policymakers took Kennan's arguments as evidence that Stalin, like Hitler, was an imperialist despot who threatened global security, and that the Soviet Union sought global dominance. In 1947, President Harry Truman requested a $300 million aid package for Greece and Turkey to prevent the emergence of communist regimes in those countries. Known as the Truman Doctrine, the policy became a precedent for how the United States could deter communist threats in a postwar environment. The European Recovery Program, or Marshall Plan, followed the Truman Doctrine, providing more than $13 billion in economic relief to European countries after 1948 to stave off communist parties, which, policymakers argued, thrived on economic collapse. The United States and the Soviet Union also came into conflict over food aid to Berlin, when Stalin contemplated shooting American planes out of Soviet airspace because they encroached on his sphere of influence.

After communists led by Mao Zedong took control of China in 1949, the Soviets tested their atomic bomb that same year, and the Korean War broke out in 1950, U.S. policymakers such as Paul Nitze and the secretary of state, Dean Acheson, championed the militarization of U.S. foreign policy to roll back communism under the auspices of a National Security Council policy paper known as NSC-68. Economic power and diplomatic threats were insufficient to stop communism from metastasizing further into Asia; the United States must build up its military and nuclear arsenals to deter communist aggression, Nitze and Acheson argued. The United States would come to rely upon a "preponderance of power," according to the historian Melvyn Leffler, to prevent the spread of communism beyond Eastern Europe and China. By the end of the Korean War in 1953, the United States had committed itself to stamping out communist incursions wherever they threatened capitalist economies or democratic governments.

The Cold War created a new model of great-power competition. Unlike the great powers of the eighteenth and nineteenth centuries that sought territory and financial influence to bring "backward" civilizations into modernity through religion and conquest, the United States sought to lead by example rather than violence. The United States would seek both global stability and liberation of oppressed peoples. There would be no "white man's burden" in America's empire. American military force would provide equilibrium—a bulwark against communism—and hope to those who suffered under tyranny. American values would be absorbed by nations rather than enforced by coups and corruption, as the British had done. A messianic zeal to preserve global freedom motivated U.S. policymakers, but religion and religious values would not be forced onto foreign populations as the French and Spanish did. "Liberal internationalism," rather than "liberal imperialism," would drive the mission of the United States abroad.

But liberal internationalism masked the continuities between the old and new great-power competition. The benevolent intentions behind U.S. primacy belied the reality of its effects on the world. Like the advocates of great-power competition against China today, policymakers told themselves a story that aligned with America as a great power doing good in the world. American exceptionalism presupposed that the ends of the Cold War (the defeat of communism) justified the means (overthrowing democratically elected governments, engaging in torture and execution of civilians on the battlefield, risking mass nuclear death). The moral dimensions of U.S. foreign policy since World War II are belied by the historical record of how that moralism justified immoral actions abroad.

Cold War Paradoxes

America's Cold War relied on two paradoxes. In the name of security abroad, it compounded risks of global nuclear annihilation and laid waste to millions of lives. In the name of democracy at home, America's grand struggle did more to impede racial and gender equality than to promote it: the national security state surveilled, harassed, jailed, and even killed many of its own citizens—often for unjustified reasons.

The first paradox had to do with how America waged its Cold War abroad. The most generous interpretation is that, after the American monopoly on the atomic bomb ended in 1949, policymakers worried that miscommunication and fear between the two major superpowers could spiral out of control, resulting in a nuclear holocaust. This fear thwarted U.S.-Soviet bilateral negotiations—or any attempt to reconcile tensions—until the 1960s. The prospect of nuclear war motivated an arms race between the United States and the Soviet Union after 1952. The United States secured its sovereignty through ever larger nuclear arsenals, from almost three hundred nuclear weapons in 1950 to more than eighteen thousand by 1960, seeking to ensure that the Soviets could never obtain an atomic monopoly. The contorted logic of the arms race—the proliferation of nuclear weapons to deter communist aggression—led to the policy of "mutual assured destruction" by the 1960s. Should nuclear war materialize, each superpower would doom the other, and the world, to annihilation.

In a bizarre (but logical) turn of events, the threat of nuclear war checked the most aggressive hawks in both Washington and Moscow, yielding mostly stable relations. Policymakers anticipated nuclear war but could not fathom its inevitability. Indeed, the potential destructiveness of nuclear war proved so overwhelming that it seemed preposterous. Leaders would never dare condemn their people—and their own lives—to doom.

In the most basic sense, the threat of nuclear weapons articulated the stakes of making a Cold War a hot one. As the historian Jeremi Suri has written, nuclear weapons "helped draw the main lines of conflict and stability in the Cold War."[9] Relations between the United States and the Soviet Union remained frozen in the 1950s, caught between two extremes:

nuclear escalation or global destruction. But this led to a precarious status quo where both the Soviet Union and the United
States sought to outcompete each other in nuclear and conventional power.

But this stability proved fleeting, even illusionary. In 1953,
the secretary of state, John Foster Dulles, declared that the
United States would rely on a "deterrent of massive retaliatory
power" if threatened with a nuclear attack. His speech became
the precedent for a policy of "massive retaliation" against the
Soviet Union. The development of thermonuclear weapons in
1952 erased parity in the minds of some U.S. policymakers. The
United States once again had atomic technology that the Soviet Union would not possess until 1955. President Dwight Eisenhower and Secretary Dulles both felt in 1953 that "somehow
or other the tabu which surrounds the use of atomic weapons
would have to be destroyed."[10]

The conundrum posed by nuclear weapons—how to es-
cape global destruction while relying on nuclear weapons as
tools of deterrence—produced the first generation of the foreign policy "blob," the interventionist foreign policy establishment. The nuclear era created America's "military-intellectual
complex," and the country's first think tanks, such as RAND,
emerged from this moment. So-called defense intellectuals such
as Hans Spier, Edward Teller, Herman Kahn, and Henry Kissinger leveraged their academic pedigrees and intellectual trade to
advise the U.S. government on how to best navigate a new era
of great-power relations. Operating in private-public networks,
they became, or at least thought of themselves as, the modern
Machiavellis: the court counselors whispering in the ears of
the sovereign about how best to manage the empire. Great-
power competition in the Cold War bred a new era of "peacetime" war planners. Cozy relations between social scientists and
the Pentagon became the norm. Foreign policy thinkers worked

in tandem with presidential administrations, going into and out of government service. Together they generated a group-think that furthered careers outside the government and the existence of a permanent national security bureaucracy that operated outside of democratic checks and balances.[11]

These "wizards of Armageddon" told the Eisenhower administration that nuclear conflict could be managed—that America should not fear war with the Soviet Union.[12] This was the argument of Henry Kissinger's book *Nuclear Weapons and Foreign Policy* (1957). Kissinger, then a Harvard professor, ar-gued for the selective use of nuclear weapons in the event of a superpower conflict. Kissinger wrote that "a limited nuclear war would approach all-out war in destructiveness only if it should be conducted with the tactics of World War II." This passed for a revelatory insight in the late 1950s. The absurdity of "limited nuclear warfare," and the fact that it was promoted as an in-genious policy, tells us much about the state of commentary on U.S. foreign policy in the early Cold War. The dearth of al-ternatives to accepting nuclear war reflected a lack of creative thinking about the state of the world; policymakers were intel-lectually paralyzed by a great-power competition determined by an arms race. And while Kissinger's comments captivated attention, they failed to change the stalemate that persisted between the two superpowers.

That is, until the 1960s. Senator John F. Kennedy, a Dem-ocrat from Massachusetts, ran for president in 1960 decrying a "missile gap" between the Soviet Union and the United States. When he squeaked out a narrow win against Vice President Richard Nixon, Kennedy requested a $650 million increase in defense spending—an eye-watering sum at the time—including expansion of nuclear bombers and nuclear submarines, even as he professed his "earnest desire for serious conversation" on nuclear disarmament.[13] Even though a "missile gap" with the

Soviet Union did not exist—as the secretary of defense, Robert McNamara, later admitted in 1961—the Kennedy administration accepted the truisms that had inspired the missile-gap paranoia: nuclear strength was national strength; the only way to win a war with the Soviet Union was through military and nuclear deterrence.

Kennedy courted a coterie of defense intellectuals to his administration. Encouraged by McNamara, these defense intellectuals told Kennedy and his national security team that the world remained dangerous and survival depended on making an art and science of threatening planetary extinction. RAND consultant Albert Wohlstetter, whose paper "The Delicate Balance of Terror" had fueled Kennedy's claims of a missile gap in the 1950s, assured Kennedy that the Soviet Union still sought the defeat of the West. Although Nikita Khrushchev, who succeeded Stalin in 1957, had allowed some reforms in the Soviet Union, he was not a reformist. A nuclear exchange remained possible, if not certain. Could the United States eliminate the possibility of its defeat? Although officials understood the horrors of nuclear war, they accepted what they saw as their new reality. They worked accordingly, trying to impose order and rationality on an otherwise irrational world through American military hegemony.

Thomas Schelling and Henry Rowen, economists from RAND and advisers to President Kennedy, pioneered simulations and war gaming that were meant to quantify how to achieve an American victory. Schelling and Rowen wanted to take the vagaries out of war. They constructed scenarios related to Berlin, the European center of the Cold War conflict. Schelling designed his simulations as "games of chicken, games of daring, games of attempting to put yourself where the next dangerous move was up to the other side, who would then back down, rather than take that dangerous move." Schelling hoped his war games created empathy for the enemy, so that policy-makers would accept the interconnectedness of Soviet and American fates in a nuclear conflict. Some officials thought war games could be a tool to de-escalate hostilities in the event of a real-life nuclear scenario. But war games created the opposite effect, forcing policymakers to test conflicts until they could get it "right"—achieve a U.S. victory. They also reaffirmed a bleak reality: that nuclear war was both "extremely unlikely" yet inevitable.[14]

Then came the Cuban Missile Crisis. Chastened by the Berlin Crisis in 1961, feeling disrespected by Kennedy at their first meeting in 1961, and embattled by critics in the Politburo, Nikita Khrushchev decided to send missiles armed with nuclear warheads to Cuba in the summer of 1962. Khrushchev hoped to send a message of resolve to the Kremlin and to counter the presence of American missiles in Europe aimed at Moscow. When American intelligence discovered the missiles in October 1962, Kennedy convened his national security advisers and received a torrent of advice, some of it contradictory. The chairman of the Joint Chiefs of Staff, Maxwell Taylor, advised an air strike on Soviet missile installations. Others argued for a naval blockade. The attorney general, Robert Kennedy, and Secretary of Defense McNamara contemplated an amphibious invasion of Cuba. The Air Force chief of staff, Curtis Lemay, wanted Kennedy to bomb Cuba with unrelenting force, saying that a blockade would be "a pretty weak response" to the missiles. "This is almost as bad as the appeasement at Munich," Lemay argued.[15]

Lemay and the military hawks seemed reasonable at the time. They had the consensus of the national security establishment and fifteen years of government assessments of Soviet behavior on their side. Why would the Soviets be in Cuba, they reasoned, unless they sought to shift to a first-use nuclear posture or solidify control of the island? American experts had told Kennedy since 1961 that Khrushchev had a vision for the Global South that entailed "a comprehensive, tested doctrine for conquest from within."[16] If the Soviets established a nuclear deterrent on the island of Cuba, it would be one step toward the hemispheric spread of communism.

As much as the United States had prepared for a crisis like the one in Cuba, the Kennedy administration did not recognize that a series of CIA attempts at regime change and assassination in Cuba set a context that precipitated the crisis. It also had no clear answers to resolve it. Schelling's simulations proved to be just that—simulations. They erased historical context in favor of abstruse social science abstractions. They could not predict, or comprehend, an event like the missile crisis. One Kennedy official reportedly said that "this [Cuban] crisis sure demonstrates how realistic Schelling's [war] games are." This generated the response, "No, Schelling's games demonstrate how unrealistic this Cuban crisis is."[17] Indeed, the Cuban Missile Crisis was both unprecedented and entirely predictable. Cold War competition had brought the two countries to this point. All of Kennedy's advisers urged the president to maintain military resolve, no matter the costs. Two days before U-2 spy planes discovered the missile sites, Schelling submitted a report to Kennedy suggesting that the United States continue its arms race focused on the production of intercontinental ballistic missiles (ICBMs). "The principal thing to make evident to the Soviets is that we shall have not only a large and diversified strategic force in the mid-sixties but a capacity to expand it rapidly," wrote Schelling and the members of his working group on "Strategic Developments Over the Next Decade."[18] And when the crisis was over, the lesson that subsequent officials took from it focused on brinkmanship and the contest of resolve, not the reassurances and back-channel diplomacy that actually stabilized relations by de-escalating the confrontation.

Kennedy's statements on a missile gap, policymakers' faith in the arms race, and the consensus on Soviet expansionism all suggest that Kennedy could have adopted a hard line toward Khrushchev. He initially favored a targeted air strike against the missile sites but could not be convinced a strike would take out all of them.[19] Kennedy soon pulled back from an air strike and navigated a fine line between not showing "weakness"— capitulation to Lemay and Taylor—and not escalating the conflict. He was, above all, confused by Soviet decision-making. Why would Khrushchev do this? Communication between the two nations had broken down since the Berlin crisis. Kennedy had only his first impressions of Khrushchev to go on—they met for the first and only time in Vienna in 1961—along with the conflicting recommendations of his advisers. He remained uneasy about doing anything to provoke a Soviet response but felt he had to do something.

In the end, Kennedy decided not to listen to the hawks. The president announced a blockade on October 24th, but he withheld air strikes on Cuba. Khrushchev called the blockade an "act of war," but by that point he knew he was in over his head. Khrushchev privately reached out to Kennedy on October 25th, hoping for a deal. If the United States pledged not to invade Cuba, the Soviets would take their missiles out of Cuba. The United States also agreed (secretly) to withdraw its Jupiter missiles from Turkey as part of the deal. Khrushchev hoped that the agreement showed Soviet strength, that Kennedy capitulated to Soviet demands—he had set the terms of the compromise. Kennedy could walk away from the crisis looking like a leader who chose to remain calm yet resolute in the face of nuclear war. Both men saved the lives of countless individuals.[20]

The Cuban Missile Crisis became a turning point in the

Cold War. First, it showed the merits of cooperation and concession, the need for hostile leaders to have empathy with each other in times of crisis. Contentious relations between the United States and the Soviet Union could not fester; heads of state should not let events spin out of control. The missile crisis introduced the merits of nuclear diplomacy as diplomacy rather than coercion, leading to a series of negotiations on strategic arms. The United States and the Soviet Union entered negotiations over the testing of nuclear weapons in 1963, with both countries eventually signing the Limited Test Ban Treaty of 1963 that banned atmospheric testing of nuclear weapons. The LTBT laid the groundwork for the Non-Proliferation Treaty in 1968, which provided steps for nuclear disarmament and the sharing of nuclear energy for the purposes of peace.

In addition to making headway for diplomacy, the crisis proved the defense intellectuals wrong. The Soviet Union was not ten feet tall and bulletproof. Its leaders were at least as rational as ours. The arms race did not have to be our future. Nuclear war could not be "won." Khrushchev's actions disproved the apoplectic RAND reports by Wohlstetter and his colleagues. Although Cold War hawks continued to warn American policymakers about the military and nuclear capabilities of the Soviet Union, they had less sway in the Kennedy and Johnson administrations. To be sure, communism remained an existential threat to this milieu, and the national security state continued its mission of puzzling how to win the Cold War—particularly in Vietnam, the Dominican Republic, and the Global South—but the idea that the Soviets yearned for a nuclear confrontation was no longer mainstream opinion. Even though the United States and the Soviet Union remained enemies, they pursued diplomacy and international agreements on nuclear weapons up through the administration of Ronald Reagan.

Competition, U.S. and Soviet leaders recognized, invariably creates confrontation.

These lessons, this history, seem lost amid the rush to rivalry with China. Cold War competition brought the United States and Soviet Union to the Cuban Missile Crisis. And now similar issues—heightened by the fact of rivalry—dividing Washington and Beijing could lead to military escalation between the two countries.

Great-power competition forbids prioritizing the issues on which the United States can cooperate with China over the means and ends of confrontation. Every issue gets filtered through a lens of "competition"—zero-sum actions, like the CIA attempting regime change and assassination without any concern for how that creates a context in which epochal crisis becomes inevitable. The competition mindset harkens back to a rigid and ossified era in U.S.-Soviet relations before the Cuban Missile Crisis. When officials and pundits invoke a "New Cold War," it is this history they imagine. They ignore the long sweep of the Cold War, its evolution into a détente after 1963, and they presume the Cold War represented an enduring, static competition for more than forty years.

PEACE FOR WHOM?

As the Cold War arms race invited global destruction, it simultaneously encouraged proxy wars around the globe. The "long peace" of the Cold War between the Soviet Union and the United States was anything but peaceful. The historian Paul Thomas Chamberlin has done the math and argues that more than twenty million people were killed in conflicts during the Cold War, an estimated twelve hundred people a day from 1945 to 1990. Most of these people—seven out of ten—were killed on the continent of Asia; many others died in Latin America.[21] Unwilling to wage war against the Soviet Union within its borders, the United States deployed its military power in countries across the Global South. Intervention in these countries provided little risk to the United States—the Soviet Union was unlikely to wage nuclear war on behalf of small powers. A hot war in the Global South existed within a Cold War among the superpowers.

U.S. foreign policy during the Cold War rested on the deterrence of communism around the globe, on the presumption that the Soviet Union sought to occupy and annex countries beyond its sphere of influence in Eastern Europe. The Soviets could spread their influence in distressed states without firing a shot. Communism held appeal among nations with widespread inequality, weak governments, and social unrest. Once a nation became communist, it became a de facto satellite of the Soviet Union. And communism, like a disease, would spread. If France or Italy went to the communists, England and Austria would follow. It did not matter if a country was weak or strong. Weak countries grew stronger through Soviet assistance and could entice other weak powers to the side of the communists. A communist nation anywhere was a threat to free peoples everywhere.

President Truman based his foreign policy—the "Truman Doctrine"—on this presumption. President Eisenhower gave it a name: the "domino theory." Eisenhower took office with the Korean War still raging and the fear of communism looming. But the Chinese revolution in 1949 and the Korean War proved that economic and diplomatic power would not be enough to stop communism in Asia. "Asia, after all, has already lost some 450 million of its peoples to the Communist dictatorship, and we simply can't afford greater losses," said Eisenhower in 1954.[22] If deterrence failed to keep communist movements out of nations through alliances with the United States, the U.S. military would intervene in these nations on behalf of stability and democracy.

Eisenhower appointed Allen Dulles—brother of John Foster Dulles, the secretary of state—as director of the Central Intelligence Agency in 1953 and let him run that agency with impunity. While John Foster Dulles prepared for "massive retaliation" in the State Department, Allen Dulles used the CIA to overthrow regimes that impeded America's economic and military interests. These interventions took the form of the conventional and the covert. Many of them occurred in the Global South—in non-nuclear states to avoid the prospect of nuclear escalation.

Iran became the testing ground for Dulles's covert tactics. Access to oil and control over Iran's economic development motivated CIA intervention in the country. Britain controlled Iran's oil production under the Anglo-Iranian Oil Corporation, consolidating oil profits while occupying Iranian land for decades. Then, in 1951, the Iranian president, Mohammad Mossadegh, announced the nationalization of Iran's oil, provoking concern in western companies. Oil politics motivated the CIA-led coup against Mossadegh, as did Cold War anxieties. Dulles and Eisenhower wondered if Mossadegh had communist sympathies and if his plan for oil nationalization represented a faith in socialism. Dulles prodded the shah of Iran to support a coup overthrowing Mossadegh, pouring hundreds of thousands of dollars into Iran, bribing anti-Mossadegh activists. Ultimately, as the historian Gregory Brew points out, the United States overthrew Mossadegh because of a combination of these factors. Mossadegh's rule spelled an "uncertain future" that policymakers feared could lead to an "ill-defined collapse of Iran's internal stability through economic and political disintegration" in the years to come.[23]

Plans for the coup materialized over the summer of 1953. Dulles's CIA orchestrated a mob to overrun Mossadegh's residence, forcing him to flee Tehran. The shah of Iran displaced Mossadegh without immediate repercussions for the United States—effects of the coup would come twenty-five years later. Fearing threats to his regime, the shah banned Mossadegh's political party, the Tudeh Party, arrested thousands of partisans, and tortured and executed Tudeh Party members. From 1953 to 1978, the shah regularly executed political prisoners; his military fired upon protesters during uprisings in 1963 and 1978. Despite this record, the shah of Iran's ouster in 1979 by Ayatollah Khomeini is still widely viewed as a "devastating strategic loss" for the United States.[24] The shah and the causes of the Iranian Revolution in 1979 shape the hostilities between Iran and the United States today—a classic case of what the CIA has called "blowback."

Mossadegh's ouster set a precedent for Dulles to continue his strategy. A coup in Guatemala followed, as did rigged elections in Vietnam. In 1951, the Guatemalan president, Jacobo Arbenz, sought to nationalize fruit production—not oil—and redistribute land owned by the United Fruit Company to Guatemalan farmers. That move triggered a campaign by Dulles to discredit Arbenz and remove him from power. As he did in Iran, Dulles paid off the opposition to the democratically elected Arbenz, this time led by Carlos Castillo Armas, a small, reserved man who sported a Hitleresque mustache. The CIA then orchestrated a campaign of propaganda and psychological warfare to discredit Arbenz and boost the image of Castillo Armas among Guatemalans. Castillo Armas soon gained the sympathies of the Guatemalan military. And when Colonel Enrique Díaz León pushed Arbenz out of power in 1954, Castillo Armas replaced him. The CIA also had plans for targeted assassinations of communists after the coup, but Castillo Armas did this work for them, murdering thousands of suspected communists during his three-year autocratic rule before he was assassinated in 1957.[25]

A similar story unfolded in Vietnam, or French Indochina, as it was known until 1955. France launched a counter-revolutionary war in 1945 to defeat Ho Chi Minh and the Vietnamese communists who had taken over the northern part of the country. After a nine-year campaign and a decisive loss at the valley of Dien Bien Phu in 1954 when the French were overrun by communist forces, France signed the Geneva Accords dividing Vietnam along the 17th parallel, pulled out its forces, and promised elections between North and South Vietnam in 1955. The prospect of elections in Vietnam spelled disaster for America's efforts to stop the spread of communism. Any elections held in 1955 surely meant a victory for Ho Chi Minh, who would consolidate his control over the entire country. To prevent this fate, Dulles's CIA sent in Ngo Dinh Diem, who had been in exile in New Jersey during the First Indochina War. Diem fit the bill for an American ally: he dressed in three-piece white suits and was an ardent Catholic and anti-communist. The CIA sent Diem into South Vietnam with American cash and personnel to help stuff ballot boxes and inflate voter rolls during a 1955 referendum to determine who would rule over South Vietnam. Diem won 98.2 percent of the vote, a clear sign that the election was anything but fair and democratic. Diem then suspended elections between the North and South, and the Americans created a permanent state in South Vietnam.

Eight years later, Diem's rule came undone as a result of his autocratic tendencies and reliance on nepotism. His brother-in-law, Ngo Dien Nhu, a well-known opium addict and sociopath, ran the secret police. Nhu arrested, tortured, and killed hundreds of Buddhists and communists—the main opponents of the Diem regime. Diem also created government-run farms,

so-called *agrovilles,* that rounded up Vietnamese peasants, cor-
ralled them with barbed-wire fencing, and prevented free movement in and out of the farms. All in the name of preventing
communism. The Americans became dependent on Diem,
to their detriment. "Shit man, he's the only boy we've got out
there," said Lyndon Johnson, then vice president, about Diem.[26]
Diem's leadership grew tenuous by 1963, and the Kennedy administration gave the green light for a coup to overthrow him,
which led to his assassination on November 2, 1963. Kennedy
himself was killed three weeks later. Diem's death failed to prevent the Americanization of the Vietnam War in 1965—the
main point of the coup. Covert action did not prevent overt
action. And successive South Vietnamese leaders proved just
as unmanageable and authoritarian as Diem. The country went
through a series of corrupt, ineffectual presidents until South
Vietnam collapsed in 1975.

American interventions continued throughout the 1960s.
President Lyndon Johnson sent the 82nd Airborne Division
and the 6th Marine Expeditionary Brigade into the Dominican
Republic in 1965 to squash suspected communist forces during
the Dominican Civil War. Johnson feared that the constitution-
alists who supported the reformer Juan Emilio Bosch Gaviño
(ousted in a military coup in 1963) were taking orders from the
Cuban president, Fidel Castro. Johnson thought that the Dominican Republic would be the next Cuban revolution. "I sure
don't want to wake up . . . and find out Castro's in charge," said
Johnson to his national security adviser McGeorge Bundy.[27] The
invasion left eight Americans dead and proved unnecessary—
Bosch's supporters lost at the ballot box in 1966. Johnson also
supported the massacre of communists in Indonesia. Johnson
let General Suharto massacre members of the Indonesia Communist Party, or the PKI, for months. The United States sup-
plied the weapons and monies for Suharto's men to slaughter

roughly fifteen hundred people a day from September to December 1966.[28]

None of these covert interventions led to ideal outcomes for U.S. grand strategy. Either the United States stabilized the targeted country (and region) for a period before its anointed leader left power or was deposed (in Vietnam or Chile, for instance) or the interventions produced dissent and uprisings that undid the regime and American intentions (in Guatemala, Indonesia, and Iran). The political scientist Lindsay O'Rourke has closely studied U.S. attempts at regime change—and efforts to influence election outcomes abroad—and concluded that they are largely ineffective, if not counterproductive. "US leaders pursued covert regime change based on the assumption that the missions would provide a cheap and permanent solution to their problem, but these outcomes were seldom delivered," she argues.[29]

This history reveals many things: the U.S. government's litany of human rights abuses during the Cold War, the near century-long impunity of decision-makers in the national security state, the hypocrisy of the "liberal world order," and the short-sightedness of a Cold War strategy that discounted the lives of many to serve the interests of a few.

This is far from the full catalog of violence perpetrated in the name of great-power rivalry. The Cold War was also the pretext for America to chemically poison foreign land and waters, forcibly displace populations, and deny self-determination to individuals. In the Pacific, for example, residents of America's territories were denied full sovereignty and exploited for nuclear and missile testing.[30] The United States also supported the overthrow of more than sixty foreign governments, and forty-four of these actions involved taking the side of autocracy.[31] Much more could be said, but the point is clear: the Cold War was not a boon to global democracy.

This history foreshadows the realistic costs and risks of rivalry with China today. Contemporary policymakers cannot elide the failures of Cold War foreign policy, cannot ignore Cold War abuses in imagining a future great-power competition. Panic over the Chinese "spy balloon" in February 2023—Secretary of State Antony Blinken called it a "violation of U.S. sovereignty"—implied a condemnable ignorance of U.S. covert actions during the Cold War and their ramifications. As the historian John Delury argued, the spy balloon incident represented "a kind of farcical reversal of what Communist China faced for decades after its founding in 1949: unrelenting efforts by the United States to spy on—and even subvert—their country." Apoplexy over Chinese balloons will ramp up hawkishness at home, giving comfort to further covert actions.[32]

THE DOMESTIC COLD WAR

The second paradox of the Cold War was the way Americans waged war against political and economic democracy at home in the name of anti-communism.

Among supporters of great-power rivalry, the popular memory of the Cold War is that it produced technological progress and economic growth on an unprecedented scale. It put a man on the moon. It birthed Silicon Valley as an innovation hub. The Cold War created rapid breakthroughs in the arts, science, and medicine—federal dollars financed important research into eradicating diseases such as smallpox. And it even helped Congress pass the Civil Rights Act and the Voting Rights Act. The Cold War forced the United States to confront its racist past and make amends for its injustices. Seen in this way, it is easy to understand why Washington has come to find a "New Cold War" with China not just necessary but good for the United States. Many policymakers earnestly believe that the "arrival of an external competitor has often pushed the United States to become its best self; handled judiciously, it can once again."[33] Or as Hal Brands has suggested, competition resulting from the Cold War "brought out the best in American democracy."[34]

These judgments have some basis in truth, and we do not deny historical facts. But like Washington's memory of how the Cold War was fought abroad, they are ultimately dangerous half-truths. Unlike previous great-power conflicts, democratic concerns—or the perception of democracy—prefigured policymaking. But whereas America's liberal world order departed in some ways from the British model of "liberal empire," it did not always serve democratic ends at home.

Take the issue of the American economy and its growth after World War II. It is true that the United States saw unprecedented growth after the war. Aided by the G.I. Bill in 1944, which spurred rapid rates of homeownership and access to college degrees, Americans increased their disposable incomes by 15 percent. Unemployment averaged 4.6 percent in the 1950s, with more than a third of working-class Americans enrolled in unions. After a brief recession in the late 1950s and early 1960s, U.S. economic growth came roaring back until the late 1960s. Wage growth and disposable income created mass consumption, increased population in cities, and created new jobs and housing developments, particularly in the suburbs.[35] This new era of prosperity meant that many middle-class households—classified as those making more than $5,000 a year—could live on one income. Indeed, the Cold War led to the rise of the male "breadwinner" in many white American families.

But this model had its flaws, and it ultimately fell apart by the 1970s.

The Cold War economy brought fortunes to many, but it also heightened racial and economic inequality. Most of the economic gains of the Cold War went to white Americans. Although

Black Americans were technically eligible for benefits under the G.I. Bill of 1944, they faced redlining by real estate agents and banks reluctant to allocate loans to them, forcing many out of the housing market that promised economic mobility to many whites. Until the passage of the Civil Rights Act in 1964 and the Fair Housing Act of 1968, Blacks had no legal recourse for widespread discrimination in jobs and housing. When employment prospects for Blacks faded because of demobilization after World War II, Blacks scrambled for good jobs and good housing, often falling short of both.

The growth of the Cold War military contributed to this problem. The emergence of the Soviet threat became a question of geography: how could the United States position its military bases in strategically isolated areas, away from industrial centers? Policymakers decided to spread the defense industrial base around the country to resolve this problem. Companies moved out of the Northwest and Mideast and into the rural South and West—into areas where whites were the dominant racial group. Missile silos were installed in remote parts of the Dakotas; undeveloped areas of rural South Carolina were chosen as ideal sites to make fuel for atomic weapons.[36] America's defense industrial base soon became dependent on the production of expensive weaponry, such as intercontinental ballistic missiles and space satellites. This required skilled work by people with advanced degrees. Fewer factories were needed to make these weapons, and fewer jobs were available for Black Americans— who historically had fewer opportunities for education and the skills-building required to obtain jobs in defense.

In Levittown, Long Island, the quintessential postwar blue-collar suburb, many white, skilled workers found jobs in the defense industry after World War II, while most Blacks were excluded from the industry by discrimination in hiring and housing. Defense spending created one out of six jobs on Long Island, but Blacks found few jobs in the industry outside of unskilled positions. Until the Civil Rights Act of 1964 barred discrimination in hiring practices, Blacks had little recourse other than the service industry and sometimes public employment, as police officers and teachers. As a result, Levittown became a haven of racial and economic inequality. Similar patterns were repeated in defense industries in the South and West.[37] The military-industrial complex proved to be—then and now—ineffective at creating diverse jobs for a broad range of workers (compared with other industries such as education and health care) but effective at creating high-level jobs for the already well-to-do. In sum, the Cold War generated economic progress for some, but not for those who needed help the most.[38]

Cold War anti-communism compounded the material difficulties that confronted Blacks. Black Americans delicately navigated the political climate of the Cold War, knowing that challenges to Jim Crow segregation and racial inequality led to charges of being "communist," a term tantamount to "traitor." The first speech of Martin Luther King, Jr., in Montgomery, Alabama, to launch the Montgomery bus boycott in 1955 reflected this new era of politics. King was careful to say that if Blacks in Montgomery "were incarcerated behind the iron curtains of a Communistic nation" or if they "were dropped in the dungeon of a totalitarian regime," their plans for change would be squashed immediately. "But the great glory of American democracy is the right to protest for right," King argued.[39] In this rendition, Black Americans were not interested in revolution; they did not seek to overthrow the system. They simply wanted what the Declaration of Independence granted them in 1776: the recognition that "all men are created equal." King gained a reputation as an "insider," someone who worked alongside Lyndon

Johnson to ensure passage of the Civil Rights Act of 1964 and the Voting Rights Act of 1965 before breaking with LBJ over American involvement in Vietnam.

That didn't stop the federal government from trying to silence King and the civil rights movement. The director of the Federal Bureau of Investigation, J. Edgar Hoover, made it his personal mission to uncover King as America's "most notorious liar," in Hoover's words. Hoover believed with every fiber of his being that King was a communist, that he was a clever subversive, an American Lenin. Hoover wiretapped King's residence, blackmailed him, and tried to force him to commit suicide. The Cold War provided the means for Hoover's threats and surveillance of King. Anti-communism gave Hoover the opportunity to rule without regard for civil liberties. The justification of "national security" gave license to Hoover's rabid anti-communism, his racist tendencies, and his personal animus toward King. Without the Cold War, Hoover could not accomplish what he wanted—he could not erode democracy to save it, in his view.[40]

Besides King—falsely charged as a communist, even as he disavowed ties to communists—there were other prominent, long-standing critics of the federal government who were targeted, such as Paul Robeson, W. E. B. Du Bois, Lorraine Hansberry, and Malcolm X. Some were open socialists. They faced widespread FBI surveillance and public antipathy throughout their lifetimes. Robeson, a renowned singer and actor, held communist sympathies that led to the revocation of his passport and blacklisting in Hollywood. Hansberry, the playwright and novelist, also suffered for her anti-colonialism and Marxism in her short life. Like her compatriots, Hansberry experienced extensive FBI monitoring, with the FBI opening an investigation into her now lauded play *A Raisin in the Sun*, fearing it might be "controlled or influenced by the Communist Party" and probing "whether it in any way follows the Communist line."[41] Du Bois was tried and eventually acquitted for being a "foreign agent" after setting up the Peace Information Center in New York, but the damage was done. The trial forced the closure of the Peace Information Center and the delegitimization of his peace efforts, which were caught in a larger state repression of peace activism in the early Cold War.[42] Malcolm X, meanwhile, was thought to be a communist, in Hoover's view, as far back as the early 1950s. Hoover blamed Malcolm X for the 1964 Harlem riots, saying he inspired "hoodlums" to violence.[43]

One may be tempted to say that Hoover's decisions were unrepresentative of the federal government's approach to the civil rights movement. Hoover's legacy is in tatters; the FBI has learned from its mistakes. The FBI's defenders would point out that presidents and congressional figures had more impact than Hoover—both Democratic and Republican presidents believed the problem of the color line impeded the egalitarian "image" of American democracy during the Cold War, and they acted accordingly. Eisenhower sent the 101st Airborne into Little Rock to desegregate Central High School in 1957 over fears that the incident would be fodder for *Pravda* and Soviet media. John F. Kennedy criticized Governor George Wallace's tactics to stop the integration of the University of Alabama because they contradicted America's "worldwide struggle to promote and protect the rights of all who wish to be free."[44] These decisions are important benchmarks in the history of the civil rights movement, but they ignore the point that creatures like Hoover thrive in the boggy waters of Cold War rivalry. These more pro-democratic moments are also far from the whole story.

The Cold War often hindered rather than furthered racial progress. Until World War II, a broad coalition of left-leaning activists, artists, bureaucrats, lawyers, and intellectuals held sway under Roosevelt's New Deal. Known as the "Popular Front,"

this coalition mobilized around social democratic policies—
what would now be called "democratic socialist" policies—that
saw cooperation and organizing between liberals and leftists,
between New Dealers and communists. At a time when capitalism seemed doomed—mass unemployment, business failures,
and homelessness during the Great Depression—liberals ap-
preciated communists' utopian visions, while communists saw
liberals as useful allies who could influence New Deal policy.

    For much of the 1930s and 1940s, the top priorities for
Black Americans were equal access to jobs and to the ballot
box. The Popular Front helped organize Black Americans in
unions, including the Congress of Industrial Organizations and
the United Auto Workers, to achieve these goals. Black membership in trade unions soared after the mid-1930s, with five
hundred thousand Blacks having joined unions such as the
CIO. Union membership provided wage growth and job stability to large numbers of African Americans, with communists
and radicals leading the way with their vision of racial equality
beginning at the workplace but spreading to the voting booth
and social life.[45] The Popular Front also provided momentum
to the Democratic Party. Black socialists including A. Philip
Randolph rallied behind President Franklin Roosevelt and
his New Deal in the mid-1930s alongside Black liberals in the
National Association for the Advancement of Colored People
(NAACP), such as Walter White. FDR's vision of social democracy, one that included Black Americans, despite the racial barriers to federal employment and monies, made the 1936 election the first time in history that most Black Americans voted
for a Democratic president.[46] The Popular Front provided vital
support to Franklin Roosevelt during the interwar years, cam-
paigning for racial equality and a restrained foreign policy. Indeed, alongside communists in groups such as the American

League Against War and Fascism, the theologian and future Cold War liberal Reinhold Niebuhr critiqued the "capitalist forces" behind American power. The outbreak of World War II created fissures in the Popular Front, particularly among communists, but support for Roosevelt and the defeat of fascism (at home and abroad), the two pillars of the Popular Front, endured.[47]

But the Cold War killed off the Popular Front and its vision for a multiracial democracy. The Red Scare of the late 1940s and 1950s—the creation of federal loyalty programs, the suspicion that communists occupied positions in government and schools, the pervasive fear of "socialism" in all its forms—decimated the ranks of the left, particularly the Black left. Fears of communism forced civil rights organizations into repudiating leftists they once considered allies. Black leaders in the NAACP publicly dissociated themselves from reported communists in the pages of their newspaper, *The Crisis*. White liberals pulled out of coalitions with communists, including political parties such as the Minnesota-based Democratic Farmer-Labor Party.[48] Many Americans lost jobs, had their reputations sullied, or were ostracized from public life, but the Red Scare most affected social movements and social progress for Black Americans.

And while the Cold War encouraged presidents and congressional officials to intervene on behalf of racial justice, it also deprioritized the Popular Front's—and the larger civil rights movement's—focus on jobs and voting, on universal programs, on cross-racial organizing, in favor of other issues such as school desegregation. Well-minded but elite Supreme Court justices ruled unanimously for school desegregation in *Brown v. Board of Education* in 1954 because it had no effect on their lives—and because they believed the integration of schools represented an enlightened and moral act. Fraught and contentious, bound up in the politics of children and the family, the goal of integrated schools was at the bottom of the civil rights agenda until 1954. When school desegregation became the preeminent issue after *Brown,* it produced a backlash that expedited federal involvement in the civil rights movement (in Little Rock to support the Black children attending Central High School in 1957 and in Tuscaloosa to enforce the desegregation of the University of Alabama in 1963). But the focus on school desegregation meant it took ten years for voting rights to rise to the forefront once again.[49] The Cold War controlled the pace of progress, the nature of change—and indeed, campaigns for more high-paying, unionized jobs for Black workers and for fair and affordable housing have yet to be realized. The history of the civil rights movement might be radically different had it not been for the Cold War.

Blacks were not the only minorities to suffer from communist witch hunts. After the Chinese Communist Party took hold over China, self-interested and self-righteous politicians took advantage of the situation to claim communists lurked everywhere: in government, in academia, and in the halls of public schools. A new Red Scare, McCarthyism, named after the most vocal proponent of red-baiting, swept over American life, ruining the reputations and careers of many Americans. After the Chinese Revolution of 1949, Chinese Americans were accused of fraudulently entering the United States, of being alien citizens, "illegal." If Chinese Americans "confessed" to their illegality, the U.S. State Department promised to help them change their citizenship status "if at all possible under the law." Many did become legal, but that did not change cultural perceptions that the Chinese were traitors. As the historian Mae Ngai has argued, "Cold War politics . . . reproduced racialized perceptions that all Chinese immigrants were illegal and dangerous" no matter their citizenship status.[50]

And the Cold War reinforced inequality for women too. Whereas World War II brought the entry of large numbers of white middle-class women into the workforce—poor women, predominantly of color, had always worked in the United States—the Cold War pushed women back into the domestic sphere. Women were told to be consumers, child bearers, the stalwarts of American values. The good living wages paid to the highly unionized industrial working classes depended on keeping women out of the workforce, making labor artificially scarce. The reproduction of Cold War economic life up through the 1970s was based on a social order that encouraged women to stay at home doing "hidden" labor that the economy simultaneously relied on but did not value.[51] Women were to support the fight against communism by "teaching and preaching the values of individualism and personal freedom."[52]

The limits to women's freedom in the United States led Betty Friedan to publish *The Feminine Mystique* in 1963 and to found the National Organization for Women in 1964. The women's movement organized around the premise that Cold War America reduced their opportunities outside of motherhood, stifled their creativity, and did violence to their potential as full human beings. Cold War ideas of "womanhood" limited their autonomy. "Who knows what women can be when they are finally free to become themselves?" asked Friedan.[53]

Women employed a critique of the Cold War as part of asserting their agency and obtaining rights in the United States after the 1950s. Women weaponized the gendered politics of the Cold War to campaign for jobs and opportunities outside the household. In 1961, two years before Friedan released *The Feminine Mystique,* fifty thousand women protested to stop nuclear testing, arguing that radiation from atomic weapons was getting into their children's milk. Women also played important roles in the New Left that formed in the early 1960s. The New Left opposed not only the Vietnam War but also the way the United States fought against communism. Through groups like Students for a Democratic Society (SDS), the New Left argued that U.S. "paranoia about the Soviet Union" threatened the "preservation of peace."[54]

Women in the New Left saw their struggle for equality as one conjoined with the anti-war movement. Women organized and turned out in the streets by the thousands for the Women Strike for Peace march in January 1968, seeking an end to American involvement in Vietnam but also greater representation for women in the public sphere.[55] The Women's Strike for Equality in 1970 had similar origins. One of the strike's organizers, Ruthann Miller, was, in her words, "a nonpolitical ballet dancer who joined the anti–Vietnam War movement" in the 1960s. From there, she went on to organize the Strike for Equality with Betty Friedan, advocating for three demands: access to abortion, universal childcare, and equal employment for women.[56] As Miller's experience proves, only by rejecting gendered tropes about women's "roles" and "responsibilities" during the Cold War, and aligning them with a critique of Cold War foreign policy, did the women's rights movement make headway in American politics.

In the aggregate, this history presents a more complicated, and dire, picture of how rivalry has shaped American democracy. The Cold War bestowed good jobs, excellent housing, and social mobility for the already fortunate. When it did provide economic uplift to the working class, it did so in unequal, racialized terms. American policymakers only intervened on the right side of history when they feared that civil rights gave fodder to Soviet claims of American hypocrisy. And the

Cold War actively disenfranchised women in the United States until the 1960s.

If we are looking for great-power competition to provide democracy in the broadest sense, to disenfranchised groups, we should look elsewhere. Those who believe that great-power competition will invigorate domestic life ignore this history at their peril.

Conclusion

President Biden rested his domestic and foreign policy agenda on rivalry with China. He hoped, like Cold War presidents before him, that rivalry would invigorate domestic policy through a foreign enemy. Biden officials imagined a political economy that shaped the fortunes of the middle class through federal spending—a rising tide lifting all boats. By confronting China the way a previous generation confronted the Soviet Union, two of President Biden's foremost Asia experts asserted in 2020, "American leaders can begin to reverse the impression of U.S. decline."[57] In an environment of highly fractured domestic politics, "China may be the last bipartisan issue left in Washington."[58] Some commentators have looked to the Cold War to save American democracy, noting, "George Kennan's strategy of containment is not a bad model" for confronting China today.[59] But, as we will show, this worldview is profoundly misguided. Treating the Cold War as a template for great-power relations—implicitly or explicitly—is freighted with unacknowledged problems that policymakers have thus far ignored.

Critics of our argument might point out that ideology (anti-communism) no longer plays a role in great-power rivalry (untrue). No one has lost a job because of the U.S. rivalry with China (untrue).[60] Joseph McCarthy has no equal today (he has been replaced by a sea of demagogues). The worst excesses of the Cold War (Vietnam, the Red Scare, coups in Iran and Guatemala) are behind us; the U.S. acknowledged its errors abroad before and after the Cold War ended (mostly untrue).

Putting aside that this is all incorrect, these premises imagine that the United States can do great-power competition better than it did before. But even if such claims were true, and even if China rivalry is the best version of great-power competition (less rapacious and colonial than the great-power rivalry of the eighteenth and nineteenth centuries, fewer misguided proxy wars and rigged elections in the Global South than there were in the Cold War era), it will not yield better results for democracy.

In fact, the current incarnation of great-power competition presents an even greater problem for democracy. Anticommunism led to disastrous repercussions for Americans at home, proving deleterious to shaping the material conditions that could foster greater racial and economic equality. But anticommunism still provided a patina of social democracy. U.S. leaders pursued some social progress because formalized apartheid in the U.S. South imperiled the perception of American liberal democracy. Rivalry with the Soviet Union was not the goal of the United States. Rather, competition became the means to what American policymakers thought would be democratic ends. American primacy, devotion to the "liberal world order," they mistakenly believed, would create a better, more peaceful world. When Soviet propaganda pointed to the Jim Crow South as evidence to the contrary, policymakers felt that they had to acknowledge that reality and neutralize the Soviet's line of argument by improving American democracy.

Those motivations for building social democracy are gone now, leaving only competition as the sine qua non of China rivalry.[61] But U.S. grand strategy must not conflate its means with ends. The justification for competition (preventing China's ascendancy) cannot be the ends of competition. If rivalry with

China is the reason to rebuild American infrastructure and expedite advances in dealing with climate change, then when rivalry goes—because China declines or a new challenger distracts us again—so will the reasons for investing in good jobs and saving the planet. And in the meantime, our way of life is made to rely on the perpetual preparation for extinction-level war.

Finally, even though the fevered anti-communism of the 1950s is gone, politicians and bad-faith actors continue to employ Cold War tropes to silence those pushing for domestic reform. Joe Biden, no card-carrying socialist, was pilloried as a "puppet" of the Chinese Communist Party by members of the Republican Party, including Donald Trump. Cold War attacks have outlasted the Cold War.[62] We can expect these broadsides to continue if the United States hangs the future of global democracy on rivalry with China.

Fears of losing American democracy to communists led to the abuse of democratic rights during the Cold War. We cannot expect a new era of great-power competition to be different.

2

The Fall and Return of Rivalry

The fall of the Berlin Wall in November 1989 meant the world no longer needed to fear communism. In his State of the Union address in 1992, President George H. W. Bush told Americans that the "biggest thing that has happened in the world in my life, in our lives, is this: By the grace of God, America won the cold war." Sixteen months before this address, on another September 11th—September 11, 1990—Bush spoke of a "new world order" that promised cooperation between the two former rivals. Bush foresaw an era of global relations ruled by collective security, with the dominance of the United States—and democratic capitalism—unquestioned, even celebrated.[1] A Pax Americana was here to stay.

As Bush indicated in his State of the Union speech, U.S. policymakers believed they had outright "won" the Cold War. The fact that the United States had single-handedly caused the demise of global communism seemed irrefutable. How else could the Soviet Union have met its end? The line of thinking went as follows: the Soviet Union depleted its coffers trying to outspend the United States on defense during the presidency of Ronald Reagan. The allure of democracy and free expression enticed the East Germans, Poles, and Russians to revolt against autocracy. Globalization created access to American consumer goods that Russians wanted and could not obtain, so they rejected state socialism. The American example—what George Kennan envisioned as the backbone of "containment"— prevailed over the Soviet model. These factors—the United States—collectively brought down the Soviet Union.[2]

The feeling that the United States—and by extension, the world—had won the Cold War created a triumphalist spirit that pervaded American politics and culture in the 1990s. Francis Fukuyama proclaimed an "end to history" in the pages of *The National Interest;* the fame of this declaration captured the zeitgeist that it crystallized. Experts and pundits wrote book-length obituaries for great-power war. Americans were told to expect an enduring "unipolar" era, one unique to global history.[3] The United States had become the most powerful country in both economic and military terms; it had no rival on the horizon. Few in the United States wanted to believe, let alone contemplate, the reality that the Soviet Union imploded due to its internal contradictions and inabilities to modernize its government and economy; that ineffectual leadership handicapped Soviet progress; that the Politburo tore its own house down.

The myth of an all-powerful United States, of a beacon of liberty vanquishing its ultimate foe during the second half of the twentieth century, proved too powerful. This version of the Cold War's demise prepared policymakers for a new era of global relations in which they would "lead" the world. The zeal with which U.S. policymakers rushed into a "New Cold War" did not occur in a historical vacuum. The interregnum following the U.S.-Soviet Cold War encouraged romantic memories of the Cold War while laying the groundwork for the return of geopolitical rivalry.[4]

Cold War triumphalism had its upsides. Many Americans thought the end of the Cold War allowed the United States to put its domestic house in order. President Bush spoke of a "peace dividend": the federal dollars that could be used for non-military purposes given the absence of the Cold War. Democrats and some Republicans (including President Bush) requested cuts to military spending. Civil rights activists in the United States hoped that international peace meant a renewed commitment to the social welfare state. John E. Jacob, president of the National Urban League, called for an "Urban Marshall Plan," echoing visions of a "Marshall Plan for the Cities" first announced by Vice President Hubert Humphrey in 1967.[5] A national consensus took hold that the past could not be our present in terms of how the government spent its dollars on defense. There would be a greater focus on housing, poverty, and racial justice. With no more monsters to destroy, there had to be.

But faith in a new world order and a peace dividend dissipated during the 1990s and altogether disappeared after the 9/11 attacks. The War on Terror demanded that Washington wield its power on behalf of humanity once more, to extirpate terrorism from the world. That project proved disastrous. The idea of defeating terrorism proved, as some predicted, illogical and outright Sisyphean. But the United States tried nonetheless, expending $8 trillion that led to more than nine hundred thousand deaths.[6] Throughout the 1990s and up until the 2010s, the United States planned to be the sole superpower, the only actor capable of making world order. The War on Terror nullified the idea that the United States could, indeed should, be overseeing global affairs, that the "unipolar moment" stabilized the world. Critics of the War on Terror could point to two failed wars (in Afghanistan and Iraq), indiscriminate drone attacks on populations in the Middle East that led to civilian casualties, and a culture of xenophobia and anti-Muslim sentiment that inflamed right-wing zealots like Donald Trump.

But by the end of Barack Obama's administration, the War on Terror had waned, and China materialized as the ultimate threat. The United States went from being preoccupied with nation-building in Afghanistan and eliminating ISIS in Iraq to confronting China in little more than five years. In 2009, President Obama argued that "the security of the United States and the safety of the American people were at stake in Afghanistan"; but in 2011—amid the United States' efforts to "withdraw its forces from Afghanistan"—a shift to the Indo-Pacific became essential "to secure and sustain America's global leadership."[7] And by 2015, Washington seemed to be laying the groundwork for a future containment policy aimed at China.

In time, the PRC rejected American unilateralism and the political implications of the unipolar moment. A series of economic crises in the 1990s, compounded by distrust and opposition to the Bush Doctrine's claim of a right to preventive military attacks, the Iraq War, and the evolution of the War on Terror, made Chinese leadership skeptical that a U.S.-led, unipolar world would serve its best interests. After the Great Recession in 2008 and the quagmire in Iraq, China took subtle but concrete steps to create economic and political alliances in the Global South, where American influence was ebbing. Chinese leaders looked at the international crises in the West and saw them as making the world less stable.[8] China would have to venture out on its own to avoid succumbing to the downfalls of Western markets and confronting the United States' mismanagement of international affairs. China's rise as an economic and political power heightened tensions between the two countries and was a necessary condition for the return of rivalry.[9]

How did rivalry return, and why so quickly? Part of the

answer has to do with internal changes to China during the late 1990s and 2000s. China's rapid and exponential growth—its GDP increase of 3.9 percent in 1990 rose to 14.2 percent in 1992, before dipping to 7.7 percent in 1999—allowed the country to exert greater influence on the world stage. China's capital accumulation bankrolled the industrial policy and military modernization that gradually shifted the balance of power in the Taiwan Strait—raising fears in Washington that China could become America's principal rival in future years.

Another part of the answer lies in the spectacular failure of the War on Terror. By 2012, Iraq and Afghanistan seemed beyond repair—or the closest they would get to stability. When the War on Terror fell apart, national security agencies found their opportunity to redirect U.S. foreign policy to their new "great power" priorities (specifically China, and to a much lesser extent Russia).[10] The collapse of the War on Terror allowed a select group of U.S. policymakers, ones who had planned for rivalry with China since the 1990s, to rise to the fore. Indeed, the much touted "pivot" to Asia had been the vision of some officials well before the Obama administration.[11]

These events collectively reveal how the unipolar moment institutionalized great-power rivalry in the twenty-first century. Well before China became the major rival to the United States, a section of American policymakers assumed it would be. National security officials did not will the China threat into existence—both the Clinton and the George W. Bush administrations mostly avoided the language of "competition" and "threats" when it came to China. Rivalry became our present because U.S. preeminence became the sole lens through which to see our future, of what was possible, making us alert to anything or anyone that might challenge our ability to dominate. This did not happen overnight and at many points could have been prevented.

From Cooperation to Engagement

The 1990s represented a time of rethinking, of reimagining U.S. foreign policy. Not since World War II had policymakers dealt with a world without major enemies. A paradigm shift in U.S. grand strategy seemed necessary, even inevitable.

President George H. W. Bush, somewhat reluctantly, recognized the political moment and sought to meet it. In addition to his references to a "new world order," Bush knew that the U.S. military would not fight conventional wars for the foreseeable future. No equivalent power could challenge America's status in the world; the United States didn't need—and many Americans didn't want—its Cold War military. "There is almost euphoria about the declining threat and talk of a $60 billion peace dividend," Bush told the British prime minister Margaret Thatcher in January 1990. "There are a lot of weirdos over here who have all sorts of crazy ideas," he added.[12]

Bush knew the status quo would not stand. Republican stalwarts like Dick Cheney, then secretary of defense under Bush, also conceded to the "new world order" in terms of defense strategy. Cheney proposed a 10 percent cut to military spending in 1990, which included a 25 percent reduction in military personnel.[13] Many Democrats thought Cheney could go further. Democratic representative Les Aspin said the Pentagon needed "fundamental new thinking" about the size and purpose of the defense budget. Even former Reagan officials like Fred Ikle, once responsible for the largest peacetime buildup in history during the 1980s, felt that massive cuts in defense were warranted.[14] "Stalin has been buried twice in Moscow, but his ghost lives on in the Pentagon," said Ikle. In a statement that now seems unfathomable, the longtime defense intellectual William Kaufmann said in 1990, "I reject the argument that the Navy performs some pacifying function by floating around

the South China Sea or something." Kaufmann wanted to see
military spending reduced by half.[15]

These statements, this history, all occurred before the Soviet Union formally collapsed. When the Soviet Union did fall
in December 1991, Bush capitulated to proponents of additional
defense cuts, requesting $7 billion for fiscal year 1993 with an
additional $50 billion over the next four years. The next threats
appeared amorphous, uncertain. For the Pentagon, the lack of
a superpower rival meant U.S. primacy would not be especially
at risk; there were no peer competitors, so even with cuts the
United States would remain preeminent. But whatever threats
lay on the other side of the Cold War, Bush knew that Americans' "long drawn-out dread is over." With "imperial Communism gone, that process [of defense cuts] can be accelerated."[16]

Congress, again, thought Bush too conservative on defense cuts. The Republican John McCain, no dove on defense
in his lifetime, complained about Bush's recalcitrance. "The Administration is behind the curve," said McCain in 1992. "The
fact is that we all know, beyond any possible doubt, that the
Soviet Union isn't about to launch an attack." Democrats continued to push for further reductions in defense, wanting the
peace dividend promised to Americans. Some fought for 70
percent of the cuts in the military to be reallocated to creating
jobs, improving housing and education, and fighting pandemics like the AIDS crisis. Bush stonewalled on this plan, but the
final version of his defense budget reflected the inevitable conclusion that cuts were politically necessary.[17]

In 1992, Bush lost the presidency to Bill Clinton, who
inherited Bush's reluctance to make rapid changes to military
spending. Although Clinton avoided mention of a "new world
order," he knew that he needed a foreign policy for a post–Cold
War era. Clinton announced plans to close military bases (and
convert them to shopping centers and civilian purposes) but

had no vision for defense conversion—to remake the political economy of military spending. And his administration remained aloof from the National Commission for Economic Conversion and Disarmament, which had detailed plans for how to build a post-military Keynesian economy—plans with little traction so long as the United States persisted with global primacy as its mission.[18] Clinton's national security strategy pivoted to preventing "failed states," to ensuring humanitarian ends. With no singular threat but rather a series of destabilizing actors and events, Clinton sought, through the barrel of a gun if necessary, to spread liberal values and prove the liberal world order had indeed prevailed. With a hammer, every crisis looked like a nail.

Pentagon planners feared that the United States lacked sufficient urgency and preparation to confront the next great power, the future Soviet Union. National security officials engaged in long-term strategic planning dedicated their time to finding the next Soviet counterpart. The skeptics, if not detractors, of the peace dividend wanted the United States to remain vigilant, to prevent new threats rather than waiting for their formation.

Staff from the office in charge of drafting the Defense Planning Guidance (DPG) emerged as the most influential of the Pentagon hawks. Led by the future architect of the Iraq War, Paul Wolfowitz, Zalmay Khalilzad authored a strategic planning document in February 1992—three months after the Soviet Union fell—with the purpose of articulating a strategic path forward for the Pentagon in a unipolar age. The mission: prevent other nations from competing with the United States. "Our first objective is to prevent the reemergence of a new rival . . . that poses a threat on the order of that formerly posed by the Soviet Union."[19]

Americans should not rest on their laurels. Don't enjoy

peace. The United States "must now refocus on precluding the emergence of any potential future global competitor."[20] Other recommendations emerged from this Cold War–like mutation in thinking about the world: maintain military and nuclear deterrence, ensure global markets remain favorable to U.S. interests, shore up alliances in Asia—expressions of U.S. dominance presented as if the United States had ignored these goals for decades. In an era of unrivaled American primacy, the aim of foreign policy would be to ensure it. This was tautology disguised as grand strategy. The DPG's recommendations were not wholly embraced by the Bush White House, but they still represented a potent strand of thinking among national security officials who went on to occupy key positions in future Republican administrations. As the historian Hal Brands has argued, the DPG did "incite much controversy" in the immediate aftermath of its publication, but "its core elements would prove quite enduring."[21]

The DPG had no specific country in mind as potential aggressor to the United States. That task, naming a belligerent, eventually fell to Andrew ("Andy") Marshall. Marshall oversaw the Office of Net Assessment (ONA), which operated as the Defense Department's equivalent to the State Department's Policy Planning Staff. Founded and headed by Marshall since 1973, the ONA had a prestigious record of anticipating the evolution of Soviet capabilities, of showing policymakers "how to plan for long, open-ended conflicts."[22] Critics pointed out that Marshall also engaged in a great deal of guesswork, that his pessimistic if not cynical view of the world led him to find prospective threats so they could become real, or that he was uniquely positioned to know what Washington insiders wanted to hear.[23] And since ONA's mandate was studying "long-term competition" and the balance of military forces, it could never see international politics outside of a competitive framework. Nevertheless, Marshall became a guru to many in the national security establishment, a sage of sorts.[24] Colleagues and friends, even President George W. Bush, referred to him as a "Yoda."

Marshall posited in 1987 that China would rival American preeminence in thirty years. As Mikhail S. Gorbachev rapidly eroded the foundations of the Soviet state, Marshall did not hesitate to single out China as its replacement. Only China had the economic dynamism and foreign policy background to challenge the United States.[25] Much of Chinese domestic policy in the 1980s seemed, if not haphazard and experimental, then at least very far from indicating hegemonic ambitions; the China of the late Cold War bore little resemblance to the Washington image of China today as a great-power totalitarian with visions of global dominance. Indeed, Deng Xiaoping had only Chinese stability in mind in the 1980s; he had "no grand plan" for the country's economic growth.[26] But this did not matter for Marshall, who traded in predictions masquerading as "strategic assessments" for a living. China, Marshall argued, would soon have the means and capabilities to become a rival great power. The ongoing "structural changes connected with the rise of China" put the country on a crooked but certain path to great-power status. And, by definition, the existence of other great powers presented an automatic challenge to a grand strategy of primacy. For net assessment thinkers like Marshall, the likely "changes in warfare," including new technologies and the appearance of informational war, alongside China's countervailing views to liberal world order, exacerbated the potential for conflict.[27]

Marshall's prophetic acumen coincided with a Clinton administration that facilitated China's rise in an era of economic globalization, even as some of the president's advisers had lingering anxieties over China's growing power. Clinton recognized that China exceeded all rivals for the status of "the fastest growing economy in the world." This startled some Clinton officials, who wondered if China could emerge as a great power in the immediate future.[28]

But a meaningful challenge from China seemed a distant possibility at the time, and China never held Clinton's attention for very long. When it did, he vacillated between lambasting China's human rights record and preaching the inevitability of China's pending political reforms, which were thought to follow its economic reforms. Clinton embraced liberal humanitarianism as the cornerstone of U.S. foreign policy without relinquishing a position of global primacy. Clinton believed deeply in "democratic peace theory," the idea that democratic countries do not wage war against each other. To him, democratic peace theory was perfectly compatible with military and economic preeminence. With the Cold War gone, the United States could fulfill a strategy of "democratic enlargement" that allowed "democracy and market economies [to] take root in regions of greatest humanitarian concern." American power could provide protection for freedom and liberal values to all the world, unfettered by fears of nuclear war or Soviet counterattack.[29]

China was a fly in the ointment of Clinton's grand strategy. The United States had no military ambitions in China and no interest in curtailing Chinese growth, but it would not allow the "butchers of Beijing" to threaten American power, said Clinton. When China tested ballistic missiles and conducted military exercises near Taiwan in 1996, Clinton responded by sending U.S. aircraft carriers toward the Taiwan Strait.[30] The Chinese took the confrontation no further, but Republicans still thought Clinton should hew a tougher line on China. In later years, members of the GOP accused Clinton of "outright appeasement" toward China, even going so far as to claim that "the United States has actually helped create a new superpower threat."[31] The brief military confrontation over Taiwan did give impetus to the People's Liberation Army to modernize its military to fare better in future conflicts and crises with the United States. But there is no reason to think a different (especially Republican) president would have navigated the crisis any differently.

Sanctimonious language from the GOP failed to change the structure of U.S.-China relations in the 1990s. Posturing over the Taiwan Strait aside, Clinton sought collaboration with China on most issues. Clinton did not fear China. Clinton officials believed that China would shift toward economic and political liberalization, that the PRC could not ignore the tide of history but would be swept up by it. China would not be a belligerent superpower, not in the long term. It would remain a "strategic partner," as Clinton called it.[32] Republican attacks on China continued in the 1990s but failed to influence U.S. foreign policy. In opposing the renewal of Most Favored Nation (MFN) status for China in 1996, the Republican representative Frank R. Wolf, from Virgina, argued that China posed an existential threat to global freedom: "This is fundamentally an evil group of people. This is the evil empire of modern times." But a renewal of MFN status sailed through Congress.[33]

Still, to those at the White House and the Pentagon, China's human rights record—alongside threats from terrorism, acts of genocide, and coups—demonstrated that the world remained a dangerous place. Clinton felt he must act accordingly. He removed American troops from Somalia in 1993 after a failed military operation that led to the deaths of eighteen soldiers—immortalized in the Ridley Scott film *Black Hawk Down*—but then sent troops into Haiti in 1994 to restore the ousted leader Jean-Bertrand Aristide under "Operation Uphold Democracy." Clinton also launched a bombing campaign against Iraq in 1993 that he periodically halted and resumed throughout his presidency. Progressive officials including Congressman Ron

Dellums from Oakland did not want to give up on the promise of a better America, of a new era of peace. "There can still be a peace dividend," Dellums claimed in 1994. "The question is whether we have the political will to do it."[34]

Intellectuals and activists also hoped the peace dividend would endure. Members of the National Commission for Economic Conversion and Disarmament organized conferences and wrote reports arguing that more needed to be done to support laid-off defense workers. The committee comprised economists such as Ann Markusen, Christine Evans-Clock, and Seymour Melman, representatives from labor unions like the AFL-CIO, and Democratic politicians. It was not partisan, it avoided grandstanding, and it relied on technocratic knowledge and academic studies to ground its advocacy. The commission held conferences and panels on the layoffs of employees in the defense industry, the lack of federal assistance to defense communities, and Congress's hostility toward additional funding for conversion. The federal government needed a comprehensive strategy for conversion; it could not be handled piecemeal. The question of "what economic stimulus will replace the role once played by military spending in the economy" remained open. Given "there's little likelihood of catastrophic war," the United States must reimagine its economy and whether the current size of the defense industry served the interests of workers and economic growth in the United States.[35]

Clinton knew that "catastrophic wars" were unlikely, but he also believed that activists' vision of a peace dividend, as they conceived of it, would be impossible. Obsessed with preventing "failed states" (Haiti) and spreading liberal values, Clinton refused any reform that left the United States unable to patrol the globe to stamp out threats to democracy or to allies in democratic countries. The United States also faced increased threats from Islamic terrorists at the time, including the bombing of the World Trade Center in 1993, the bombing of American embassies in Kenya and Tanzania in 1998, and the attack on the USS *Cole* in 2000. Indeed, Clinton bombed Afghanistan in 1998 in retaliation for the embassy attacks and launched a comprehensive campaign to find Osama bin Laden, the mastermind of many of the attacks. Clinton then supported an aerial assault by the North Atlantic Treaty Organization (NATO) on Kosovo in March 1999 to overthrow Slobodan Milosevic and stop the ethnic cleansing of Albanians in the country. The air campaign achieved its ends—Milosevic was ousted in 1999. American power liberated Kosovo. The Kosovo bombing tested Clinton's vision of militarized liberal humanitarianism—channeled through institutions of collective security like NATO—and it passed, with international backing.

Domestic politics also intervened to kill the peace dividend. A fiscal hawk, Clinton allocated most savings from defense to deficit reduction. His choices on how to spend the peace dividend, combined with his foreign policy of threat reduction and democracy promotion across continents, meant the end to any future without massive military spending. Add to this the sense among Clinton officials that market-based policies and solutions would heal what ails the economy, and the result led to a malformed, half-hearted effort at conversion.[36]

But when terrorists flew commercial planes into the World Trade Center and the Pentagon on September 11, 2001, killing three thousand Americans, it changed everything. Prior to the 9/11 attacks, national security officials saw threats in the homeland from dirty bombs and biological weapons originating from rogue states like North Korea, Iraq, Iran, and Libya.[37] The method and origins of the 9/11 attacks took officials in the U.S. government by surprise and refocused U.S. foreign policy on eliminating Islamic terrorists. President George W. Bush, who defeated the Democrat Al Gore in the presidential election of

2000—decided by the Supreme Court in a 5–4 ruling—declared a "War on Terror" days after the attacks.

The United States sought revenge for the 9/11 attacks. Angry, scared, and motivated by fear, the United States sent troops into Afghanistan the next month with the aim of finding Bin Laden and the other masterminds behind the 9/11 attacks. Bush also hoped to oust the Taliban regime that harbored Bin Laden and other members of Al Qaeda. The events of 9/11 also created a surge of patriotism and nationalism in the United States that revived instinctual, visceral animosity to Muslims. Bush outwardly tried to quell the raging xenophobia in the country—Americans were not at war with Islam, he said. But his policies—militarizing police departments, global primacy, multiple wars, heightened global surveillance, a CIA "enhanced interrogation" torture program, and the creation of a Department of Homeland Security obsessed with borders, immigration, and "insider" threats—ensured that fear won the day.[38]

The response to 9/11 also revealed the dominance of asymmetric warfare. The fight against Al Qaeda would rely on the "Revolution in Military Affairs" (RMA) model first promulgated by Andy Marshall. Marshall believed that the United States was in the middle of a rapid shift in technological capabilities that rendered old ways of fighting obsolete and overwrought. Guided missiles and the quest for "information supremacy" determined the victors.[39] The militaries used in D-Day and Vietnam—hundreds of thousands of ground personnel—were for history books. The RMA meant depending on a light military footprint, innovative weaponry to ferret out terrorists in hiding, and precision aerial assaults to bomb terrorists—or suspected terrorists—without risking American casualties. The secretary of defense, Donald Rumsfeld, embraced the tenets of the RMA, and it dominated America's vision for fighting the

global war on terror. In Iraq, Afghanistan, Yemen, and Syria—
the major sites of the War on Terror—the United States avoided
a Vietnam-like war relying on half a million troops. Instead,
the United States used air power to "shock and awe," armed
proxies and insurgents, and relied on technology and intelligence to win wars against terrorists.

The ascendance of asymmetric warfare meant that the
probability of great-power war faded into the distance. Islamic
terrorism, as a phenomenon, became Washington's number
one enemy. Terms like "balance of power," "spheres of influence," or "nuclear parity"—terms associated with the Cold War,
with great-power conflict—meant little when fighting guerrilla armies whose main weapons were improvised explosive
devices (IEDs) and Kalashnikov assault rifles. The United States
had faced guerrilla armies during the Vietnam War, and that
conflict loomed large over how the United States should fight—
and avoid losing—this new era of asymmetric warfare. But as
with Vietnam, a global war on terror demanded supremacy,
which some Bush-friendly intellectuals, such as Michael Ig-
natieff, Niall Ferguson, and Donald Kagan, thought should constitute a new liberal empire.[40] Most were not so brazen, prefer-
ring hegemony without the appearance of empire, showing a
commitment to a global military presence but a rhetorical reluctance to wage war indefinitely, while still knowing that the
"war against terror will be long."[41]

George W. Bush's cabinet wanted a different foreign policy before 9/11. Bush's "Vulcans," his collection of neoconserva-
tive advisers and officials—many of them veterans of the Reagan administration—prioritized China. They believed China
should be viewed with genuine skepticism, if not outright hostility. China menaced Taiwan with displays of military power,
devalued the yuan to weaken the dollar, and disregarded

human rights. Clinton had acknowledged these realities, too, but thought China could be reasoned with, like any other state with rational leadership.

How the War on Terror
Primed Great-Power Rivalry

Bush wanted to pursue a tougher attitude than his predecessor toward China. On the campaign trail in 2000, Bush said that China should be "viewed as a competitor, and a strategic competitor." This statement provided the backdrop for the president's early positions on China. As president, Bush made ambiguous comments about abandoning "strategic ambiguity," saying that he would do "Whatever it took to help Taiwan defend theirself [*sic*]." The deputy secretary of defense, Paul Wolfowitz, a student of Andy Marshall, called China "the major strategic competitor and potential threat to the United States." The deputy assistant secretary of defense, Peter Brookes, relentlessly warned policymakers about "unacceptable" actions by the Chinese toward Taiwan. Brookes argued that the United States should constrain China before disaster occurs, before China becomes a larger power. The "consequences of not confronting China today might mean a far more dangerous world in the years to come," Brookes contended. Conciliatory voices like Colin Powell tried to downplay the prospect of "turning China into an enemy," challenging the neocons' fretful, near apocalyptic vision of a Chinese colossus. Although the administration's policy had yet to take shape by September 2001, all signs pointed to a more hawkish approach toward the PRC. The administration looked to adopt a policy of strategic "rebalancing," from acceptance and accommodation with China to a more conspicuous defense of Taiwan's sovereignty as an independent nation.[42]

But the War on Terror threw Bush's China policy out the window. The War on Terror initially had a limited mission but grand purpose: eliminate Al Qaeda in Afghanistan and the Taliban regime. But the ends broadened by 2002, as did the means to fight the War on Terror. By November 2001, the United States had seized Kabul and displaced the Taliban regime. Most of its leaders were captured and killed, with only twelve American casualties by March 2002. But Bush wanted to make Afghanistan a thriving democracy, a haven from terrorist activity. It was not enough to defeat the Taliban; the United States had to stamp out any revival of terrorism in Afghanistan. Osama bin Laden was a fugitive; Bush, and all Americans, needed him to meet justice.

The Americans installed Hamid Karzai as president with the United States a permanent security force in the country. Karzai had significant support among Afghans, and the Americans hoped he would stabilize Afghanistan while the U.S. military rooted out Bin Laden and eliminated the last vestiges of the Taliban. The United States would remain in Afghanistan indefinitely. By April 2002, Bush implied that the United States was carrying out a "Marshall Plan" for Afghanistan—"an Afghanistan that is free from this evil." A limited invasion had turned into a full-scale occupation.[43] In this context, Bush made countries like China a vital partner in what he saw as a clash between civilized states and barbarian terrorists, declaring, "civilized nations find ourselves on the same side—united by common dangers of terrorist violence and chaos."[44]

Then the Bush administration turned its attention to Iraq. President Bush searched to implicate Iraq in the 9/11 attacks only hours after the Twin Towers fell. "See if Saddam did this," Bush told Richard Clarke, his head of counter-terrorism. Bush also instructed Secretary of Defense Rumsfeld to reexamine military options in Iraq, to plan for something "creative," in the words of Rumsfeld. The president did not want a "massive land force" in Iraq but needed to explore the range of military possibilities.[45] Rumsfeld did not need much prodding to find an excuse to go after Hussein. Like Bush, Rumsfeld wanted his subordinates to "judge whether good enough hit S.H. [Saddam Hussein] at same time. Not only U.B.L. [Osama bin Laden]. Go massive. Sweep it all up."[46] Rumsfeld told his associate Doug Feith to start gathering intelligence to make a case against Iraq. Feith and his counterpart Richard N. Perle led, respectively, the Office of Special Plans and the Defense Policy Board, which accumulated the first collection of—dubious—evidence to support the administration's push for war in Iraq.

Planning for Iraq consumed much of 2002 and the winter of 2003. Vice President Cheney and Condoleezza Rice, the national security adviser, joined Rumsfeld and Bush as the main spokespersons touting war as the best answer for dealing with Saddam. In newspapers and Sunday talk shows, Rice warned of a "mushroom cloud" if Hussein remained in power. Cheney argued that "the United States may well become the target" of biological and chemical weapons originating from Iraq; Hussein had violated international norms and was likely developing nuclear weapons, said Rumsfeld.[47] Bush officials fearmongered their way to a consensus that Saddam had to go. Democrats capitulated to Bush's war plans in Iraq, fearing they would appear "soft on terror." Democratic senators Hillary Clinton and John Kerry voted in support of potential war with Iraq, even if they later claimed to be enforcing the United Nations' program of weapons inspection in Iraq.[48] Leading liberal intellectuals like George Packer, Christopher Hitchens, and Thomas Friedman joined Republicans and Bush officials in the case for ousting Hussein with military force. Even if Saddam Hussein had no direct involvement in 9/11, his presence contributed to terrorist activities, destabilized the Middle East, and could threaten U.S.

interests, they argued. As Friedman said in September 2002, "Saddam Hussein is a really bad guy who is doing really, has done really bad things and will continue to do them."[49]

When war did come in March 2003, the Bush administration relied on—at first—a limited ground presence and superior air power to defeat Saddam Hussein's Baathist regime. Rumsfeld's Iraq would be won, he argued, through the RMA: a minimal ground campaign backed by overwhelming air power and supported by the latest innovations in military technology. This would reduce both American and Iraqi casualties. In theory. "Shock and Awe," the name given to Bush's air assault against Iraq, led to 30 percent of the civilian deaths during the first two years of the war.[50] Civilian casualties would mount as the Iraq War spiraled out of control. Exact figures are murky and will never be obtainable, but estimates run between 280,771 and 315,190 total Iraqi deaths.[51]

The Iraq invasion also cost the United States its international credibility and support following 9/11, including from major allies. Although Bush had support from the United Kingdom and its prime minister, Tony Blair, France and Germany opposed the war. The president of France, Jacques Chirac, said that the invasion inflamed terrorism in the Middle East and that the justifications for preemptive war were slippery and could be appropriated for malicious ends. In a moment of prescience, Chirac wondered aloud, "what would you say in the entirely hypothetical event that China wanted to take preemptive action against Taiwan, saying that Taiwan was a threat to it?"[52] Bush did not fear the repercussions. As the sole global superpower, the United States could act unilaterally without challenge to its hegemony. The United States must wage war preemptively when threatened by aggressors with the capability and willingness to attack; it had done so in the past.[53]

After Saddam fled Baghdad (he was eventually captured

in December 2003) and the United States took control of the reconstruction of Iraq, it became clear that the administration's postwar plans consisted of a blind faith in democratic capitalism—that a thousand democratic flowers would instantly bloom from the ashes of Hussein's regime. The Bush administration had no provisional government in place when it overthrew Saddam. It also had no economic vision for Iraq, other than that prospective oil revenues would be the basis for the country's reconstruction. As the United States remained in Afghanistan trying to pursue a "Marshall Plan," Bush's advisers hoped to create a New Deal–style Civilian Conservation Corps in Iraq to employ former Baathists to reconstruct the country after the American bombardment.[54] It looked, at first, like the United States would be funding "the greatest financial commitment of its kind since the Marshall Plan," according to President Bush.[55]

But it had no vision for how to create or fulfill any Marshall Plan project either. Lieutenant General Jay Garner, who led the Coalition Provisional Authority (CPA) that controlled Iraq after the invasion, wanted to hand Iraq back over to Iraqis before the administration had a chance to find Saddam and install a regime friendly to U.S. interests. This would not stand. Bush removed Garner and replaced him with Paul Bremer, the former counter-terrorism tsar for Reagan and adviser to Henry Kissinger, as head of the CPA. Under Bremer, private companies had a field day in Iraq. A day after Bush announced a "Marshall Plan for Iraq," Bremer signed Order 39 to allow "foreign investment through the protection of the rights and property of foreign investors in Iraq," which awarded billions in contracts to U.S. contractors, with much of the funds unaccounted for two years later. If there was to be a Marshall Plan for Iraq, it would rely on private, profit-seeking companies. As could be predicted, the private-sector funds never materialized. "We were never intending to rebuild Iraq," said the head of the U.S.

Army Corps of Engineers in Iraq, General William McCoy, in 2006. "We were providing enough funds to jump-start the reconstruction effort in this country."[56]

Security in the country collapsed in late 2003 after Bremer disbanded the Iraqi military under a policy of "De-Baathification" that purged Baathists—essentially all Iraqis in the military and government—leaving many Iraqis without employment or prospects. Violence spread as former Baathists joined the militias and insurgents. Attacks on American troops in Fallujah followed in 2004, as did sectarian violence between Sunni and Shiite Muslims. By 2005, the premise that U.S. military power could create a democratic Iraq proved to be deluded, as hubris and profound mismanagement flung the country into a downward spiral.[57]

The United States then tried to fight its way out of mission creep. As the War on Terror unraveled in Iraq and Afghanistan, the United States doubled down on its nation-building projects, hoping the War on Terror—and a democratic Afghanistan and Iraq—could be salvaged with the right strategy, with the right individuals at the helm. By 2006, Rumsfeld was out as secretary of defense, and his plan to win Iraq through the RMA discarded. American troops hovered between 130,000 and 140,000 "boots on the ground" in Iraq between 2003 and 2006, but violence worsened. The failure to secure peace in Iraq over three years proved that this number was insufficient, Bush reasoned. Even though it wanted to avoid repeating the history of Vietnam, the United States fell into the same fallacies and assumptions that led to the outcome of the Vietnam War. Technological prowess, overwhelming military capabilities, and sheer numbers of forces alone would be no match for insurgents fighting with old Russian machine guns and without air support. Bush called for a "surge" of an additional ten thousand to twenty thousand troops in Iraq in 2007, with

General David Petraeus leading a new counterinsurgency strategy that sought to win over the Iraqi population and quell sectarian violence.[58]

Fighting a global war on terror meant that Bush had to rethink or sideline his other foreign policy priorities. The Bush administration treated its original enemy, China, more cautiously, and propitiously, after 2003. Indeed, the Bush administration nearly reversed course on China after 9/11. Bush called China and East Asian nations "important partners in the global coalition against terror" when he met President Jiang Zemin for the first time on October 19, 2001, at the conference for Asia-Pacific Economic Cooperation. Jiang also expressed sympathy with the United States following the 9/11 attacks. Both the United States and China sought to leverage the 9/11 attacks to achieve comity on areas of mutual benefit, particularly trade and commerce.[59]

Bush knew that Chinese growth could not be reversed or halted by U.S. efforts. "America wants a constructive relationship with China," said Bush. Bush encouraged Chinese membership in the World Trade Organization and multilateral organizations. Secretary of the Treasury Henry Paulson, who took office in 2006, was chosen partly because he had made more than seventy trips to China as an executive at Goldman Sachs. Paulson's appointment sent a message: the United States wanted a cordial relationship with China, to create pathways of economic cooperation. Bush made a strategic choice not to try to rein in Chinese growth, let alone the Chinese state. No good would come from an "effort to encircle China or turn the region against it." Bush acknowledged "that China's strategic future remains uncertain" and made contingency plans if China engaged in "military adventurism"—an amphibious invasion of Taiwan—but he did not want to escalate competition without cause. Bush had a more jaded view of China than that of Bill

Clinton, who believed that China would liberalize its economy and, perhaps, its state. Bush sought a strategy that "encourages" China to peace through integration in the global community. He still held out hope that China would volunteer to abide by the "rules-based" liberal world order; but if not, the United States should not force its will on China. The same went for military affairs. The United States recognized that China's "growing military power" did not mean, ipso facto, that war would come to the Pacific soon.[60]

Retrospective analysis of Bush's strategy toward China has divorced this context from Bush's decision-making. In 2019 Paul Blustein argued in *Foreign Policy* that "the U.S. response [to China] can be fairly described as sluggish." Blustein blamed the "persistent optimism in Washington that China would continue to shed the vestiges of Maoism and open its markets" for permitting China's rise.[61] But Bush did not have blind faith that China would reform. Quite the contrary. Bush knew that the status quo also served U.S. interests. There was no need to take preemptive, punitive action against China. Playing up the threat of China would be anachronistic and misplaced while the national security apparatus remained fixed on eradicating Islamic terrorism.

China also avoided entanglement with what it saw as America's evolving War on Terror, beyond hijacking the narrative to persecute the ethnic Uyghur population in the Xinjiang region as "terrorists" and separatists (which we address in Chapter 5). Chinese leadership opposed the Iraq War and turned against the Bush Doctrine, the idea that preemptive war was necessary to defeat terrorists. The former foreign minister Qian Qichen wrote a scathing indictment of Bush's war in Iraq in 2004, arguing that it "has made the United States even more unpopular in the international community than its war in Vietnam." He implied that the United States had fallen victim to its

Cold War mistakes, to the hubris of the unipolar moment. China's break with Bush over the Iraq War coincided with its efforts to create countervailing institutions that challenged America's control over global affairs, based on the view that U.S. unilateralism worked against Chinese interests. China signed the Association of Southeast Asian Nations' Treaty of Amity and Cooperation in 2003 (despite being a non-ASEAN nation) and opened talks to resolve the issue of North Korea's nuclear program. China aimed to build a multilateral cooperative security framework that challenged the United States' willingness to go it alone in global affairs.[62] It was here, in 2003, in response to the Iraq War, that we can see the fissures between the United States and China, the coming of a disjuncture that would lead to a conflict between the two countries. Had the War on Terror not happened, the United States might have jumped straight to great-power competition during the Bush years.[63]

But Bush handed his mistakes and failures—his wars, and his China policy—over to President Barack Obama in 2009. When it came to the Middle East, Obama cared more about Afghanistan than Iraq. Obama had opposed the Iraq War in 2003, a fact that made him an attractive political candidate when he ran for president in 2008, after the Iraq War had been deemed a resounding failure—his Democratic challenger, Senator Hillary Clinton, had voted for the Iraq War. Obama thought Iraq distracted from the U.S. effort to find Osama bin Laden, who remained on the run in either Afghanistan or Pakistan. And while General Petraeus led the surge in Iraq, the Taliban reemerged in Afghanistan in 2006, setting the table for Obama's foreign policy vision of reallocating troops and material from Iraq to Afghanistan to refocus on the Taliban.

Obama then launched his own surge in December 2009, announcing that he had "determined that it is in our vital national interest to send an additional 30,000 U.S. troops to Af-

ghanistan." The president pitched the increase as the necessary, and final, effort to secure peace in Afghanistan. "These are
the resources that we need to seize the initiative, while building
the Afghan capacity that can allow for a responsible transition
of our forces out of Afghanistan," said Obama. "Today, after
extraordinary costs, we are bringing the Iraq war to a responsible end." The president also announced that he would wind
down America's involvement in Iraq, that all combat troops
would be out of the country by December 2011.[64]

But Afghanistan did not get Obama elected to the presidency. The 2008 financial crisis, and the so-called Great Recession that followed, made Obama's victory possible. Obama
promised to right the economy and rectify the errors of neoliberalism—although he did not use that term—after the housing market collapsed, banks failed, and international markets
plummeted, leaving many with foreclosed homes and without
jobs. By December 2009, the date Obama made his speech on
Afghanistan, unemployment in the United States was at 9.9 percent, its highest rate since 1982.

The Great Recession may have originated on Wall Street,
in the collapse of the subprime mortgage lending markets, but
it had broad ramifications for the global economy. As the historian Adam Tooze reminds us, "the idea of an 'all-American
crisis' obscures the reality of profound interconnection" among
global markets and economies that existed by 2008.[65] The effects of the 2008 crash rippled across the world. In the Euro-
zone, as in the United States, housing markets plummeted, debt
escalated, and consumption fell off dramatically. Smaller European economies, such as Greece, were thrown into prolonged
recessions that were intensified by strict austerity measures. Many
sub-Saharan African countries have never fully recovered from
the Great Recession in terms of their sovereign debt rates.[66]

China also faced obstacles. Its economy was surging up

until the fall of 2008, with exports increased by 25 percent and imports by 30 percent. Consumption had gone up 20 percent a year. Some even worried that China's growth would prompt it to adopt a policy of "decoupling" from Western markets. Then the Great Recession came and put millions of Chinese, both white collar and agricultural workers, out of work. In response, China launched an ambitious stimulus program under "Central Document Number 18," one that outshined other infrastructure projects in the West, including the United States. China launched new infrastructure investment in high-speed rail, health care facilities, schools, and housing. This spending allowed China to weather the crisis. A rebirth of central planning—through state-party mobilization—proved to be an effective model for dealing with the crisis.[67]

China's response to the 2008 crisis helped preserve and stimulate its economic growth; it also created a "Chinese model of development—featured by a strong role of the state in economic development, stress on the real rather than the virtual economy, a high savings rate, measured financial market liberalization."[68] Alongside an industrial policy dependent on infrastructure expansion—which went from a domestic to an international project in 2013 under the Belt and Road Initiative—China offered something different to markets (and countries) in the Global South where many felt that the United States and Europe had left them behind after 2008.

China also took steps to reject the Western-led economic order that had jeopardized its growth since the 1990s. In 2009, China proposed a "new Bretton Woods" to supplant the post–World War II foundation for global economic relations that put the dollar at the helm of currency markets. Chinese officials were jarred by "America's fiscal recklessness," according to Tooze. To restrain future financial hubris, the world economy should be pegged to a universal currency, not a national one. China wanted to protect its export-driven economy and the surpluses it enjoyed from its model of growth. It hoped this would be a first step to making sure that China's currency became an important factor in shaping reserve markets. The message was clear: China thought it could be the preeminent economic power of the twenty-first century.[69]

Foreign policymakers under Obama took notice of China's maneuvers and saw them as risks to U.S. power. In 2010, the Department of Defense published its Quadrennial Defense Review (QDR) to assess new threats and retool its military capabilities. It delivered, albeit elliptically, the first major appearance of the idea that Chinese economic growth, coupled with its military power in the Pacific, was cause for concern. "China's growing presence and influence in regional and global economic and security affairs is one of the most consequential aspects of the evolving strategic landscape in the Asia-Pacific region and globally," wrote its authors. But the QDR also implied that China had pursued A2/AD, or an "anti-access, area denial" operational concept, designed to inhibit the free movement of U.S. military forces in Asia. America, the QDR argued, will "counter the proliferation of anti-access and area-denial threats, which present an increased challenge to our maritime, air, space, and cyber forces." Although the Pentagon hoped U.S.-China relations would remain sound, the "lack of transparency and the nature of China's military development and decision-making processes raise legitimate questions about its future conduct and intentions within Asia and beyond."[70]

Hillary Clinton's *Foreign Policy* article on the "pivot to Asia" followed in 2011, and in 2012 the "Defense Strategic Guidance" report codified Clinton's messaging. At this stage in history, the War on Terror had reached its diminution. Osama bin

Laden had been killed by U.S. Special Forces on May 2, 2011. The central hub in America's War on Terror—the mission to capture or kill Bin Laden—had been achieved. Al Qaeda was no longer a tightly coordinated group that could plan major attacks against the United States. Its leaders were spread out across the Middle East. The Defense Strategic Guidance recognized this new reality and recommended a shift in military resources and attention to an Asia that some were starting to call the Indo-Pacific.[71] Indeed, "while the U.S. military will continue to contribute to security globally, *we will of necessity rebalance toward the Asia-Pacific region*" (emphasis added).[72]

Chinese economic growth continued apace after 2012, as did its military standing—in naval destroyers, aircraft, long-range precision missiles, and its overall military capabilities—in relation to America's fears of a revanchist PRC.[73] Over Obama's second term, it appeared to some commentators that "China sees the competition in the region as more of a zero-sum game," as the PRC looked to establish naval control of the South China Sea.[74] By the end of Obama's term, "strategic competition" had become the new and only mode of viewing future relations with the PRC. In February 2016, the secretary of defense, Ash Carter, announced the "return to great power competition" with the threats presented to the United States from Russia and China. Carter's speech signaled a return to a bipolar world, even as the United States operated in a multipolar context. Once again, deterrence was back on the table, the same Cold War tropes (and terms) revived for a new contest. The United States, Carter said in 2016, must "be able to deter our most advanced competitors. We must have . . . the ability to impose unacceptable costs on an advanced aggressor that will either dissuade them from taking provocative action or make them deeply regret it if they do."[75]

Great-power rivalry was back.

Conclusion

Washington is quick to blame great-power competition on China's behavior. Officials cite the fact that Xi Jinping's ascendance to power in 2012 led to a more belligerent China, a China that flaunted the rules of international engagement and looked to push the United States out of the region. The changes to U.S. policy we describe—the quick turnaround from strategic cooperation to strategic competition—are, they would argue, due to China and China alone. Great-power competition is our only recourse.

This is wrong. We do not dispute that China has changed for the worse under Xi. But Xi's behavior does not absolve the United States from examining how its history and its policy choices steered China into making the decisions it did, or how China's position in the world system favored the selection and empowerment of a dictator like Xi. The combined events of the War on Terror and the 2008 financial crisis spurred China to eschew Western-led institutions and resist U.S. oversight of the economy out of concern that America aimed to preserve its hegemony in the region at all costs and at China's expense. Primacy under unipolarity threatened global security, which, in turn, cajoled China into adopting first a defensive and then a more offensive strategic posture. The U.S.-China rivalry is bound up in this history and the tensions it produced.

The United States cannot simply point to China as a bogeyman and hope that its domestic and international problems will be solved through rivalry. If the bipolar competition between the United States and the Soviet Union during the Cold War did not lead to peace, and if the unipolar era did not rectify the blunders and hubris inherent to American primacy, we must look to new solutions, new frameworks, new models—underwritten by new diagnoses.

But before we do that, we must examine how the presidencies of Donald Trump and Joe Biden compounded, rather than resolved, the problems we face. The legacies of the past are in our current attitudes toward geopolitical rivalry, and they do not serve the purposes of peace, equality, or greater democracy.

3

How Rivalry Poisons
American Politics

"China is a key part of the new conservative movement moving forward," remarked Republican congressman Jim Banks in 2021. "If Republicans are going to win the White House in 2024 . . . we need to preserve a tough-on-China message, make that a key part of our platform and expose [Democrats] for being a pro-China party."[1]

Banks, who had been a vocal advocate of the far-right, Trump-aligned, Make America Great Again (MAGA) movement in the Republican Party, represents the dark future of American politics in a context of geopolitical rivalry. In a society riven with conflict, a painful irony of treating China as the threat that "brings us together" is that it does the opposite: it is further dividing America against itself, as Banks's comment suggests. Politicians claim, and some likely believe, that the path to American renewal runs through unifying the country against an external foe.

But that is a bunk theory.

Many of the same politicians insisting that the China

threat will unite America also wield it to polarize society, weaken civic life, attack voting rights, and silence political opponents.

China rivalry cannot ameliorate what ails the United States. It cannot rectify polarization, tribalism, or racial and economic inequality. As we saw during the Cold War, rivalry inspires paranoia and witch hunts for domestic enemies. Far from birthing a new political consensus, a new unity, what instead follows is the suspension of civil liberties for targeted groups, the empowerment of extreme reactionary and anti-democratic political voices, a climate of racialized fear that tips into societal violence, deflection of political accountability, and the diversion of public resources away from public welfare. These symptoms are already making an appearance in contemporary politics, to the long-term detriment of American democracy.

The Politics of the "China Threat"

Less than two weeks after taking office, President Biden went on CBS's *Face the Nation* to say China would face "extreme competition" from his administration.[2] Biden vowed not to let China "eat our lunch." China had territorial ambitions in the South China Sea; it looked to nullify Taiwanese independence; it showed signs of wanting to displace American power. Viewing the China challenge in Manichean terms, Biden suggested the struggle was, again, one between "democracy and autocracy."

There was some basis for thinking that China had become a greater threat under President Xi Jinping. Xi quickly consolidated the CCP bureaucracy around his rule—and around his vision for China. China launched and expanded its "Belt and Road Initiative" (BRI) under Xi, funneling its surplus capital into infrastructure projects in the Global South. BRI was unprecedented in Chinese history: an infrastructure project that exceeded U.S. modernization in the first two decades of the Cold

War. Flouting international law, Chinese officials adopted a bellicose posture regarding its dominion in the legally contested South China Sea, and Xi escalated China's repression of human rights and democracy in places including Hong Kong and Xinjiang. Xi also ramped up domestic surveillance of Chinese citizens, policing society, culture, and personal behavior in China with discomfiting efficiency.

As we discuss later, Xi's actions could be taken as evidence of many things: his personal quest for power, a means to ensure fealty to his regime, a way to force rapid increases in China's gross domestic product and secure global dumping grounds for excess production—or a combination of these factors. But to American officials they were construed as evidence of global ambitions, a sign that China looked to subvert the "liberal" or "rules-based" international order. Xi's actions fortuitously aligned with national security officials' desire to fight the next threat, to move on from the War on Terror. China was the only evident and available peer competitor to the United States. These attitudes toward China did not begin during Biden's presidency; they emerged years earlier, taking on new life during Donald Trump's presidency.

Donald Trump ran for office in 2016 arguing that "We can't continue to allow China to rape our country."[3] As Trump prepped for his trade war with China, defense intellectuals and China hawks debated the relevance of Cold War policies to Sino-U.S. relations—and had done so as early as 2010. Writing in 2019, the author Robert Kaplan declared that China's various forms of espionage and assertive foreign policy "constitute war by other means. . . . The new Cold War is *permanent . . .* the negative organizing principle of geopolitics."[4] The rhetoric parroted a familiar line of thinking, one that began to inform U.S. foreign policymaking.

Republicans hyperbolized the China threat during and

beyond Trump's election. China hawks like Elbridge Colby, Nadia Schadlow, and H. R. McMaster occupied the highest echelons of national security policymaking in Trump's administration and were key architects of Trump's National Security Strategy (NSS) in 2017. They argued that the days of thinking the United States could coexist with China were gone. China did not just manipulate its currency and conduct unfair trade practices for nationalist purposes or to expand its industrial power. China sought world influence—even "domination"— to displace the United States from the global stage. Trump's NSS stated this outright: "China and Russia challenge American power, influence, and interests, attempting to erode American security and prosperity." The winner of this war would determine who controlled the "free world."[5]

For national security officials in the Trump administration, the danger posed by China exceeded the threat of global communism during the Cold War—even as they adopted Cold War frameworks for understanding China's behavior. "What's happening now isn't Cold War 2.0. The challenge of resisting the CCP threat is in some ways worse," said Secretary of State Mike Pompeo.[6] The State Department's Office of Policy Planning issued a counter-China strategy document in 2020, *Elements of the China Challenge,* that compared Xi's China to the Soviet Union, arguing that China now has "a kind and quantity of economic power of which the Soviets could only have dreamed."[7] Marco Rubio, a Republican senator from Florida whose bellicose rhetoric on China propelled him to influential status on foreign policy, said, "in Beijing we are faced with an adversary that has a nuclear arsenal, but also control of critical supply chains, and an influence over global markets not even the old Soviet Union had."[8]

These actions and statements influenced Biden's approach to foreign policy. By the time he took office in 2021, most Democrats had become vocal participants inflating the China threat. Even Bill Burns, a career diplomat whom Biden named as CIA director, remarked that the China challenge would be greater than what the United States faced during the Cold War. "We have to buckle up for the long haul in competition with China.... This is not like the competition with the Soviet Union in the Cold War. . . . This is an adversary that is extraordinarily ambitious in technology and capable in economic terms as well."[9]

Trump's foreign policy did not determine Biden's positions on China, but it certainly made them possible. Officials in the Biden administration repeatedly echoed the sentiments of his predecessor—China was "the only country with both the intent to reshape the international order, and, increasingly, the economic, diplomatic, military, and technological power to do it."[10] As Biden's FBI director, Christopher Wray, warned, China was the "biggest long-term threat to our economic and national security."[11] The nature of the China threat, at that point, did not need litigating within either political party.

But domestic politics, above all, made Biden embrace rivalry. The Biden administration ultimately decided that the China threat could galvanize its foreign and domestic policy in the face of concerted right-wing opposition. Indeed, during the 2020 election, Biden enjoyed widespread support from Republican national security officials as a result of his China policy out-hawking Trump. "U.S. President Joe Biden has implemented the broad outline of his predecessor's strategy," Robert C. O'Brien and Arthur Herman, former national security advisers to Trump, noted approvingly. Republican support for U.S. foreign policy, it was thought, might allow Biden to carry out a policy agenda without partisan friction.[12]

The other argument, embraced by many Democrats, was that the politics of *long-term* rivalry was a way of delivering short-term public goods—everything from national infrastructure to public education funding could be yoked to outcompeting China. As Congress had done with the National Defense Education Act of 1958, which allocated federal dollars to U.S. universities in a bid to boost employment in science and technology to defeat the Soviets, Democrats thought they could use competition with China to pass bills that created employment, rebuilt America's crumbling infrastructure, and invested in adaptations to climate change.

Republican backing on infrastructure—as a necessary investment in good jobs, safe roads, and bridges—proved elusive. But the China threat gave Biden's push for progressive legislation some momentum. The original announcement for the infrastructure bill contained no mention of China. But when the bill finally passed in November 2021—right before Biden met with Xi Jinping for a virtual summit—China overshadowed the bill's success. "This is not designed to be stimulus. It's designed to be the most strategic, effective investments so that we can continue to compete against China and other countries that are making bigger investments in their infrastructure," said the chair of the Council of Economic Advisers, Cecilia Rouse. And China helped win GOP support on bills that explicitly targeted China. Republicans, for example, eventually supported the CHIPS Act and the Bipartisan Infrastructure Bill to outcompete China. The lesson from these legislative victories for Democrats and liberals was evident: Rivalry could be marshalled for political ends.[13]

Perhaps rivalry could even bring the country together and heal the wounds opened during the Trump years. As Biden remarked in his State of the Union Address in 2023, "winning the competition with China should unite all of us."[14] By imagining the Cold War as a unifying force, by ignoring the price many Americans and populations in the Global South paid to wage the Cold War, and by believing that the Cold War was a struggle against another singular superpower that the United States "won," Democrats and Republicans could see the Cold War as not just necessary but good. "The arrival of an external competitor," Biden officials insisted, "has often pushed the United States to become its best self; handled judiciously, it can once again."[15]

The idea that competition brings out the best in a nation is romantic, but wrong. American politics has become even more divisive and caustic in the age of China rivalry. China features as an object fueling that polarization, not ameliorating it.

Seeing this, the Biden administration tried at times to temper enthusiasm for "strategic competition" with China while nevertheless clinging to it as a policy. Secretary of State Antony Blinken met with Xi and other Chinese officials in June 2023 to soften the conflict and perhaps avoid Chinese retaliation for U.S. measures to impinge on Chinese influence abroad. The national security adviser, Jake Sullivan, claimed that the Biden administration did not seek a Cold War; comparing China rivalry to the Cold War was anachronistic, he suggested. "The Cold War is just not a particularly useful analogy in fundamental respects," said Sullivan.[16]

But it was hard to take that rhetoric seriously, given the direction of U.S. policy since 2021.[17] That same year, the House of Representatives founded a new Select Committee on China, and its Republican chair, Mike Gallagher, defined its purpose as "to win this new Cold War with Communist China. . . . China and Russia have been waging a Cold War against us for the better part of a decade."[18] With the Cold War as its explicit point of comparison and "winning" it the raison d'être, only sixty-five House members (a minority of Democrats) voted against the committee's formation. The issue was not *whether* analogies to the Cold War made sense; it was which analogy to the Cold War made sense—the glossy history of struggle, resolve, and triumph was inappropriate . . . but the history of control, exclusion, paranoia, and militarism would have been an apt warning.

As we write this, it looks as though great-power competition is not going away. Certainly not in Congress. The Republican senator John Cornyn judged that "China has risen to the top of everyone's concerns. . . . I think there is a bipartisan consensus" in Congress.[19] Cornyn had company among Democrats. Senator Chris Murphy, a progressive Democrat, explained that great-power competition was "going to be the primary organizing paradigm for the United States and the world over the next few decades."[20] Stephanie Murphy, a Democrat who represented a purple district in Florida, acknowledged in 2022 that "no politician, Republican or Democrat, can be seen as soft on China, and so that pushes us in the direction of not [discussing] smart policy, but politics."[21]

Any politician trying to make public policy must do so within the constraints of the moment, and the current moment presumes that "only bipartisanship can defeat authoritarian aggression."[22] External threats, some believe, can engender a "rally-round-the-flag" effect.

But that is a bad bet.[23] It disregards the history of how great-power rivalry hurts workers and the disenfranchised.[24] The past decade alone provides ample evidence that rivalry undoes democratic progress.

The Political Costs of Rivalry

Scapegoating China allows politicians to spend their time circumventing democratic accountability. It also encourages them to ignore the real problems faced by everyday Americans—and the planet—beyond the China threat.

Our Exhibit A: Donald Trump. Trump ran for reelection in 2020 after four years of fearmongering and hate-slinging, tanking America's global standing in opinion polls, flirting with nuclear war, overseeing widening economic inequality, ratcheting up military spending to absurdist levels (which Biden surpassed), and botching the government response to the Covid-19 pandemic that led to the deaths of more than 250,000 people by November 2020. Trump, along with Republican Party candidates up and down the ticket, sought to distract voters from his record in favor of blaming China for America's woes. "Don't defend Trump," directed the National Republican Senatorial Committee, "attack China."[25] Without China rivalry, the GOP had few electoral hopes.

But China-bashing is not confined to the Republican Party. In 2022, the Democratic congressman Tim Ryan ran for the Senate in Ohio against J. D. Vance, a polarizing, billionaire-funded candidate who openly associated with far-right politics and conspiracy theories—and who enthusiastically backed Trump and expressed sympathy toward the Capitol insurrection of January 6, 2021. Vance's extremism made him, in theory, an easy target for criticism. The race remained close, but Ryan maintained a steady lead from July to September.

Vance had roots in Ohio. But he also had a law degree from Yale and a career working in venture capital firms. Ryan had neither. Ryan positioned himself as a champion of Ohio's working class, whom he claimed had been victimized by outsourcing. Ohio's economic insecurity, in his campaign's telling, was not the result of U.S. corporations deciding to offshore and automate jobs. Nor was it the fault of prior Republicans and Democrats, who collaborated in the 1970s and 1980s to deindustrialize Ohio.[26]

No, China took Ohioans' jobs. "It is us versus China," Ryan said. "America can never be dependent on Communist China. . . . it is time for us to fight back."[27] When rights groups called him out for repeatedly using discriminatory rhetoric, he doubled down, refusing to apologize and continuing to stake his claim to the Senate on a fusion of anti-China politics with pro-union credentials. Ryan lost to Vance—a dark-horse, far-right candidate—and his anti-China politics shares some of the blame for that.

Ryan was one of several centrist Democrats in 2022 who ran—and lost—on campaigns that focused overwhelmingly on hyping the China threat.[28] As their fate demonstrates, scapegoating China is a bad political strategy, but more important, it redirects politicians' focus away from more systemic and pressing issues. China rivalry forces politicians to expend energy on fruitless pursuits—like banning TikTok, a Chinese-owned social media app—that needlessly whip up hysteria and divert scrutiny from other issues that demand national attention.[29]

The climate crisis—a widely recognized global threat—is a case in point. It is hardly surprising that Trump's National Security Strategy ignored climate change. But Biden seemed poised to reverse Trump's failures on climate. Biden's National Security Strategy acknowledged that, "Of all the problems we face, climate change is the greatest and possibly most existential for all nations."[30]

But Biden's federal budgets failed to reflect his auspicious rhetoric. Biden's spending priorities ignored climate change in favor of funding the Pentagon at eye-watering levels—$860 billion annually by FY 2023. Worse, the Department of Defense was the "largest fossil fuel user in the federal government, and consequently, its largest greenhouse gas emitter . . . the world's single largest greenhouse gas emitter."[31] Defense contractors have also been among the most powerful actors lobbying against a pending requirement to disclose the greenhouse gas emissions they generate and to publish plans for how to reduce them down to levels that comply with the Paris Agreement.[32] So while Biden's rivalry-anchored infrastructure bill sought to remediate climate change through investment in electric vehicles and clean energy, his federal budget submissions not only ignored the problem but empowered the most environmentally toxic portion of the economy. And even though, in principle, the U.S. discretionary budget is large enough to take on the climate crisis on a scale proportional to the threat it poses, in practice the majority of that budget goes to defense instead of limiting carbon emissions.

One could argue that defense spending does not come at the expense of other federal spending and that Biden was constrained by political realities—a divided Congress would not support sustained spending to deal with climate change at a level commensurate to the challenge. Undoubtedly true.

But geopolitical rivalry is a key source of those constraints. A divided Congress could not muster support for confronting climate change on a grand scale because, in its members' own reasoning, those resources were needed to combat China. Republicans—and centrist Democrats—opposed the Green New Deal because of its price tag. But they also invoked the specter of China. A Green New Deal would not stop Chinese aggression, they said; in fact, it would strengthen China. "The Green New Deal, surprise, serves China and China only," said Representative Marjorie Taylor Greene in 2021.[33] And even while Biden was busy yoking his vision of a green economy to the China threat, China became the reason for politicians in his own party, like Senator Joe Manchin, to reject more ambitious approaches to mitigating climate change.[34]

Sacrificing Equality

Great-power rivalry not only deflects from long-term, potentially existential problems. It also poses clear dangers to equality in the United States.

The idea that, in a functioning democracy, all individuals deserve equal rights and protections under the law should be uncontroversial. However, as we saw in the first chapter, invoking national security has been used in the past to erect barriers to societal progress.

A similar situation is playing out today. Politicians are using international rivalry to inhibit civic democracy and political equality. Democrats use the China threat with hopes of securing bipartisan support for domestic reform—risking their political futures in the process. But Republicans rely on it to scare voters with fantasies of a China takeover.[35] Mike Pompeo, Trump's CIA director and secretary of state, shamelessly warned, "The Chinese Communist Party is coming for your kids."[36]

Because both Democrats and Republicans agree that competition with China is necessary—albeit in different terms— rivalry foments fears of the enemy "other." During the Cold War, paranoia about subversion, espionage, and disloyalty turned citizens against one another. And panic over Chinese subversives is, once again, rampant in the United States. Under Trump, the White House's Office of Trade and Manufacturing Policy— run by longtime Sinophobe Peter Navarro—issued a highly polemical report purporting to document Chinese "economic aggression."[37] It included an entire section labeling Chinese nationals potential "non-traditional information collectors"— spies.[38] In 2021, the Conservative Political Action Conference held an event specifically titled "China Subverts America," during which participants contemplated how various groups and citizens in American society—especially progressive groups and organized unions—might really just be Chinese spies.[39]

For years, Tucker Carlson, whose Fox News show reached between 3.3 and 4.5 million viewers before he was fired in 2023, wielded the China threat against American citizens and American companies. He implied that Anthony Fauci, the leading scientist on the White House's Coronavirus Task Force, was a Chinese agent who manufactured the virus with China's help; he accused Apple of covering up CCP oppression; and he said the Biden family had ties to Chinese businesses that helped Joe Biden cover up the origins of Covid-19.[40] He also intermittently indicted "U.S. companies like Google, Facebook, and Twitter, along with Hollywood and other elites, as complicit in what they call 'a Chinese takeover.'"[41] And he insisted that Americans "are missing . . . a massive expansion of Chinese hegemony around the world."[42]

Carlson is not alone. Trump himself led the charge by insisting that "almost every [Chinese] student that comes over to this country is a spy."[43] Heightened fear of Chinese subversion has devolved into "accusations that one is a 'useful idiot' or 'Chinese spy'—or perhaps 'promotes a Chinese narrative'"; these are ways of shutting down debate and delegitimizing any non-hawkish analysis of China and Sino-U.S. relations.[44] Senator Ted Cruz frequently demagogues against Democrats via the China issue with remarks like, "Joe Biden has been great for enemies of America. . . . China is waging a 1,000 year war against the United States. . . . And still the Biden White House and the Democrat Party are structurally pro-China."[45] Congresswoman Judy Chu, one of the sixty-five Democrats to vote against the formation of the House Select Committee on China, was not only openly accused of disloyalty and working for Chinese intelligence but also subjected to calls from sitting members of Congress for her to be denied access to intelligence as a consequence; this indignity forced Democrats into the awkward position of closing ranks behind her and condemning Republican racism even as they fostered a rivalry with China that catalyzed the hunt for "internal enemies."[46]

Anti-Chinese racism is not just a Republican problem. Biden's FBI director, Christopher Wray, has cast blanket aspersions of potential disloyalty on politicians who maintain ties to China. He implied that Chinese citizens could become an enemy within, "called on to do Beijing's bidding when their power and influence grow."[47] Director Wray made the thinly veiled accusation that Chinese students in the United States are primed to be intelligence collectors for the CCP, and this meant Americans should be urged to see "the China threat as not just the whole-of-government threat, but a whole-of-society threat. . . . it's going to take a whole-of-society response by us."[48]

The pervasive rhetoric about fifth columns and subversion exploits and worsens a climate of racialized fear and resentment toward not only Chinese citizens but also those who simply look Asian, denying them the ability to experience political equality as it is enjoyed by others.

The problem of anti-Asian violence predates Covid, but politicking on a fear of China since the pandemic dramatically inflamed racial violence.[49] More than 9,000 incidents of anti-Asian racism—which range from racial slurs to being spit on to beatings, stabbings, and shootings—were reported in the year after the pandemic started, with more than 2,400 additional incidents being recorded in the succeeding months, through March 2022.[50] In San Francisco alone, where Asian Americans are overrepresented in the population compared with the country at large, hate crimes against Asians reportedly increased 567 percent in 2021.[51] By April 2023, more than 75 percent of Chinese-Americans had reported experiencing racial discrimination or hate crimes over the prior year.[52] Moreover, experts widely believe that, because of the methods used to collect the data, hate crimes in the United States are vastly underreported.[53]

Many of these attacks have clear documentation—including video footage and racial slurs spray-painted at the scene of crimes—indicating that they are overwhelmingly about hate directed toward China.[54] And the overall trend shows that the societal price of rivalry is not limited to ethnically Chinese Americans; it is a Pandora's box of racial exclusion and oppression that ensnares "Asian-looking" people too. Only 43 percent of hate crimes targeted at Asians involved victims of Chinese descent.[55]

Furthermore, racial hierarchy does not assert itself only through vigilantes and reactionary members of civil society; it is a project of the state.

In May 2020, the Trump administration issued Presidential Proclamation 10043, which restricted student visa and immigration access to the United States for Chinese students with ties to any Chinese university known to work with the People's Liberation Army. Such an impossibly wide scope meant that, in the first six months of the proclamation alone, the Trump administration revoked more than one thousand visas for Chinese nationals over "national security concerns."[56] The Biden administration kept this restriction in place despite a student-led class-action lawsuit and letters of outrage from dozens of educational associations, including the Association of American Universities and the American Council on Education. In addition, federal decisions have trickled down to the states. In 2023, seizing on earlier Trump-era accusations painting Chinese students as spies, Texas Republicans filed a bill to ban all Chinese citizens from attending Texas colleges and universities.[57]

In November 2018, the Justice Department also launched the China Initiative, a counter-espionage effort to deal with the very real problem of PRC assets engaging in intellectual property and technology theft. But the initiative not only criminalized associations with China, it engaged in racial profiling at scale—close to 90 percent of investigations were against Asian Americans.[58] One year after the China Initiative launched, the Justice Department acknowledged that, after two thousand investigations, it had managed to prosecute only twenty-eight cases as of 2021, with only eight criminal convictions.[59] And most of the convictions were for crimes unrelated to espionage—research "integrity" problems, non-declaration of Chinese income or Chinese bank accounts, giving inconsistent testimony to federal investigators, and the like.[60]

So when six Chinese researchers were arrested in the United States in 2020 as part of the China Initiative, it did not matter that the Justice Department ultimately dropped its charges against five of the six. The damage had been done—the arrests triggered a swift exodus of more than one thousand Chinese scientists who also feared persecution.[61] Of Chinese American scientists surveyed in 2021, 42.2 percent reported feeling racially profiled by the U.S. government. Nearly that same percentage (42.1) reported that FBI investigations had affected their plans to remain in the United States. And 78.5 percent of respondents "wanted to distance themselves from collaborators in China" because of the FBI's China Initiative—blowback in the form of a scientific brain drain.[62]

In 2022, the FBI abandoned the label "China Initiative" under withering public criticism, but fears of widespread Chinese espionage lingered. The China Initiative's track record was more than "got the wrong guy" incompetence; it was an expression of pervasive state-driven xenophobia.[63] It reflected an undeniably racist policy and approach to China, in consequence even if not in intent. And its racism was inseparable from the repressive politics that come with heightening geopolitical rivalry.

Fueling Extremism

Great-power rivalry feeds reactionary politics beyond issues of foreign policy and national security. It emboldens society's antidemocratic fringe and debases the quality of civic democracy.

Anti-intellectualism and xenophobic nationalism are widespread in American history.[64] But under conditions of rivalry, xenophobia more readily spreads through the body politic, pervading all aspects of life if politicians find it advantageous. When there is a named foreign enemy in the American imagination, portions of the public become more receptive to preachers of hate and conspiracy. By interweaving what in any other time might be dismissed as paranoid hate-filled rants with grossly inaccurate narratives about what China is doing to "us," extremist voices like Tucker Carlson become vectors for the proliferation of conspiracy theories that reinforce a climate of fear in the United States.

Take, for instance, the far right's use of the China threat to appropriate, distort, and subvert one of America's largest-ever social justice movements: the Black Lives Matter movement. In the wake of the rapid spread of Covid-19 and the mass outrage at the flagrant police murder of George Floyd in 2020, Steve Bannon gave an interview in which he asserted, "confrontation with the Chinese Communist Party, I believe, will be the single defining aspect of 2020. . . . whoever convinces the American people that they can confront the Chinese Communist Party . . . will be the winner. And I think that's why Joe Biden is so weak." Comparing the CCP to Germany's Nazi party on the eve of war, Bannon hyperbolized: "I keep saying Hong Kong is Austria in 1938. . . . They are truly an evil empire, just like the Nazis." Bannon went on to make the outlandish claim that the CCP was responsible for George Floyd's murder.[65] In the days following Floyd's killing, a false, right-wing meme spread online that Floyd overdosed on fentanyl (purchased from China) and that the officer who murdered him—by compressing Floyd's neck into the ground with a crouched knee, on camera, for eight minutes and forty-six seconds while Floyd cried out for his mother—should be freed.[66] Bannon, as well as

a vast network of Trump surrogates, then sought to dramatically amplify the China threat in order to win political power,
even though the process of doing so sought to deny justice to
George Floyd's family and exculpated one of the most wanton
perpetrators of police brutality ever caught on camera.

Bannon also reflected a much larger echo chamber. Char-
acters as diverse as Donald Trump, Jr., Sebastian Gorka (a former Trump White House staffer known for his obsession with
"radical Islam"), and select staff at the Heritage Foundation were
surrogates for Donald Trump who also claimed (incorrectly)
that the Black Lives Matter movement was abetting China as
part of an attempt to create "world communism."[67] Linking
their domestic fears to international threats, Republican candidates branded "critical race theory and cancel culture" as Chinese attempts at subversion.[68]

These messages were propagated widely by figures in the
right-wing media. Bannon's chief financier and disseminator
of anti-China (and anti-Biden) propaganda was Miles Kwok, a
Chinese real estate mogul who fled to the United States after
being charged with corruption in China. While China sought
Kwok's extradition, he became a member at Trump's Mar-a-
Lago resort, bankrolled extreme right-wing (Bannon-aligned)
political causes, and attempted to build an image of himself as
an enemy of the Chinese Communist Party.

Kwok partnered with Bannon to found the New Federal
State of China—a transnational lobbying group of "high net-
worth individuals" seeking regime change in China; Bannon
bragged about being one of its advisers.[69] Kwok also helped
Bannon distribute his political messaging through a series
of English- and Chinese-language media companies that he
owned, which interspersed anti-Biden propaganda with anti-
semitic conspiracy theories and hyperbole about the CCP's de-

sire for world domination.[70] The twisted irony of this was not only that Kwok stood accused of being a CCP agent even as he posed publicly as its enemy but also that Kwok was ultimately arrested in New York in March 2023 on charges of committing a billion-dollar fraud against the public, partly through his anti-CCP media channels—a grift on a grand scale.[71]

If rivalry persists, the far right will continue to deploy the "China threat" and xenophobic rhetoric to win elections and denigrate their fellow Americans—none more high-profile than Joe Biden. As Bannon proclaimed on many occasions, "He, his son, the Bidens, are corrupt and they're incompetent. They've sold out this country. He's a fellow-traveler running-dog for the Chinese Communist Party." Throughout the presidential campaign of 2020, Rudy Giuliani, Trump's lawyer, repeatedly charged that Biden was "bought and paid for by the Chinese Communist Party."[72]

This discourse aimed to sink Biden's favorability ratings in the 2020 election and to provide Trump with an opportunity to publicly contest the outcome. And it nearly worked. Bannon's plan successfully "drove up Biden's negatives" through fearmongering about China—and specifically by proliferating conspiracy theories about China's ties to Hunter Biden.[73] Worse, the "China card" created an opening for the radical right to challenge the integrity of the election outcome. Given this recent history, it is hard to imagine a greater source of *dis*unity in American politics than China rivalry.

The China threat also provided cohesion to the far right's domestic agenda, welding together the extremely disparate issues constituting the far right's politics since 2020: the opioid crisis in rural America, working-class precarity, paranoia about critical race theory, the supposed unfreedom of "cancel culture," and opposition to transgender rights. Incredibly, these

reactionary politicians—sometimes called "national conservatives"—insisted that these issues were not caused by economic
dislocation or de-industrialization, but rather China's influence
in American culture.

These fevered beliefs bleed into public policy. Missouri's
electoral politics illustrates how rivalry mixes with reactionary
politics to anti-egalitarian effect. In this it is hardly unique—
Missouri's red-scare politics bears strong resemblance to that
of locales as far-ranging as California, Arizona, Florida, Ohio,
Texas, and Virginia. Candidates up and down the "show-me
state" sought to fearmonger, racialize, and even sever ties between Missouri and China, even though China was the third
largest export market for Missouri and the state had a favorable balance of trade with China.[74]

In 2016, Josh Hawley ran a successful campaign for Senate in Missouri partly on the back of race-baiting about China,
including an affiliate group ad targeting his opponent with the
message "Stop helping the Chinese buy our farms."[75] Small
wonder that when the pandemic hit, Hawley was the sole "no"
vote on the Covid-19 Hate Crimes Act, a popular and innoc-
uous bill meant to condemn and discourage anti-Asian hate
crimes. It was a vote sufficiently galling to earn him a *Vanity
Fair* headline declaiming: "Josh Hawley Proudly Declares Himself Pro Hate Crimes."[76]

Eric Greitens, the disgraced governor of Missouri who
was forced to resign because he faced charges of sexual abuse,
spousal abuse, blackmail, and campaign finance violations, also
ran for the U.S. Senate in 2022 on a host of conspiracy theories.[77] He pandered relentlessly to the basest sentiments in
the new-right fusionism, endorsing and repeating conspiracies
about "voting irregularities" indicating that Biden "stole" the
presidential election. The Republican Party largely condemned

him, especially after he released a campaign ad in which he cocked a shotgun while claiming he was going "RINO hunting" (a RINO is a centrist conservative—a "Republican in Name Only"), implying with the subtlety of a falling anvil that Republicans who were *not* Trump loyalists should be killed.[78]

Greitens tried to revive his political career on the back of conspiracy theories, anti-China xenophobia, and support from the far right—including Steve Bannon.[79] The main political wedge between Greitens and his winning opponent, Eric Schmitt, was who could out-hawk whom on China. Greitens's campaign issued ads labeling Schmitt as "Good for China. Bad for Missouri" while Schmitt's campaign said the exact same thing—"Greitens: Good for China. Bad for Missouri."[80]

But again, Democrats also rely on red-scare tactics. Schmitt's Democratic opponent in the general election cried, "Communist Chinese buying up U.S. farms is a growing national security risk." She accused Schmitt of voting to "allow Communists from China to buy our farmland"—picking up on a theme from Josh Hawley's 2016 campaign and opening the possibility of future racially based restrictions of the sale of the most important and tangible asset in the American economy.[81]

This red-scare rhetoric translated into policy on the issue of China-related land restrictions—a national issue for Republicans. Fox News frequently spotlighted the threat of a "Chinese takeover" by way of acquiring U.S. land, sometimes with the chyron running along the bottom of the screen displaying the words "Red Threat Rising" and "China Menace." Smaller right-wing publications, like the *Daily Signal,* echoed this message.[82]

In 2021, stoking fear that China might control the U.S. food supply, Dan Newhouse, a Republican congressman from

Washington State, boasted of introducing an amendment that would "prohibit the purchase of agricultural land by the People's Republic of China," even though the threshold for prohibition was dangerously open-ended and the threat of becoming "dependent on China for our domestic and agricultural food supply" completely without evidence.[83]

In 2022, the governor of Florida, Ron DeSantis, proposed a bill "prohibiting the purchase of lands, state contracts with Chinese technology firms, and the infiltration of CCP-affiliated groups such as Confucius Institutes."[84] In 2023, the Texas state legislature filed a bill that would ban "citizens, governments, and entities of China, Iran, North Korea, and Russia" from buying Texas land, a measure which the governor, Greg Abbott, supported.[85] And at the federal level, the senators Tommy Tuberville and Tom Cotton (from Alabama and Arkansas, respectively) introduced the Securing America's Land from Foreign Interference Act, which sought to "prohibit the purchase of public or private real estate located in the United States by the Chinese Communist Party." It was written broadly enough to potentially prohibit purchases by anyone accused of links to the CCP and anyone who was not a "United States person."[86]

Republicans did not stop there. Republican members of Congress's newly formed Select Committee on China variously insisted that China was not only a threat to allies, democracy, the U.S. military, innovation, American technology, and human rights but also a threat to food supplies, public health, medical supplies, the "stability of our health care system," and the minds of children.[87] Unchecked, their fear peddling has no limits.

We need to stop empowering reactionary voices and policies—those that prevent equal protection under the law—in the United States. We need to protect Asian Americans from being attacked, surveilled, or arrested because of their ethnicity. And we need to prevent demagogues from profiting on the dissemination of China-centered conspiracy theories. Geopolitical rivalry does not just make civic democracy harder to realize; it actively favors democracy's enemies.

4

How Rivalry Worsens
Economic Inequality

Economic democracy—a term that fell out of mainstream politics during the post–Cold War era—promises public prosperity through good, stable jobs and a robust welfare state. It operates on the simple presumption that economic disenfranchisement breeds electoral disenfranchisement. The quality of electoral democracy—voting for preferred candidates at the ballot box—suffers if voters cannot pay their rent or feed their families. Democracy requires secure access to the ballot, but also maximal rates of employment, a robust safety net, manageable levels of wealth inequality through redistributive tax policies, the provision of public goods, and the possibility of economic mobility. Economic justice is the foundation of political freedoms. These were viable ideas fifty years ago, principles embraced by many Democrats. Indeed, New-Deal-turned-Cold-War liberals like Hubert Humphrey championed full employment and equal housing ("a Marshall Plan for the Cities") up to the late 1970s.[1] But when the concept of economic democracy left our lexicon, our democratic ambition languished, allowing our politicians to claim we are the greatest democracy in the world while economic inequality in our nation spiraled out of control.

What does economic inequality have to do with great-power competition? Much more than you might think. Congress and the White House currently direct resources toward the national security state and away from programs and policies that support the public welfare. There is no *inherent* compromise between investing in defense over social welfare—we have a politically imposed trade-off between "guns and butter" in American politics.

Just as geopolitical rivalry empowers extremist voices opposed to democracy, it also provides legitimacy for policies that undermine economic freedoms. Many of these policies are justified in the name of "national security," which too often functions as a euphemism for militarist policies that foment aggression while starving the welfare state. The consequences of militarism as a "doctrine of violence" stretch far beyond the battlefield, worsening economic inequality and foreclosing even the prospect of economic democracy.

Such a claim might be jarring to some because war can, sometimes, supplement economic prosperity. Mobilizing for World War II helped end the Great Depression and initially contributed to the postwar boom. The outbreak of the Korean War offered a boon to American unions and the U.S. manufacturing base during the early 1950s. So-called military Keynesianism has provided well-paying, often unionized jobs for thousands of Americans since the early Cold War.[2]

But in times of widespread and extreme inequality—which is the case today—war, or "great-power competition," creates greater economic precarity.[3] Not only does rivalry empower the already powerful; it further marginalizes the powerless. Great-power rivalry has helped concentrate wealth in the hands

of a few, rather than creating a healthy economy. It has weakened the welfare state and stymied economic democracy.[4]

This cannot be our future.

A New Era?

As we have seen, great-power competition reaches into Americans' everyday lives, into how they view domestic and international affairs and their interrelationship. Great-power competition cannot be separated from economic relations, the
future of democracy, and the state of the environment. To wit,
the effects of great-power competition have coincided with the
changes wrought by "neoliberalism"—an ideology that elevated
the protection of capital over the rights of workers—after the
1970s. The hollowing out of the manufacturing sector, the weak-
ening of organized labor, and the decline of working-class wages
followed neoliberalism's triumph in the 1980s.[5]

But by the presidential election of 2020, all of the major
candidates for the Democratic Party nomination—including
Biden—had repudiated neoliberal policies to varying degrees.
Constituencies on the left and right of the political spectrum
rejected free-market dogma and the policy prescriptions that
accompanied it: privatization of public goods, deregulation,
offshoring, weak social spending.[6] The Covid-19 pandemic also
threw the global economy into crisis, requiring dramatic fiscal
stimulus and monetary enlargement that belied the laissez-faire,
"let the market decide" rhetoric of the neoliberal order. In the
background, the disastrous din of climate change grew ever
louder, eventually becoming impossible to ignore. The growing
frequency and severity of extreme weather events, as well as
record-breaking high and low temperatures, have even shifted
many right-wing politicians away from their long-standing posture of denial that climate change is a real crisis.

All of these forces converged during the Biden presidency.[7] Key foreign policy advisers, including the national security adviser, Jake Sullivan, believed the United States had to leave the old economic order behind. Covid, climate change, and political consensus had turned the tide on the neoliberal era, they felt. Leading up to the Biden presidency, Sullivan and other Biden surrogates repeatedly touted a "foreign policy for the middle class" or the idea that "America needs a new economic philosophy."[8]

Sullivan seized on the widely acknowledged failures of neoliberalism to propose a new economic statecraft anchored in the priorities of U.S. national security. In a speech at the Brookings Institution on April 27, 2023, Sullivan even outlined a "New Washington Consensus" to displace neoliberalism. He blamed economic inequality on "complex" factors but singled out "policies like regressive tax cuts, deep cuts to public investment, unchecked corporate concentration, and active measures to undermine the labor movement that initially built the American middle class." Sullivan spoke of a revitalized industrial policy premised on technological innovation; of the need for America and its "partners" to ramp up semiconductor production; of trade agreements that strengthen supply chains while providing "protections for labor and the environment." Above all, the Biden administration sought economic growth for the middle class through "a new global labor strategy that advances workers' rights through diplomacy."[9]

There is much to appreciate in this outlook. Sullivan deserved credit for critiquing neoliberalism. The effort to discredit and dispense with policies that hollowed out the working class for a half century is a welcome attitudinal shift. The Biden administration's gesture toward global workers' rights—while largely rhetorical—also departed from Democrats' recent policy proposals.

But on second glance, Sullivan's "New Washington Consensus" looked like its intellectual predecessor—or worse—in most of the ways that matter for the well-being of Americans. Indeed, it represented what we call "national security Keynesianism": an economic logic where the American industrial base, supported with federal initiatives, sustains U.S. global primacy against its would-be challengers. In this sense, Biden's vision of a different economic order had something in common not with Roosevelt's New Deal but with Harry Truman's vision during the early Cold War. "Our national security and our economic vitality depend" upon an American commitment to "investments in infrastructure, innovation, and clean energy," said Sullivan. "Military strength is dependent on a strong economic system and a strong industrial and productive capacity," wrote President Truman seventy-five years earlier.[10]

Like Truman, Biden made the mistake of linking American prosperity to the existence of a foreign foe—rather than to the health and future of Americans' well-being. Although it might aim to serve the interests of workers, Sullivan's national security Keynesianism cannot but fall short of this goal.

There are at least two reasons why.

First, like neoliberalism, national security Keynesianism guarantees that the interests of corporations take precedence over workers. Under neoliberalism, the state insulated capital from the demands of democracy; it supported corporations through government subsides, tax breaks, and "special economic zones" that allowed chief executive officers to horde profits and marginalize unions.[11] But national security Keynesianism does the same, albeit with different intentions. It prioritizes government subsidies to manufacturing sectors that are historically anti-union and require skilled, educated workers. It does not support workers first and companies second, nor does it seek a balance of power between workers and owners of cap-

ital. What's more, national security Keynesianism offers no attempt at economic justice. Whereas economic democracy fore-
sees high corporate tax rates leading to redistributive outcomes
that benefit the poor, national security Keynesianism clings to
an approach to economic growth that obscures how its gains
get distributed. National security Keynesianism does not shift
economic *power* to workers.

Second, national security Keynesianism is not a basis for
long-term economic growth, let alone economic democracy.
Sullivan's speech offered a series of "to-do items"—tackle corruption, integrate supply chains, support collective bargaining
rights—but it was vague on how to achieve these goals. The
Biden administration would "unlock the power and ingenuity
of private markets, capitalism, and competition to lay a foundation for long-term growth," but Sullivan did not explain how
that project could benefit all citizens, whether of the nation or
the globe. Without concrete visions of economic justice or redistribution, national security Keynesianism, like the military
Keynesianism of the Cold War, relied on a rapacious logic of
geopolitics as the basis for public spending on job creation and
infrastructure—and massive defense budgets to undergird this
effort.[12] National security Keynesianism subordinates economic
equality to national security objectives that are derived from
bad strategy, corrupted interests, and political demagoguery.

Some post-neoliberal thinkers have put their faith in "productivism" or "supply-side progressivism," seemingly instead
of competition. Progressives like the journalist Ezra Klein have
touted the virtues of government-sponsored innovation in climate mitigation and pharmaceutical development. Government,
for example, can incentivize housing construction and childcare centers. These policies, by increasing production, will decrease prices for public goods. In principle, supply-side progressivism also eschews rivalry with China—no foreign bogeyman

is needed except as a political expedient. But such an expedient turns out to be necessary. They reinforce the China threat as the priority of government action because that is what politics demands. And they have no view toward global economic problems; the world is simply a nationalist blind spot.[13]

Ultimately, because national security Keynesianism optimizes the economy for war-making rather than war prevention, it makes economic policy an extension of defense policy rather than labor or fiscal priorities. Concentrating resources to thwart hyped-up national security threats does not align with ensuring workers' economic security, and in a healthy democracy threat inflation of that sort would be unsustainable. An "arsenal of democracy" is not needed if America prioritizes pragmatism over competition, and economic democracy over economic growth.[14]

So while national security Keynesianism conjures a different set of economic policies than neoliberalism, it is not an answer to the problems that have mushroomed under neoliberalism.

The Limits of "Bidenomics"

The convergence of the climate crisis, the pandemic, and China rivalry produced three major pieces of legislation: the Inflation Reduction Act (IRA), the CHIPS and Science Act, and the Bipartisan Infrastructure Law of 2021. Supporters called these pieces of legislation "landmark," and "unprecedented."[15] We were told they were a down payment on a new era.[16]

None of that has yet proven entirely unfounded, but neither is it helpful to understanding how national security Keynesianism weighs down America's social economy. "Unprecedented" does not imply "new." "Bidenomics" desired U.S. primacy in the military and the market—the same goals speci-

fied by the Trump administration and by Cold War presidents—
in relation to Beijing. As Senator John Cornyn, the Republican co-sponsor of the CHIPS and Science Act, explained, "if
America is going to maintain our preeminence, not only from
a national-security perspective but economically, a federal incentive program . . . to encourage semiconductor manufacturing is very important."[17]

But before we get to what is old—why Bidenomics was
a revival of military Keynesianism—we must address what
was new.

First, the scale of federal monies Bidenomics dedicated
to infrastructure and climate is unique to the twenty-first century. The IRA allocated some $369 billion to climate-related
initiatives over a decade, and the CHIPS and Science Act allo-
cates around $200 billion to research and manufacturing that
may or may not bolster a green economy in the long run.
CHIPS' complex system of tax credits and corporate subsidies
was, indeed, unprecedented—and encouraged corporations to
accommodate workers' rights in certain respects. Whether those
new policies will reduce economic inequality depends on how
they are exploited, and by whom.

Second, Bidenomics promised to generate better wages
and growth for workers than prior administrations. For the first
time in a long time, the United States had a self-conscious industrial policy, instead of relying on military spending as a "de
facto" industrial policy.[18] Biden's policies incentivized capital
investment in key sectors of manufacturing that could eventually lead to wage growth, higher employment, and reductions
in income inequality. Historically, "America does social policy
through investment and industrial policy," rather than redistribution, and Biden followed in this vein.[19] Bidenomics could
also help workers by imposing new regulations on corporate
behavior. The incentives for corporations to pay prevailing local

wages to low-skilled workers, provide childcare, and hire unionized labor could establish the basis for economic democracy.[20]

Furthermore, the trifecta of legislation (IRA, CHIPS, and
the Bipartisan Infrastructure law) bet on an economic future
powered by *American* production of renewable energy. The
IRA in particular sought to incubate growth in green industries, prevent corporate losses in green investments, and provide tax credits to households that purchase electric vehicles
or make their homes more climate friendly. This accords with
the International Labor Organization's belief that "transitions
to environmentally and socially sustainable economies can become a strong driver of job creation, job upgrading, social justice and poverty eradication."[21]

But conditional phrases—"could," "should," "seeks to"—
do a lot of work in the above picture. Any heavily subsidized
sector will see higher productivity and job growth as long as
the subsidies persist. But did Bidenomics improve the lives of
workers in the medium or long term? Did it roll back the oligarchic institutions and policies created by decades of neoliberalism?[22] Did it meet the climate crisis with the required for-
titude? And if social policy is done through industrial policy,
and industrial policy is national security policy, did that move
us toward a stronger welfare state, toward economic justice,
and therefore greater economic equality?

We think the answer to these questions is "no."

To begin with, Bidenomics was punitive toward China.
While it spent lavishly to increase U.S. industrial capacity, it
simultaneously aimed to decrease U.S. corporations' exposure
to Chinese firms (especially in high-technology sectors) and
weaken China's economy. As the secretary of commerce, Gina
Raimondo, said of semiconductors—a technology found not
just in missiles but also everything from toaster ovens to tele-

visions—"We are ahead of [China]. . . . We need to stay ahead of them. And we need to deny them this technology that they need to advance their military." Jake Sullivan went further, acknowledging, "we must maintain as large of a lead [over China] as possible."[23] Sullivan later stated that U.S. industrial policy is "narrowly focused on technology that could tilt the military balance . . . ensuring that U.S. and allied technology is not used against us." And he admitted that U.S. industrial policy sought to challenge China and "other countries intent on challenging us militarily."[24]

The results led to bans on specific investments in China—on semiconductor and artificial intelligence technology—with more expected to come on China's energy and technology sectors. Some experts anticipated that these investment controls mean declining growth over the next few years not only in China but also in Europe (2 percent of its GDP) and the United States. Declining wages and fewer employment opportunities for Americans will follow.[25] Controls on Chinese semiconductors were also short-sighted, given that America's share of global semiconductor manufacturing was expected to increase by less than one percent in the near term despite all the investment.[26]

Investment bans also will not allow the United States to dominate semiconductor production anytime soon. Asia is projected to remain the home to somewhere between 60 percent and 80 percent of the world's semiconductor production, even with TSMC building a factory in Arizona.[27] Moreover, America's share of global production for lithium batteries (necessary for "green" vehicles) is projected to just eclipse 13 percent by 2030, only 3 percent above pre-IRA projections.[28] Meanwhile, the "Asia-Pacific will still account for two-thirds" of battery production. And reaching the most optimistic projections for the United States requires quiescence from China, which

controls "60% of the world's lithium refining."[29] More investment controls will not reverse these statistics.

Attempts to weaken China's economy also feed Chinese
nationalism and animosity toward the United States. Although
U.S. restraints on China's economy will take years to produce
results, they provide fodder for Xi and the CCP's message that
the United States seeks to punish China and pursue rivalry,
not "competition without conflict." Protectionist policies fuel
ethnonationalism and bellicosity toward the United States,
heightening tensions between the two great powers. China's foreign ministry has labeled the outbound investment controls
"technological bullying" and has responded in the past by plac-
ing its own bans on U.S. investment.[30] This is not good for the
global economy or for global stability.

Besides its punitive aspect, Bidenomics' version of national security Keynesianism fell wildly short of meeting the
climate crisis and achieving net zero carbon emissions. As a
percentage of the U.S. share of global GDP, the United States
could have been doing much more to manage the climate crisis (at least $680 billion annually—$10.8 trillion total—to meet
what were already modest climate targets under the Intergov-
ernmental Panel on Climate Change).[31] The IRA offered subsidies for clean energy but also allowed more oil drilling permits,
to appease fossil fuel interest groups. And as some of the IRA's
strongest backers have noted, the IRA was not primarily a climate policy: "it was a plan for jobs, taxes, supply chain resil-
iency, and domestic manufacturing, lashing together groups
with competing interests."[32]

Because Bidenomics was a national policy, it had forsaken
the planetary scale of climate change. Sullivan's "New Washington Consensus" speech had little to say about climate adaptation in the Global South (which produces the largest percentage of carbon emissions and experiences greater catastrophic

fallout of climate change in the form of natural disasters and rising temperatures). Sullivan singled out a few countries (Brazil, Angola, and Indonesia) as evidence of the Biden administration's commitment to the Global South on investment in renewable energy and "climate-friendly growth," but he did not mention a multilateral effort to tackle the climate crisis, which affects all nations.[33] Indeed, the absence of multilateralism in Biden's climate policy was striking given its commitment to a supposedly new, global economic order and to a "rules-based order" whose origins lie in multilateral institutions. The paradox of environmental policy under Biden, then, was that by filtering its climate policy through China rivalry, it fell well short of the global scale and scope needed to address the problem.[34]

Defenders of what Sullivan dubbed the "New Washington Consensus" might argue that its primary intent was to increase America's share of global manufacturing—it was not a strategy for climate change. But that is our point. If the United States is to be the effective world leader that it thinks it is, if it is to tackle climate change with the bold vision doing so demands, if it is to truly win over Global South nations on climate, the United States needs to have a foreign policy premised on a green transition, full employment, wealth redistribution, and economic security outside the framework of great-power rivalry.

Bidenomics also obscured the budgetary trade-offs of an economic policy pursued through China rivalry. Even if national security Keynesianism was preferable to neoliberalism in the United States, it was nevertheless a raw deal for the average American. While we praise the Biden administration for its efforts to change economic orthodoxy, we must also ask who gains the most (or at all) under an industrial policy determined by great-power competition.

Not the average American worker. "Strategic competition" impels national investments in advanced technologies, a sector of the economy that historically has propelled society's wealth upward, subsidizing large firms and higher wages for a small technocratic elite with advanced degrees and an advantaged position in the economy. National security Keynesianism is a jobs program for the few who, by dint of their education and social networks, were positioned to succeed under Biden's industrial policy.[35] An economic strategy guided by China rivalry is no kind of fix for chronic inequality in the United States.

This is concerning given the numbers on economic insecurity. For starters, social mobility has steadily declined for more than a generation.[36] Over 30 percent of Americans earn less than $15 per hour.[37] In the United States, 87 percent of low-wage workers are age 25 or older.[38] The greatest proportion of low-wage workers are women.[39] People of color are overrepresented in the ranks of the working class, with women of color being the most overrepresented.[40] And while the average American's wages have stagnated since the 1970s, the cost of living—specifically housing—has steadily increased.[41] The crisis in affordable housing is not primarily the difficulty of owning a house but rather of having *any* place to live. According to NBC News, in 2022, "nearly 7.8 million Americans said they were behind on their rent in October and 3 million felt they were likely to be evicted in the next two months."[42] During the pandemic, the number of people who fell into poverty globally increased by 160 million people while the net worth of the ten richest men more than doubled, from $700 billion to $1.5 trillion.[43] The proportion of Americans "struggling to pay for usual expenses" increased from 80.8 million in 2020 to 90.3 million by 2023.[44] The wage share of the national income remains close to a seventy-five-year low.[45] Meanwhile, since the global financial crisis, after-tax corporate profits have been both steadily growing and at a seventy-year high.[46]

Over the past decade and a half, while wages have stag-
nated and the working class has fallen further behind, U.S. defense spending has surged. In just five years, from 2016 to 2021,
the U.S. defense budget soared from $639.86 billion to $800.67
billion. It is closing in on $900 billion annually as of 2024. If
China rivalry endures, experts expect to see a $1 trillion de-
fense budget in the next two years.[47] And by some estimates,
the defense budget already exceeds $1.537 trillion annually.[48]

Defense budgets convey the federal government's interests and priorities on behalf of the American people. But budgets are also moral documents. If we view the defense budget
in this light, Biden's budgets were not documents that reflected
a moral commitment to all—or even most—Americans. An
economy centered on national security concerns in the twenty-
first century exacerbates—not ameliorates—the problem of
growing structural inequality in the United States. The Costs
of War project at Brown University has found that defense
spending between 2001 and 2016 created 1.5 million jobs, but
that same amount could have generated twice the number of
jobs in health care or in education—a field with notoriously
low salaries relative to workers' education and skills. The "job
multiplier effect" from federal spending on the military (6.9
jobs in the defense industry and supporting supply chains for
every $1 million spent) is lower than the same amount spent in
any other industry. During the first sixteen years of the War on
Terror, the United States lost the opportunity to create between
one and three million jobs in other sectors and, consequently,
lost the opportunity to create a healthier, more educated, and
more economically secure nation. We should expect a similar
outcome from the era of great-power competition.[49]

The professional class benefits the most from national
security Keynesianism.[50] As inequality has grown, high-skilled,
high-wage people are making up a greater percentage of the

richest owners of capital in the country. The scholar Richard
Reeves has shown that as the wealth of the upper-middle class
grows, it perpetuates intergenerational wealth and steers public policy toward preferential taxation, real estate, school zon-
ing, and other privileges that accrue to them but are not accessible to the typical worker.[51] These workers, the upper-middle
class, stand to benefit the most from China rivalry. And they
will use these benefits in ways that enhance their own power
to the detriment of society as a whole.

One could argue that national security spending creates
jobs on the bottom rung of the economy too. Producing things
at scale still requires assembly line work, as well as janitorial
and other types of low-wage services that remain some of the
few occupational refuges for the mass of people without high-
priced technical degrees. And America's post-pandemic investments have coincided with real wage growth for the poorest
tenth of Americans.[52]

So why rush to conclude that Sullivan's "New Washington
Consensus" was bad for economic democracy?

Because even crude conjunctural analysis of our recent
past makes this conclusion obvious. Although IRA-related regulations put in place by executive-branch agencies aimed to
use industrial policy to benefit workers and encourage a measure of racial and gender equality in the workplace, such
"progressive" steps were neither rights nor laws but rather soft
executive-branch instructions—wholly and easily reversible by
a future administration.[53] It matters that gestures toward economic democracy in the IRA and the CHIPS and Science Act
were in absolute rather than relative terms—their durability
depends not on labor representing its own interests in preserving gains but on how acceptable those gains appear to a political opposition that shows little evidence of support for any
new Washington consensus other than the supposed existen-

tial threat China poses to America. As Biden showed when he forbade rail workers from striking for paid time off in 2022—because it would "devastate" the economy—workers are allowed to protest, but denied the tools to fight for themselves.

Federal spending on national security could, in theory, enhance worker power. Commentators have pointed to the Korean War as a relevant model for how military spending can boost the economy. But the Korean War is an anomaly. War mobilization then occurred in a context of high tax rates, sustained private investment, and high union density. The Korean War defense buildup took place in conjunction with strong worker organizing and a large labor movement, which is absent in the United States now because of restrictions on labor.

Contrast the Korean War's setting with the balance of class forces today. American labor laws have weakened since the days of Reagan, whose administration waged a war against worker organizing. Corporations have made a routine of flagrantly violating the weak labor laws that do exist because paying a fine for violations is often cheaper than giving in to worker demands.[54] The marginal and effective U.S. tax regime is far lower than it was in 1950. Union density today is still close to a hundred-year low. And even corporations reaping record profits today are not investing their accumulation or giving a greater share to employees but simply engaging in stock buybacks and dividend payments to shareholders, reinforcing wealth hoarding and secular stagnation—an economy lacking a clear growth trajectory, investment, or adequate consumption demand.

The benefits of the Korean War economic surge are also oversold. In many parts of the country "the Korean War boom strangled social democracy . . . [despite] economic expansion."[55] The Korean War is often cited as a case study in how the military can create an economic stimulus. But the Korean War was financed entirely through taxation, not borrowing.[56] The Korean defense buildup also quadrupled the size of the defense budget. These wartime levels of spending are not sustainable today—nor were they in the 1950s. But even if we ignore that we mobilized for the Korean War in a manner that pitted economic growth against economic equality, the balance of class forces at the time of the Korean War was still far more egalitarian than today.

How Rivalry Hurts Labor

Republicans have historically opposed labor unions. That is nothing new. But that ongoing political reality seriously hinders the ability to pursue economic security for the majority of Americans by way of national security Keynesianism.

Take the IRA—initially the Build Back Better Act (BBB), which the Democratic-led House of Representatives passed in November 2021. When the bill's name changed, so did its content. Before Republicans rejected it, BBB had dramatic investments for health care, welfare, and community building, in addition to ending subsidies for fossil fuel producers and banning new oil and gas drilling. The scale of BBB spending (as much as $4.9 trillion through 2031) dwarfed the amount eventually passed by Congress.[57] Several measures meant to strengthen labor rights and the National Labor Relations Board in the United States—which would have strengthened the relative position of workers—were removed from BBB. Moreover, BBB had offered a tax credit for battery-related manufacturers who hired unionized labor, which was also removed to make what became the IRA.[58]

The BBB's more ambitious elements were stripped out, and the IRA remained—massive federal subsidies for society's haves, little for society's have-nots. Given total Republican opposition, a thinned-out, corporate-friendly, and anti-China spending bill was the only kind that was feasible. Realistically, the IRA was the outer bound of the possible circa 2022. Yet that is proof that America's industrial policy remains as constrained as ever by a small political class that jealously guards the privileges of capital against the needs of the majority. To say that IRA-type industrial policy might have been radically pro-worker if only political gravity did not drag it toward protecting capital's interests is nevertheless to admit that it adapted to a new economic terrain (rather than rebalanced) the existing lopsided distribution of power.

Geography also played a role in the fate of BBB. That is, *where* national security Keynesianism invests also affects the balance between capital and labor in practice. The coalition in support of a national security–based economy has steered America's expanded investments in manufacturing, green tech, and supply chain control to states dominated by Republican politics—a potential poison pill for the entire gambit. "More than 75 percent of all investment" was committed to conservative congressional districts.[59]

Advocates talked of a burgeoning "battery belt"—most of the electro-voltaic and battery manufacturing in the United States is in conservative parts of the country in the Midwest and the South.[60] And since these were the industries of choice in national security Keynesianism and a green energy transition, they were positioned to realize large infusions of federal investment via tax credit schemes to corporations located there.

This was a good thing. People who live in conservative parts of America ought not to be starved of federal funds just because their political representatives usually oppose them. And there was logic in this "give money to your political opponents' constituents" wager. Perhaps a Democrat who built the

economy and stimulates jobs in conservative parts of the country could win over conservatives, creating future stakeholders
in national programs.

But it was a risky wager that potentially traded against
the interests of labor.

The only relevant comparison in U.S. history, the original
New Deal, also plowed investment disproportionately in conservative political strongholds along the Sun Belt.[61] That fueled
the Republican machine in places like Arizona and Southern
California—not only benefiting a political cadre that mostly
opposed the New Deal and insisted on insulating it from demands for racial equality, but also incubating the political tal-
ent who would ultimately kill the New Deal altogether.[62]

At present, the "battery belt" is sparsely unionized; the
IRA and the CHIPS and Science Act did not increase the likelihood of more union members. Most red states remain "right
to work" (anti-union) states by law. These are the portions of
the country with the worst capital-labor imbalances and the
highest levels of economic insecurity. They are places where
the tendency that "the bosses do what they will and the workers suffer what they must" is most egregious. The industries
that located there in the first place often did so to take advantage of favorable tax and weak labor conditions. And since the
investments being made through the IRA and CHIPS and Science Act are indirect to workers but direct to corporations,
they permit capital to retain its imbalance of power. *How* funding was dispersed—via tax credits routed to corporations and
individuals—ensures this.

And how Republicans respond to federal money pouring
into their areas via corporate tax credits is far from preordained.
The hope, at least for supply-side progressives and advocates
of the IRA, was that a new "green" conservative constituency
would be born that supports federal spending and climate ad-

aptation because it ensures U.S. "energy independence," thereby securing a transpartisan political coalition on behalf of investing in national power beyond just guns and bombs.[63]

But the early response of Glenn Youngkin, the Republican governor of Virginia, foreshadowed the opposite. Youngkin rejected a bid to build a Ford Motors battery plant in his state on the grounds that Ford—not just an American company but one with deep roots in American industrial history and heartland identity—was just a "front for China."[64] Exploiting groundless, racialized fears of Chinese "global dominance," he abandoned an electric vehicle company in his state because he thought Virginians "should be wary of Chinese communist intrusion into Virginia's economy."[65]

The Youngkin experience was not unique, either. In 2023, the United Auto Workers (UAW) went on strike against the Big Three (General Motors, Ford, and Stellantis) and succeeded in securing a boost in pay, benefits, and worker protections not seen in half a century. The Republican response was to oppose the UAW's demands and side with the bosses—hardly surprising—but their wedge for resisting labor power was great-power competition. Everyone from former vice president Mike Pence to Trump to senators Josh Hawley and J. D. Vance insisted that electric-vehicle manufacturing strengthened China and weakened America. The common message was, "the auto-workers' real enemy is China."[66] These are uncanny echoes of the way red-scare politics in the early Cold War facilitated passage of the Taft-Hartley Act (the key law neutering worker power) and weakened union solidarity.[67]

The Perils of a Permanent War Economy

From the perspective of economic equality, there are still other problems with relying on China to boost America's economy.

Designing an economy optimized for great-power competition has adverse implications for employment in the United States. It also perpetuates an unbalanced global economy that is a recurring cause of financial crises and widespread austerity.

Defense spending is an inefficient way to boost the economy partly due to the debt structure Washington uses to fund the military. The interest alone on U.S. financing for the first eighteen years of the War on Terror amounted to $925 billion.[68] Assuming interest rates do not radically rise, interest payments on military spending are projected to be $2 trillion by 2030 and $6.5 trillion by 2050.[69] This is money spent on debt servicing— not job creation, wages, or welfare.

The inefficiency of defense spending also has to do with the character of modern war. Compared to the old days of Fordist manufacturing, today's weapons of war are capital- (not labor-) intensive. A financialized, post-industrial economy has incentivized the United States to pursue not the largest military in the world by troop end strength but rather the most technologically sophisticated military in the world.[70] The U.S. way of war involves overmatch (battlespace domination) through technological superiority. More and more dollars are being spent on fewer and fewer exquisite platforms, leading to the joke within the industry that "in the year 2054, the entire defense budget will purchase just one aircraft."[71]

And because defense is a capital-intensive industry, it is by definition an inefficient way to reach full employment. Indeed, Nixon found "goosing" the economy through military spending for Vietnam attractive precisely because it was a way of directing federal spending for economic advantage without creating more public sector jobs (a prospect he abhorred).[72]

America's newfound obsession with semiconductor technology illustrates this problem well: 90 percent of *all* advanced semiconductors globally are made in Taiwan, and its largest semiconductor company, TSMC, employs only 65,000 people. Pouring money into the semiconductor industry makes a negligible difference to the unemployment rate or the wage share of the national income. To wit, between October 2022 and March 2023, firms seeking tax credits through the IRA and CHIPS and Science Act committed to $204 billion in spending on renewable energy technology and semiconductor manufacturing. The most generous estimate available at the time of this writing is that this grand sum will yield 82,000 jobs—a rounding error in the unemployment rate.[73] And that figure includes spending commitments by TSMC of up to $40 billion to build a new manufacturing site in Arizona.[74]

If the point of U.S. fiscal and industrial policy was primarily to achieve economic growth, employment, equality, or efficiency, it would be irrational for it to take the form of national security Keynesianism. Sustaining or recovering a position of strategic primacy—the ultimate rationale for national security Keynesianism—creates imbalances in not just the United States but also the global economy that lead to financial crises, which disproportionately harm workers and those already economically insecure.

Politicians and analysts tend to evaluate military and economic questions as if they have nothing to do with each other. This is wrong, not only because U.S. officials put economic policy in service of traditional national security aims but also because the U.S. strategy of primacy entailed pursuing both military and economic primacy; they were not severable as long as primacy remained the strategy. And the means by which these ends have been pursued fuse the military with the economy in ways that have been deleterious for the economic system as a whole.

The U.S. strategy of primacy insists on military superiority. What this standard of superiority requires to maintain it depends on its point of reference. From the end of the Cold War through 2017, a "superiority" level of domination was indexed against what was called the "two-war construct"—the ability to wage two mid-size conventional wars in different regions (for example, the Middle East and East Asia) in overlapping time frames. Since 2017, military superiority has been indexed against war with China in the Taiwan Strait—meaning out-arming a "great power" that has been rapidly expanding its military capabilities but doing so with the purpose of defeating it in a geography that gives China the greatest advantages and puts the U.S. military in the most unfavorable position imaginable, thereby requiring horizonless defense spending.[75]

But this insistence on military superiority comes at an unacknowledged price that goes well beyond the defense budget. As mentioned above, U.S. politicians have developed a habit of funding defense not through tax increases but rather deficit financing, primarily from foreign borrowing. When policymakers decide that external threats require a military buildup, they exploit America's privileged position in the world economic system to avoid the near-term domestic political friction that would come with any fight over taxes by accumulating debt, much of which goes to foreign investors.[76]

In so doing, however, the United States becomes a magnet for current account surpluses accumulated in foreign economies. That "capital flow bonanza" concentrating in the metropole leads to economic imbalances in the United States and globally—the rest of the world is uniquely exposed to imbalances in the U.S. economy because of America's unique position in the international economic order.[77] Cheap credit and procyclical economic expansion eventually lead to asset bubbles (inflated prices in, for example, real estate), creating the conditions for banking crises.

Such crises expose the frailty of the global economic

order, encouraging recurring challenges to its legitimacy, protectionist economic policies, and the search for alternatives. Military buildups for the Vietnam War, for "rolling back" the Soviets in the 1980s, and for the Global War on Terror all resulted in boom-bust crises.[78] These crises were a burden for workers and foreign economies alike because they rapidly deflated the value of assets on which workers' pensions and personal savings (for example, home value) relied. They also required dramatic fiscal and monetary policy interventions that, in practice, have amounted to subsidies for private banks and large firms to keep the system solvent. Aside from the moral hazard of rewarding banks' risk-acceptant profit-seeking, this process also socialized the costs of crisis management, both through transfers of wealth from taxpayers to corporations and through the opportunity cost of foregone support for individuals who lost their savings or livelihoods as a result of the crisis.

The paradox of our current historical moment is thus that a world system with the United States at its core encourages U.S. political elites to act in ways that repeatedly destabilize it. Washington's national security Keynesianism appears to be a willful attempt to close out the international economic order as it existed before 2020 while still "leading" the global economy, giving up the obligations of world policeman while continuing to exploit the advantages of world order so the United States can outcompete China.

This is a grim outlook for much of the world. On what grounds can we hope that the Global South will be more than a plundered battleground for the powerful? What model of economic growth and development is there in a world forced to choose between the Chinese market and the U.S. market? And if the rest of the world suffers from economic stagnation or depression, what foreign markets will be able to consume America's planned manufacturing surplus? A hegemon pursuing something akin to autarky leaves little of promise for others in the international system.

Conclusion

This chapter, like the previous chapter on America's poisoned politics, illustrates not only why it is inadvisable to use rivalry to achieve a better democracy but also how democracy is already paying a high price for the sake of sustaining rivalry. Today, as during the Cold War, rivalry is a wager that sacrifices both political and economic democracy at the altar of great-power competition. We can imagine two possible counterarguments to the evidence we have presented.

One might go like this: "Rising economic insecurity, inequality, xenophobia, racism, political repression, far-right extremism, and self-imposed brain drain—all unfortunate problems, but they do not pose immediate national security threats to the United States." This rejoinder boils down to labeling these indicators of democracy erosion as negative externalities (collateral damage) while declaring the primacy of the "national" interest or *raison d'état*. It is saying that the China threat is sufficiently grave to be worth whatever domestic price geopolitical competition incurs. This is how Democratic politicians responded to the rise in anti-Asian violence that was a consequence of Sino-U.S. rivalry—condemning racism and violence while affirming the virtues of that which gave rise to them.

This logic subordinates economic equality to great-power rivalry with little attention to who benefits and who pays for U.S. foreign policy. It sacrifices democratic society to secure geopolitical advantage, and it violates the dictates of good strategy. U.S. national security worthy of the name must reflect the needs and interests of all Americans.

The merits of this line of counter-reasoning thus hinge

entirely on two things: whether national security prescriptions fit the diagnosis of the problem, and whether the pain democratic society bears for fighting the "existential and ideological threat" of China is necessary. We deal with this question squarely in the next chapter, but we see both threat inflation and threat misdiagnosis in the policy conversation about China.

A second counterargument might be this: "Rivalry isn't the only cause of economic insecurity and political inequality. If there were no rivalry, we would still have these problems." This rejoinder rests on a counterfactual belief that if the domestic problems predated the inception point of rivalry—or if there is more than one cause of these problems—then there is no point in condemning geopolitical competition. In other words, do not blame the state for the problems inherent to U.S. political economy.

But this is not just fallacious reasoning; there is also no evidence to support it. Since the onset of rivalry with China around 2016, the severity of these problems has been rising—a trend that must be arrested if democracy is to retain its soul. We have walked through ample proof in these chapters of the direct linkage between rivalry and the myriad harms it visits upon political and economic democracy. To dismiss all of that because de-escalating or finding alternatives to geopolitical competition would not solve everything is both to ignore what is right in front of us and to make the perfect the enemy of the good. More crucially, we agree that the horizon of U.S. grand strategy should extend beyond simply making U.S. foreign policy less dependent on great-power rivalry—a topic we return to in the concluding chapter.

Above all, however, we must be unambiguous about one thing: great-power rivalry cannot generate economic equality. Rivalry's zero-sum outlook forecloses on economic democracy. It provides economic security for some by taking security away from others. Given this, we should not be surprised that undemocratic means have yielded undemocratic results—ones that shape the material lives of Americans in harmful ways. The double tragedy is that the very same conditions that inhibit economic democracy also threaten global peace.

5

How Rivalry Threatens Peace

For many Western analysts, "China and East Asia serve as empty vessels—as Rorschach tests—into which we can put whatever ideas, assumptions, fears, and guesses we wish."[1] So far, we have focused principally on the price that geopolitical rivalry imposes on American democracy and its publics. But we have said little about China's share in great-power rivalry.

In this chapter, therefore, we take on two tasks. In the first half, we outline our theory of China—the problems that China poses to the international system, and why we think U.S. policymakers have misdiagnosed the "China threat." In the second half, we explain why taking a globally confrontational, zero-sum approach to China is destabilizing. In brief, it increases the risks of war. And by empowering reactionary forces abroad, rivalry feeds rather than attenuates the CCP's ethnonationalist and authoritarian rule.

A Theory of China

Our argument in this book about the danger of great-power rivalry raises the question: How should the United States properly assess China?

We find both threat inflation and misperception in how policymakers conceive of China. This does not mean that China poses no threat to nations in East Asia or to the interests of the United States. But neither is it an existential threat, a threat to world stability, or a threat that exists in a vacuum apart from American choices. For clarity and simplicity, we summarize the China situation as follows:

- The United States does not need to retain hegemony to prevent China from realizing hegemony. For the foreseeable future, China does not have the ability or ambition to dominate the world. Even within Asia alone, it is debatable whether it has the *ambition* to create a Sino-centric order that excludes the United States, but at any rate it cannot foreseeably acquire the *ability* to do so.
- China—through the CCP and millions of Chinese workers—has benefited tremendously, though unequally, from a global economic order that substantially favors the United States. China does not sit outside world order as it actually exists; it is embedded within that order.
- China represents a version of the problems that afflict the global (and U.S.) economy generally—oligarchs and owners of capital rely on state repression of Chinese workers to keep manufacturing costs low and capture the surplus value from production. Instead of redistributing the profits from these exploitative social relations internally, they plow it into international projects, U.S. debt (Treasury securities), real estate, and high-risk financial instruments (and, increasingly, renewable energy technologies). Some of this internationalized surplus does good

abroad; some of it does harm. But it perpetuates global imbalances that are sustained at the expense of Chinese households and that risk large-scale financial crisis.

- The CCP's ability to deliver economic growth has been a major source of regime legitimacy, making it easier to sustain domestic economic imbalances that leave the majority of the population living precariously. The CCP tries to wield ethnonationalism for political ends. Without the promise of economic growth, Han nationalism becomes the primary basis for the CCP's claim to leadership.

- Ethnonationalist political attitudes favor more domestic repression (including human rights abuses), increased defense expenditures, and more assertive foreign policies. As the forces of ethnonationalism gain strength in CCP politics, China's posture toward the United States and the world becomes more belligerent.

- China's rapid expansion and modernization of the People's Liberation Army (PLA) is attempting to rectify an imbalance of power that favors the United States virtually everywhere but the Taiwan Strait. By treating the PLA as the Pentagon's "pacing threat," the United States is refusing to accept a balance of power in Asia and is instead seeking to retain U.S. primacy. This creates a qualitative arms-racing dynamic.

- The Taiwan Strait is best understood as a security dilemma. Despite an imbalance of power there favoring Chinese forces, neither the United States nor China seeks to destroy the other; neither aims to start a war; and both would prefer to manage the political status of Taiwan without war.

WHAT IS CHINA DOING?

The conventional Washington story about why China is so menacing rests on a handful of uneven, cherry-picked, but mostly accurate observations.

Xi Jinping has consolidated greater personalized control of the CCP than any Chinese leader since Mao Zedong. Largely coinciding with Xi's tenure, China has grown more repressive domestically, the most horrific and attention-grabbing practices being what some describe as its cultural genocide of Muslim Uyghurs in Xinjiang. As an extension of this domestic repression, China violently quashed pro-democracy protests in Hong Kong, effectively recolonizing it in 2019. Sino-centric institutions such as the Belt and Road Initiative and the Asian Infrastructure Investment Bank (AIIB) are not just alternatives to U.S.-centered international financial institutions; they are indicators of a Chinese sphere of influence, or worse, attempts to build a hegemonic order.[2]

The PLA and its proxies (the Coast Guard and "maritime militia") have also dramatically increased the frequency of their air and maritime intrusions into contested spaces in the South China Sea, the East China Sea, and the Taiwan Strait. Violating promises Xi made to Obama in 2013, China has been unilaterally militarizing and occupying portions of the South China Sea that remain legally contested.[3] China has made universalist claims to ethnically Chinese diaspora, because "the blood of the Chinese nation flows through their bodies," making them targets for influence by the United Front Work Department (a propagandist-action arm of the CCP overseas).[4] In a departure from the "hide and bide" era, Chinese government officials and propaganda mouthpieces have undertaken what they dub "wolf-warrior diplomacy," a transgressive, bombastic style of public messaging that is regularly laced with threats and bravado. Since the global financial crisis of 2008, China has increasingly converted its economic centrality into coercive power by suspending or disrupting the flow of certain goods from trading partners that violate its preferences. And the CCP has made a greater priority of resolving Taiwan's political status, leaving open (and preparing for) the possibility of unifying Taiwan by force if necessary.

With the exception of fuzzy and contestable claims that China seeks a hegemonic order, the concerns of U.S. policymakers described here are observable facts. What is lacking is a good understanding of the facts and corresponding prescriptions.

In accounting for all of this, the most common tendency is to boil everything down to perceiving a more assertive China and then attributing that to Xi Jinping. Yes, Xi has ruled in a more sultanistic way than his recent predecessors, consolidated control of the state, and overseen a period of growing military investment and foreign policy belligerence. But it would be a mistake to identify Xi Jinping as the principal cause.

Evidence of Chinese assertiveness—especially the frequency of air and maritime incursions into others' Exclusive Economic Zones in the East and South China Seas—was on the rise as early as 2007, and Chinese talk of a world beyond American hegemony picked up in 2008 with the global financial crisis.[5] Xi Jinping did not come to power until December 2012. When he did, it was on a promise of wiping out government corruption following a discovery in 2010 that U.S. intelligence assets had infiltrated senior levels of the regime by exploiting its culture of corruption.[6] Xi's strongman politics was an answer to what the CCP saw as an existential threat to its regime—the intersection of its own corruption and U.S. espionage. And with the exception of the Belt and Road Initiative,

China's regional institutional arrangements that Washington finds threatening (like AIIB) predate Xi Jinping's rise.

Alternative accounts of China's greater assertiveness or hegemonic ambitions—which are not the same thing—attribute these to a clash of civilizations, its superficially communist ideology, or its authoritarian regime type. All of these explanations fail on the grounds that a constant cannot explain a variable. China under the CCP has never not been authoritarian, yet, over time, it has vacillated between being an enemy and a tacit ally of the United States. Claims that "China has a 5,000 year history of cheating and stealing. . . . Some things will never change," as Senator Marsha Blackburn remarked, might sound racist, sure, but they are also analytically impoverished—Chinese civilization did not change when it started becoming more assertive.[7]

The same could be said for worries about the "totalitarian" nature of China's repressive party-state.[8] Not only is the ideology of the CCP the same pre- and post-assertiveness, but anyone familiar with China's actual conduct can see a category error. Take a comparative view: Vietnam, sitting next door to China, is also a one-party communist state, like China, yet Vietnam is a friend and partner of the United States. But there is, at any rate, little that is recognizably communist about either China or Vietnam. Whatever the rhetoric of the party, China is an ethnonationalist state operating an authoritarian model of capitalism, not communism.[9] China's material power, moreover, comes from the privileged position it occupies in the capitalist world system. And its corporate theft of the intellectual property of U.S. firms has been a known price of doing business with China that some of the world's largest corporations (and both U.S. political parties) were fine with until some weren't, typically because the costs of production there rose and profits declined as wages gradually increased.

How, then, do we account for the behaviors that inspire so much fear and loathing in Washington?

At root, the observations that animate U.S. policymaker grievances are symptoms of and worsened by extreme inequality in China—the economic, the chauvinistic, and the jingoistic are intertwined. CCP authoritarianism is instrumental to and benefits from this alchemy.

IT'S THE GLOBAL POLITICAL ECONOMY, STUPID

Washington defines the security confrontation between China and the United States in terms of the various aforementioned problems. Artificial island-building, maritime incursions, corporate espionage, human rights abuses, labor repression, sphere-of-influence building, and the like are treated as evidence of the need to confront or outcompete China. Yet not only is most of this symptomatic of rivalry itself; all of it is a political consequence of uneven and combined development (that is, the developmental constraints and opportunities that nations face depend on *when* they begin modern development and *how* they are positioned in the world system relative to more powerful governments). Any sober analysis of China's actions thus necessarily entangles the United States with it, which in turn makes "competition" at best a non-solution.

As we noted earlier, imbalances in the global economy owe partly to America's commitment to deficit-financed military primacy. But we did not explain how China relates to that problem except as the bogeyman that justifies spending on a military buildup.

The United States enjoys many of the advantages of an economic hegemon at a global level, but China's economic position in the world system makes it the dominant actor in the political economy of Asia—the world's wealthiest, most populous, and most militarized region.[10] Capital accumulation in China, which reflects this position, is the material basis for Chinese military and political power. And the asymmetrical interdependencies that form between China and other states because of Beijing's economic centrality give it both clout in its dealings with others and leverage that can be used to coerce or secure political influence (as it does with the United States).[11]

One of the ways inequality figures into this problem is that, by design, the wage share in China has not remotely kept pace with the growth of Chinese productive output the past two and a half decades.[12] So even as real wages in China (and thereby the costs of production) have increased since the 1990s, oligarchic elites are nevertheless extracting even more surplus value from workers over time. As of 2018, Chinese workers were taking home only around 40 percent of the nation's output.[13] And in 2020, Premier Li Keqiang stated that "there are still some 600 million people [whose] monthly income is barely 1,000 RMB Yuan [$245 per month]. It's not even enough to rent a room in a medium Chinese city."[14] China's high savings rate reflects accumulation by the wealthy and corporations, not high incomes among workers.

This may seem either obvious or of questionable relevance, but it is in fact central. When economists speak in terms of China's "high rate of savings" and "low rate of consumption," they are describing an accounting dimension of the surplus value that results from worker exploitation. That excess—that surplus value denied to workers—is what the state, government-owned banks, and CCP officials then deploy in various, often inefficient, and sometimes menacing ways.

Yet all of this depends on a world system that advantages Washington. Fearing that China could forge a world (or regional) order without the United States misunderstands the structures that give rise to Chinese power. A struggle for hegemony is not essential; it is contrived based on a misdiagnosis. It makes little sense to see an existential threat in Chinese conduct when the power underlying it depends on its position within a global capitalist order that overwhelmingly privileges the power of the American state.[15] The world is not really in contest, and Asia is contested only to the extent that the United States insists on a position of dominance in Asia that no longer accords with how regional relations are already ordered.

Moreover, much of Chinese conduct is *not* a contest for Asia.

Rather, it is much more productive to think of Chinese foreign and defense policy—decisions of the state that try to preserve, grow, and exploit its sources of power—as downstream of "a conflict between economic classes *within* China. . . . Systematic transfers of wealth from Chinese workers to Chinese elites distort the Chinese economy by strangling purchasing power and strangling production at the expense of consumption."[16] That same class conflict within China—the world's manufacturing hub—also feeds global economic imbalances.

Bank lending in China is decentralized—credit is generated by local banks and empowers local governments or else is routed overseas through development and import-export banks. This arrangement has been crucial to China's economic growth yet is inefficient and a site of corruption.[17] Not only has this structure of lending led to the accumulation of bad debts (non-performing loans); it has also fueled overcapacity and declining profitability in construction, manufacturing, and real estate—a problem that existed since *before* the Asian financial crisis in 1997–1998.[18] The only reason this did not explode as a globally destabilizing catastrophe the past twenty-five years is that it was offset by China's ability to export its excess capacity to foreign markets (especially the United States), coupled with a surge in foreign direct investment (FDI) flows into China.[19]

Xi Jinping's concept of dual circulation—much discussed in 2020 and 2021 but rarely mentioned since—recognized this problem but did not provide a solution. "Dual circulation" referred to expanding export markets abroad while also dramatically boosting domestic consumption (necessarily via redistribution).[20] The trouble is that the primary reason China became a grand export-based economy was the low wage share (that is, forced low consumption, forced high savings rates) of Chinese workers. The CCP never developed a plausible theory for *how* to keep exports high while redistributing surplus value back to workers.

This makes sense of projects like BRI—an initiative that systematically cultivates foreign markets to absorb Chinese excess manufacturing and infrastructure-building capacity. It also contextualizes China's post-2008 talk about its coming moment as a leading global power amid American relative decline. Washington interpreted China's boasting, which increasingly came at America's expense, as signs of Chinese hegemony-seeking.[21] But surging flows of foreign investment into China depended on a long, optimistic shadow of the future, which China's imagistic salesmanship projected. China's rise-decline narrative was self-serving, but in a manner that was essential to regime survival.

So we have in China a system of export-driven growth built on sectoral imbalances, global imbalances, and societal imbalances. Low consumption and high savings rates have translated into overproduction in manufacturing, construction, and real estate. To sustain growth, China is dependent on export markets and highly political lending practices that run up bad debt. As a mathematical reality, China's current account surpluses must entail current account deficits elsewhere in the globe (historically, primarily the United States). And squeezing households to subsidize the production of exports perpetuates societal imbalances—extreme concentrations of wealth astride tens of millions who still live in poverty and hundreds of millions more who live precariously in the informal economy. The state institutes policies that support this system of exploitation within China—a system that has powered the global economic order and boosted (or distorted) measurements of global economic development and poverty alleviation.

Because policymakers are inattentive to this reality and America's relationship to it, they fail to ask what the consequences are of a Chinese system of wealth transfer from the many to the few or to question how it is being sustained.

CCP authoritarianism, combined with China's position in the global economy, keeps an unbalanced situation going. Xi Jinping is an avatar of authoritarianism, not its cause. While Xi is portrayed as a totalitarian in Washington, he has struggled to institute a property tax and to reform the banking sector.[22] It is not even clear he wants to exercise such controls. Despite Xi speaking frequently of progressive and redistributive measures, he was brought into power by party elites who wanted to preserve the system they knew and benefited from against what at the time were bubbling redistributive reforms and grassroots demands for "common, shared prosperity."[23] Little surprise that Xi has shown no willingness or ability to act like a progressive beyond occasionally investigating and restricting the uber-rich.[24] Whatever Xi's personal motives, he has practiced a deeply reactionary politics that broadly aligns with the interests not of workers but rather China's oligarchic class.[25] And the many domestic transfer mechanisms that have sustained the system of exploitation and imbalance powering China's rise predate Xi's reign.[26]

Policies of labor repression and social control limit worker power, maintain downward pressure on wages, and preserve China's competitive cost advantage in manufacturing for global markets.[27] The ability to expropriate land when it suits the state and to downplay or ignore environmental standards in domestic production keeps costs low while leaving non-elites in China worse off. The *hukou,* or household passport registration system, makes most rural workers who migrate to cities technically illegal immigrants in their own country; furthermore, the system requires workers to pay into social welfare benefits but allows them access to benefits only if they stay living and working where they were born.[28] And the requirement to store money in a government-owned bank as the principal way for households to accumulate savings—in saving accounts that offer abnormally low interest rates—capitalizes banks, which then lend generously to the construction and manufacturing sectors of the economy.[29]

These myriad ways of transferring wealth from workers to owners of capital and well-connected elites are neither communist nor socialist, and they would not fly in a democratic society. Some of these measures and mechanisms are more directly repressive than others, but they are overwhelmingly anti-egalitarian, raising the question of how they can be sustained without mass backlash from the Chinese people.

AUTHORITARIAN CAPITALISM
NEEDS ETHNONATIONALISM

The inequalities at the heart of Chinese conduct at home and abroad are not purely economic either as cause or consequence—a repressive, ethnonationalist politics is an effect of economic inequality and economic imbalances, as well as a terrain that facilitates them.[30]

In short, Sino-U.S. rivalry is leading to "the emergence of new authoritarian state forms and the rise of the radical right" in China, as in the United States.[31] As economic growth stagnates and inter-capitalist competition becomes fiercer, the state becomes more essential because of its ability to intervene, manage fiscal crises, and occasionally direct outcomes. When that state is already authoritarian and relies on a bevy of repressive practices to preserve a status quo, we end up in situations where "neoliberals need neofascists."[32] Authoritarianism has been key to the alchemy of China's rise, but it becomes even more central as growth sputters, bad debt accumulates, and civil society agitates against state repression. Crucially, CCP authoritarianism works partly through ethnonationalist appeals and narratives about its own Han civilizational exceptionalism.

As the political scientist and Sinologist Yuen Yuen Ang rued in 2022, "The only people who are winning [Sino-U.S. competition] are the ardent radicals, the extremists, and the autocrats on both sides. It's so easy to be nationalists. . . . You just need to scream and say extreme things and get people roused."[33] Long before Xi Jinping came to power, the CCP appealed to nationalist sentiments strategically. Sometimes it was to bolster regime legitimacy, and sometimes it was to mobilize nationalism for foreign policy ends—to lend credibility to their signaling to other powers in the world.[34] The complication is not only that nationalism—particularly when grounded in ethnicity—can be a pernicious source of Manichean othering in political life.[35] It is also that nationalism takes on a life of its own; you can dial it up, but dialing it down can be difficult without domestic repression.[36]

Xi Jinping, for his part, has leaned into blood-and-soil rhetoric, evoking Han nationalism and a willingness to do violence on behalf of it, as part of cultivating his own legitimacy.[37] "Wolf-warrior" diplomacy, which Xi has encouraged, can be understood as performative nationalism for bureaucrats.

But reaching beyond state functionaries, Washington's anti-China rhetoric and the Sino-U.S. rivalry itself have led to a "wave of anti-American sentiment among China's youth"—a generational cohort that is more nationalistic than the previous one yet shares the economic precarity and societal resentments of youth in the West.[38] They are not innately patriotic fanatics of the Chinese state; they are responding to party narratives that gain credence from geopolitical rivalry.

Xi's nationalism has also accommodated a surge in racist, reactionary discourses in popular online media in China— a growth that is happening in parallel with a similar trend in Western countries.[39] The difference is that, in China, it is the Han Chinese who self-venerate as "civilized" contra the barbarism of others, both within their nation and outside it. Posters in chat forums online decry a "white left" (*baizuo*) that they conflate with "Western hegemony," seeing it as something between "an unrealistic fantasy or a conspiracy of privileged white elites."[40] As with the "national conservatives" and far right in the United States, China's online reactionaries simultaneously mock and claim to fear *baizuo* to justify their ethnonationalism.[41] The racial, the "patriotic," and the geopolitical are bound up with each other.

Seen in this way, the plight of Uyghurs in Xinjiang is not some aberrant, mysterious evil but rather a microcosm of how ethnonationalism and political repression work on behalf of economic interests. China's persecution of Uyghurs is part of "colonial-capitalist frontier making"—the convergence of authoritarian techno-surveillance, racial hierarchy, and labor repression.[42] Internment camps are exploited for corporate profit even as they fulfill ethno-political ideas about "living space" and Han identity. Even nominally free Uyghurs are subjected to "non-internment, state-imposed forced labor" at scale in support of national economic growth targets.[43] Xinjiang's land, like its people, is a resource meant to enrich the metropole; Xinjiang is governed as a colony within an empire-nation.

Many Beltway lawmakers and pundits are rightly concerned about large-scale human rights abuses against Muslim Uyghurs in Xinjiang. But the causes of such abuses are not taken seriously in Washington at all. If they were, U.S. officials would see that during the War on Terror, U.S. policy was actively complicit in Chinese exploitation and repression of Uyghurs— and not just because the War on Terror furnished the meta-narrative that China used to label its own Muslim population "terrorists."[44] Moreover, Chinese officials studied U.S. counter-insurgency doctrine in developing their internment and intelligence collection system in Xinjiang, including General David Petraeus's famed handbook.[45] And until recently, U.S. firms were directly benefiting from forced labor in Xinjiang. Despite attempts to cleanse supply chains of human rights abuses, it remains the case that "behind Seattle stands Xinjiang"—the surveillance used to control Xinjiang's population comes out of China's surveillance technology industry, which has only built up with investment from U.S. capital.[46]

Conservative politics is eclectic, but its darkest varietal— simultaneously xenophobic, racialized, and narcissistically zero-sum—demands and justifies inequalities. In the United States, it does so with deference to the judgment of the national security state on all things military and, increasingly, with a peculiarly MAGA valence. In China, it does so with the "Chinese characteristics" of Han civilization, conflating the CCP with the nation. This is what it means to recognize that geopolitical rivalry—occurring in a world economy of declining profitability—is nurturing forms of state capitalism that cultivate a reactionary political bent.

China's ethnonationalism, moreover, dovetails with jingoism beyond the rhetorical domain of the wolf-warrior diplomats.

Coincident with China's military expansion, Xi Jinping has also promoted encompassing concepts like "comprehensive security," "indivisible security," and "military-civil fusion" that incentivize bureaucrats to self-consciously shape policy in favor of national power and warfighting considerations.

In this landscape of creeping militarism, the ongoing recognition of rivalry with the United States has fueled the rise of China's military-industrial complex in the CCP. The PLA and its supporting defense industry has occupied a privileged place in Chinese politics for decades.[47] And the log-rolling, quid pro quo nature of the state's bureaucratic institutions has made it hard to check the PLA's growth over time.[48] But Xi has overseen much greater growth: over one-third of the party's Central Committee now consists of members with backgrounds in defense technology or national security (a 35 percent increase just since the Trump years).[49] This defense-technocratic social milieu prefers, benefits from, and steers national resources toward China's security competition with the United States—geopolitical rivalry gives them purpose, and it is their domain of competence.

Rivalry as Dystopian Geopolitics

Blind to the causes of Chinese "influence" and growing military power, the United States has set out to combat and contain it all the same. But by approaching China neither historically nor relationally—that is, as a problem of uneven and combined development and a security dilemma—U.S. choices are making the world a more dangerous place. The resultant rivalry is fueling reactionary politics abroad, eroding any pacifying effects that might be gained from economic interdependence, justifying arms-racing dynamics, and increasing crisis instability risks.

STRENGTHENING ANTI-DEMOCRATIC
FORCES ABROAD

The moral perversions that once made a mockery of American ideals about freedom and democracy during the Cold War have returned. Great-power rivalry now threatens democracy abroad in at least two ways. One is the power-politicization of the economy, which makes more likely nationalist and revanchist appeals—not just by China but by developmental and developing states generally. The other way that rivalry puts the United States on the side of autocracy is more literal and direct: U.S. policy lavishes arms, aid, and political capital on regimes that are hostile to democracy and rob their people of security.

The United States finds itself in the awkward position of waging limited economic war against a country on which the global economy relies. Even bracketing off thick Sino-U.S. interdependencies, China is the largest trading partner for much of the developing world. It represents a greater share of global GDP than any other nation in the world (18.2 percent as of 2022).[50] It is "the world's largest official creditor, surpassing the World Bank, IMF and 22-member Paris Club combined."[51] And the World Bank projects that China's share of "growth in developing East Asia and the Pacific" is only going to increase, in part because it is deeply woven into Asia's financial architecture in ways that no other large economy is.[52]

Despite this, U.S. economic statecraft has prioritized imposing tariffs on a growing list of imports from China, enhancing export controls that shrink the number of U.S. technologies China can access, increasing the number of Chinese firms blacklisted from doing business in the United States, tightening restrictions on inbound investment from China, and expanding a global diplomatic campaign to persuade key governments in

Europe and Asia to divest from technology firms such as Huawei. Add to this the Biden administration's industrial policy,
which conditioned its lavish semiconductor tax credits on firms'
willingness to halt or reverse plans for advanced manufacturing investment in China. Even America's carrots were meant as
a stick.

U.S. economic policy is thus at odds with the world's—
and especially Asia's—economic reality, promising nightmarish
prospects for democracy in the developing world. Responding
to China in a manner that propels geoeconomics exacerbates
rather than improves upon the burgeoning global crisis of economic development.

The East Asian "tiger" economies of the 1970s through the
1990s buoyed regional stability, but their "miracle" was predicated on state subsidies, extreme export dependencies, and reli-
able prospects of future growth. That development model did
not work nearly as well outside of East Asia, and in the twenty-
first century it has gradually come undone anyway, leaving
"fiscal insolvency [as] a live possibility for countless poor governments."[53]

The later an economy jumped on the developmental lad-
der, the greater difficulty it faced climbing up the value chain,
partly because it vied against earlier entrants and partly because of shrinking global demand since the 1970s. The economic historian Tim Barker lamented that in the Global South,
"the peaks [of economic growth] are coming at a lower level
. . . than they did in the now-rich countries that industrialized
earlier."[54] Secular stagnation—a long-term period of low investment and sputtering global economic growth—afflicts developed and developing economies alike. Since the global financial
crisis of 2008, it is clear that no realistic development model
exists for the Global South and that East Asia's recipe for success is delivering diminishing returns for that region too.

When it comes to China, the United States has been trying to secure its economic interests at the expense of the global
majority. But doing so harms U.S. interests as well. The United
States cannot turn itself into a global manufacturing power-
house without undermining other countries' export-reliant economic strategies, and, in so doing, it undermines the ability of
the rest of the world to absorb American productivity.

Failing to offer a substitute economic model, while making choices that demolish the old one, keeps developmental
states reliant upon debt accumulation—most of which now
comes from China—to keep their economies running. Much
of this debt has failed to catalyze economic growth, and servic-
ing the interest on it continues to consume public expenditure
in developing nations. In 2021, developing countries spent twice
as much on interest payments on existing debt ($400 billion)
as they received in new loans.[55] Some governments are spending more on interest than they are on health care or education.
The inevitable result is a debt crisis in emerging economies.
According to the International Monetary Fund (IMF), 60 percent of low-income developing countries are facing debt distress (at risk of defaulting on the debt) as of 2022.[56] The World
Bank estimates that between 2023 and 2030 the developing world
will require $2.4 trillion per year on average simply "to address
the global challenges of climate change, conflict, and pandemics," even apart from national development or economic security.[57] And the default international response only worsens the
problem: "for every dollar that the IMF provides to a poor
country for social spending, it requires the country to cut four
times more through austerity measures."[58]

This is a huge strategic problem for the United States,
and for the world.

In 2022 and 2023, Sino-U.S. rivalry actively impeded the
ability to work with the Paris Club and IMF on debt restructuring

for countries at risk of debt default. China's willingness to take losses on the debt it is owed is contingent on the degree to which it sees itself under economic siege from U.S. policy—rivalry and forgiveness are inversely linked. As long as the U.S. tariff regime on Chinese goods—which dates to the Trump years—remains in place, China is reluctant to write down and meaningfully restructure developing-nation debts.[59]

More generally, a geopolitical economy that insists on shunting smaller actors into a U.S. or Chinese "camp" only worsens the development problem, cutting them off from one or the other sources of investment and market access. Troubled, listless economies, in turn, are uniquely vulnerable to autocratic solutions, domestic repression, and demagoguery. Reviving global bloc politics, as U.S. policy has been doing since the Trump years, amplifies the conditions of depredation that give rise to the global far right and makes living conditions too austere and precarious for the populace to agitate for democracy. The regime change and street violence Sri Lanka experienced in 2022—the result of years of neoliberal mismanagement of the economy and unserviceable debt—portends what an "America First," anti-China economic strategy will yield in extremis.

ARMING AUTOCRACY

Great-power rivalry tilts in favor of reactionary politics abroad in more direct ways too. Since the onset of rivalry around 2016, the United States' China policy has strengthened oligarchy and kleptocracy in the Global South by compelling the United States to align and collaborate with foreign despotism as long as it has a prospect of inhibiting Chinese power or influence.

In the name of supposedly balancing against China, the Obama administration overlooked a genocide in Myanmar, supported flagrant kleptocracy in Malaysia, and actively aided a fascistic presidency in the Philippines. Under Trump and Biden, this self-defeating hypocrisy has not just continued but worsened.

Not only have both presidents sided with autocrats across the Middle East in symbolic ways like photo ops and White House summits, but in addition their administrations have spent (and made) hundreds of billions of dollars via weapons and training for militaries across the region. Under Biden, the U.S. government sold arms to the majority of the world's autocracies (57 percent), eclipsing even Trump-era highs in total value of transfers (over $205 billion).[60] And the reasoning, in almost every case, was great-power competition.

Nowhere is this more flagrantly power-political than in Saudi Arabia. For decades, the Saudi monarchy has been responsible for countless crimes against both humanity (publicly executing women seeking equality) and the United States (incubating with impunity the terrorists who conducted the 9/11 attacks). Despite this, and despite the monarchy's unrepentant murder of the *Washington Post* journalist Jamal Khashoggi in 2018, the United States actively helped Saudi Arabia prosecute a brutal war in Yemen that had yielded more than 350,000 casualties as of 2022.

Why? We could point to oil, or perhaps paranoia about a nuclear-armed Iran, but Washington has come to routinely justify this overall pattern of pro-autocratic engagement in terms of great-power rivalry. Trump's secretary of state, Mike Pompeo, explained that the United States cannot afford to view the Middle East and North Africa "in isolation" but rather must see the region in terms of how other great powers benefit, counseling that the United States "mend relations with the Sunni Arab Gulf States, and embrace them as the allies they wish to be."[61] Adam Smith, a Democratic congressman, warned that if the United States suspended arms sales to Saudi Arabia for even one year, "You will see Saudi Arabia turn more and more to Russia and China. . . . China would have greater entrée to the Middle East."[62] Even Biden declared, "We will not walk away [from the Middle East] and leave a vacuum to be filled by China."[63] So in 2022, the White House celebrated convincing Saudi Arabia to allow U.S. firms, not China-owned Huawei, to build 5G telecommunications in the kingdom.

Equally a problem was Washington's courtship of the Narendra Modi regime in India, which prominent Indian intellectuals ranging from Arundhati Roy to Salman Rushdie have decried as Hindu fascist.

Since at least 2002, American strategists in the Pentagon have fantasized about the potential for India to serve as a "natural" counterweight to a rising China. India looms large on a map and abuts China along a massive, contested border spanning the Himalayas. In the Trump era, Secretary of Defense James Mattis internalized this view to argue that arming and supporting India was "a way to expand the competitive space" with China.[64] As with so much China policy, Washington in the Biden era embraced this Trump-era outlook and took it much further.

Not only was Modi feted with a White House summit and state dinner in 2023, but he was also given the honor of addressing a joint session of Congress. The Biden administration also announced dozens of U.S.-India defense-related cooperation initiatives ranging from combined military exercises and the sale of armed drones to co-development of engines for fighter jets and joint advanced weapons-related technology research in areas including artificial intelligence and quantum computing—some of the very technologies that the United States has been trying to prevent China from developing.

The benefits of all this symbolic and material support for

India are demonstrably illusory. India has not needed help balancing China, and the Sino-Indian conflict in the Himalayas has proved to be best managed without U.S. involvement; expanding Sino-U.S. rivalry to the Indian Ocean region benefits nobody. But India is also proudly non-aligned and has been so since the Cold War. There is little evidence that India will change its foreign policy based on U.S. preferences. After all, lavishing praise and weapons on India failed even to influence its U.N. sanctions votes for Russia's invasion of Ukraine in 2022.

And yet, furnishing aid and comfort to the Modi regime has put the United States on the wrong side of the most problematic security trend about which U.S. policy has been all too aloof—democratic erosion and the growth of the global far right. "Strongmen" like Jair Bolsonaro in Brazil, Rodrigo Duterte in the Philippines, Victor Orban in Hungary, and Donald Trump lean into anti-democratic political rhetoric, but they are also nakedly aligned with sectional corporate interests in their own countries and have accumulated track records of using the state not only to punish political enemies but also to oppress their civil societies. Modi and his party, the BJP, are emblematic of this resurgence of reactionary ethnonationalist politics around the world, which confronts us with a problem of militarized violence that is not in any nation's interest, but especially not that of the United States.

Under Modi, the Indian state has not just cast a pall on press freedoms, ignored an epidemic of violence against women, and used force to disrupt workers' rights to organize.[65] It has also persecuted ethno-religious minorities and moved troops against its own people, leading to violence in Punjab that increases secessionist conflict and the prospect of outright civil war.[66] It also ran an extraterritorial assassination program that only came to light with the shooting in 2023 of a Sikh dissident on Canadian soil.[67] And in 2019, India unilaterally revoked the political autonomy of Jammu and Kashmir, deploying an additional 35,000 troops to the region and forcing Kashmiris to live under de facto martial law.[68] That same year, China unilaterally revoked Hong Kong's political autonomy too, but it did not put Hong Kong under military occupation. Both cases involved territorial revanchism, a kind of re-colonization. The difference was that India's fait accompli was more violent and oppressive than China's. Nonetheless, it was China's recapture of Hong Kong that led to Western crowing about the "rules-based" order and eventually sanctions, whereas India got little condemnation and eventually received a White House summit and U.S. arms.

In short, an outsized sense of the China threat has compelled the United States to emulate the invidious choices it made during the Cold War, most infamously by the Reagan doctrine—to prop up dictators materially and symbolically around the world in the name of playing clever games that are thought to make life harder for one's adversary. This is not just ironic; it is self-defeating. Every fighter knows you cannot launch an offensive without exposing yourself to new vulnerabilities. As in martial arts competition, so too in geopolitical competition. "Cost imposition" strategies and the moral sacrifices they entail also create strategic vulnerabilities.

Societies that become pauperized, or suffer kleptocratic governance, or are otherwise repressed by their autocratic leaders end up developmentally stunted in some way and therefore need Chinese aid and investment for lack of alternatives. Taking an ends-justifies-the-means attitude toward the globe in the name of rivalry creates the conditions that make Chinese power and influence more attractive, even essential, whereas U.S. policy seeks the opposite result. As James Baldwin noted during the Cold War, "the only real advantage Russia has . . . is the moral history of the Western world. Russia's secret weapon is the bewilderment and despair and hunger of millions of people of whose existence we are scarcely aware."[69] If the aim of confronting China is to protect democracy, then undermining democracy—whether at home or abroad—makes no sense.

Coexistence with illiberal regimes, or enjoying diplomatic relations with all nations, is one thing. Providing illiberal regimes support against their political enemies and helping them build security apparatuses capable of waging war—or actively aiding their military adventurism—is quite another.

TURNING ASIA INTO A POWDER KEG

The rivalry threat to peace is intimately tied to competition between the PLA and the U.S. military, which follows from the preceding analysis because ethnonationalism and jingoism are never far apart. Ethnonationalism in both nations' capitals creates false certainties about the good intentions of the self and the aggressive intentions of the other.[70] The risks of great-power war—directly or by proxy—then compound as both sides feel justified in seeking to secure themselves at the expense of the other.

Failing to take a relational view of China also leads policymakers to opt for responses that do not properly take into account Chinese leverage and plausible Chinese responses to U.S. competition.

Trade wars, barriers on technological production, and selective decoupling are a direct assault against Asian stability. East Asia and the Pacific have known a relative peace for more than forty years, and a substantial share of that stems from economic interdependence. Policy elites across Asian and Pacific governments have long embraced economic growth and cross-border interdependencies as a way "to continue banking political legitimacy on development and trade rather than revanchism or ethnically divisive demagoguery."[71] The choice of Asian governments in particular to prioritize nation-building is important in a region rife with both florid nationalisms and numerous unsettled territorial disputes.

Yet the ability to avoid great-power war is in conflict with the ratcheting requirements of U.S. primacy. Durable stability requires regional cohesion, inclusion, some level of interdependence, and above all military restraint. Primacy necessarily calls forth regional fracture into rivalry blocs, economically and militarily.

America's embrace of rivalry disincentivizes Chinese restraint. Because U.S. policy has shelved restraint in favor of what any reasonable person can see is limited economic warfare, Beijing has reciprocated. In the Trump years, U.S. tariffs on imports from China were answered by Chinese tariffs on certain U.S. goods. In the Biden years, China warned it could ban technologies required for solar energy production.[72] In May 2023, China declared it would restrict Chinese technology firms from doing business with Micron—a major U.S. memory chipmaker. And in July that year, China announced a new export-control regime on germanium and gallium—critical minerals needed to produce everything from fiber-optic cables to electric vehicles. It was, according to a Chinese official, "just a start"—a warning salvo about how mutually destructive economic warfare could become.[73]

Encouraging China to establish new restrictive licensing regimes punishes U.S. firms like Micron, but it also puts in place the infrastructure for China to more effectively coerce the dozens of countries in the Asia-Pacific that rely on it. Even beyond Sino-centric structures like the AIIB and the Belt and Road Initiative, China is fully imbricated in Asia's densely woven economic architecture, including the Regional Comprehensive Economic Partnership (RCEP), the Chiang Mai Initiative for intraregional currency swapping, the Asian Bond Markets Initiative, the Association of Southeast Asian Nations Plus Three (China, Japan, and South Korea), and the Trilateral Cooperation Secretariat. Washington, by contrast, belongs to none of these.

China thus has tremendous unexploited leverage over the global economy, Asian powers, and U.S. interests. The greening of the American economy depends on continuing access to critical mineral resources over which China has a near monopoly. China also produces most of the world's steel and owns 56 percent of global casting production (crucial to manufacturing ammunition) in contrast with America's 10 percent share.[74] China, moreover, is the world's largest electric vehicle market, in addition to being the lifeblood to both Apple and Tesla—two of America's largest firms.

China is too embedded in the world system to harm it without blowback on the world, but the more autarkic China becomes—which is the direction that U.S. policies encourage it to move—the more China will purge the United States from its supply chains, catalyze the very technological innovation U.S. policy seeks to inhibit, and accelerate rather than diminish its subsidies for favored industries as it chases indigenous innovation even faster.

If the CCP is not bent on foreign conquest—and we assess it is not—then U.S. policy should be encouraging its restraint rather than antagonizing it. Yet even if U.S. officials believe the CCP is an aggressive power on the march, which it could be in the future, the last thing they should want is for China to be cut off from the United States' and other countries' markets. A strategy of U.S. primacy does not respect the reality of a changing distribution of power and influence, especially in Asia; this clash between U.S. aims and global power realities is a threat to peace.

Military Competition Heightens
Security Dilemmas

The most acute and high-profile dimension of the China challenge is the PLA's rise as a military power of the first rank. The
most tangible danger comes from policies that encourage China
to grow or use that power. Over roughly the past two decades,
Chinese industrial policy has evolved from an emphasis on
economic development to national security and autonomy.[75]
In parallel, the PLA has been increasing its military capabilities and shaping its force structure in a manner that garners
alarmist headlines from Western media and pundits. The two
most important changes in China's military are its navy and
its nuclear arsenal—both have expanded to degrees that are
undeniable and highly complicating for Western military analysts seeking military solutions to what are deeply political
problems.[76]

The purpose of the PLA's naval expansion must be understood in relation to U.S. military primacy. The operational
concept at the heart of PLA warfighting, what U.S. analysts call
"anti-access/area denial" (A2/AD), aims to keep the U.S. military pinned down or out of a theater of combat while the PLA
undertakes a mission against some third territory in Asia.[77] It
is not a military doctrine capable of facilitating global conquest
or even regional domination. And it is not designed to take
over the United States or U.S. territory. Rather, A2/AD is a
concept that aims to counter the advantages of U.S. power pro-
jection in the event that U.S. and Chinese forces clash in the
latter's geographic periphery.[78]

China's nuclear expansion, meanwhile, has a similar relational quality. For a generation, China sustained a posture
of nuclear "minimum deterrence"—a term of art referring to a
strategy of having just enough of a nuclear arsenal to be capa-

ble of assured nuclear retaliation in the event China is attacked
with nuclear weapons.[79] In effect, China's nuclear weapons are
primarily for deterrence of nuclear attack. Over the past decade, however, China has rapidly accelerated its nuclear modernization. Since the Trump years, China has constructed more
than 200 missile siloes (we do not know how many have warheads and how many are simply intended to complicate U.S.
targeting) and upward of 350 nuclear weapons as of 2023. The
Pentagon estimates that, at its current pace, the PLA could have
1,000 warheads by 2030.[80] It is also improving the lethality of
its arsenal, testing hypersonic missiles and a fractal orbital bombardment system (FOBS)—a way of delivering warheads that
defeats early-warning radars and missile defenses.[81]

At the nuclear level, scholars judge that neither country
has the desire to launch a first strike, yet the nature of today's
technologies and Sino-U.S. nuclear postures have locked the
two countries in a structural security dilemma. Recent research
shows that "the shift in the conventional balance of force in the
region and the U.S. development of lower-yield nuclear weapons
has led to greater fears in China of U.S. limited nuclear use in
a conflict. Chinese strategists increasingly believe that U.S. non-
nuclear strategic capabilities threaten China's nuclear forces."[82]
As the U.S. Office of the Director of National Intelligence as-
sessed in 2023, "Beijing worries that bilateral tension, U.S. nuclear modernization, and the PLA's advancing conventional
capabilities have increased the likelihood of a U.S. [nuclear]
first strike."[83]

China is thus expanding its nuclear arsenal because it
fears Washington might launch nuclear strikes first. The modernization of its nuclear program is a rational response to this
situation; more, and more diverse, nuclear capabilities are necessary to ensure the PLA can retaliate with nuclear weapons
to U.S. nuclear first-use. Expanding nuclear capabilities from

a position of inferiority, in other words, serves the same prior goal of "minimum deterrence" but in a context where U.S. nuclear modernization (priced at more than $1.7 trillion over thirty years and dating back to the Obama administration) changes the minimum capability required for deterrence. What makes all this a security dilemma is that, like Chinese officials, most U.S. policymakers have no desire to escalate to nuclear first-use, and yet the prospect of it remains all the same.

To make sense of the risks of nuclear and conventional war, we need to hold in our minds two truths at once. At a global, abstract level, the United States enjoys a favorable balance of power—overwhelming military dominance relative to all other powers. However, at a local, concrete level in Asia—specifically across the Taiwan Strait—the balance of power shifted in favor of the PLA over a decade ago.

The correlation of forces across the Taiwan Strait tilts against the United States because of geography. Taiwan sits just off China's coast but it is 5,200 miles away from Hawai'i and 6,600 miles away from California. Moreover, all of Taiwan is within range of China's integrated air defense systems (IADS), meaning there is no possibility of the United States achieving air superiority in Taiwan without disabling China's IADS. And given China's large surface and undersea fleets, there is no way to establish sea control or sea denial off China's coast without attacking ports and critical infrastructure on the Chinese mainland.

These must be design constraints on U.S. defense strategy, not opportunities for arms-racing. Any traditional war-fighting scenario in Taiwan is a loser, requiring a massive number of missile strikes against targets on the Chinese mainland. Despite obsessive war-gaming, the United States has never come up with a plausible scenario in which it can launch repeated salvos against Chinese territory without escalating to nuclear war. No matter what weapons the United States buys or builds, it cannot dominate the Taiwan Strait militarily the way it can elsewhere in the world.

But it does not necessarily need to. The United States has been living with an unfavorable correlation of forces in Taiwan for some time and the situation has been stable, because the calculation of the balance (who has the upper hand in a night-mare scenario) is a separate analytical question from what a state does with its share of the balance at any given point. Xi Jinping has said a U.S.-led campaign of "containment and sup-pression" of China has "brought unprecedented, severe chal-lenges," rallying Chinese citizens to "dare to fight."[84] It is a clear expression of resolve—a willingness to fight, even jingoism—but not a willingness to launch a preventive war. China is in-hibited—deterred—from launching an invasion of Taiwan be-cause it would be costly in even the best case. The United States is similarly deterred from wish-casting for war in Taiwan be-cause that would be unwinnable in any conventional sense.

The situation is thus a security dilemma, which military policies can escalate but cannot remedy. Arguments that the United States needs to proliferate weapons to allies, build more bases, or accumulate missiles to fire from standoff range in order to "hold China at risk" are missing the forest for the trees—you do those things either for an unwinnable nuclear war, or you do them in the name of deterrence. But while the risks of such moves are obvious, the benefits of "more deter-rence" are not. Even without a U.S. military buildup, China has remained deterred—despite it retaining a favorable balance of power over Taiwan—for more than a decade. If deterrence holds as a status quo, then America's foremost priority ought to be not putting deterrence itself in jeopardy.

Instead, U.S. policy is seeking primacy—that is, to retain a favorable imbalance of power, including in the Taiwan Strait,

where that is not possible. It is positioning U.S. forces to encircle China—an accusation that China had been making against
the United States for more than a decade but that, since the
Trump years, has become a reality. And it is proliferating weapons to allies and partners throughout Asia, buoying—rather
than arresting—the military modernization trend across the
region that heightens mistrust and confuses war preparation
with war prevention. The United States may be undertaking all
of this with defensive motives—rational U.S. officials do not
seek open conflict—but these moves are as bad for deterrence
as they are for democracy. Individually and collectively, they
exacerbate security dilemma dynamics and encourage all the
choices from China that the United States claims not to want.

Conclusion

Our theory of China has focused on the inequalities sustained
by China's statist regime of capital accumulation in the world
economy. That regime is powered by a complex of exports, labor
exploitation, and ethnonationalism that do not exist in a vacuum but rather are intimately tied to U.S. choices.

   As a source of rivalry, these problems date to the global
financial crisis in 2007–2008—a moment of not just a narrative shift but also a growing reliance by Asian governments on
the Chinese economy, as well as a growing perception in Washington and Beijing that a world seen as less bountiful and more
precarious than before would entail more national economic
competition. By 2010, in both societies, a certain cross section
of corporate interests sought insulation from global competition by currying favor with the state.[85] Thus began an imperial
contest for state-backed growth, geopolitical allegiances, and
international rule-setting.

   These are the foundations from which the proximate concerns of military confrontation arise. That military competition—especially in the Taiwan Strait—is best understood as a security dilemma. As a day-to-day matter, the situation is best managed not through confrontational policies but through restraint. U.S. policy should be giving the CCP the fewest excuses possible to bang the drums of war or lean into blood-and-soil nationalism.

Instead, by pursuing rivalry with China—punishing it with symbolic gestures of rebuke, denying its influence abroad, inhibiting its economic growth, and containing its technological and industrial development—the United States encourages China's already hawkish foreign policy. Washington, alongside Beijing, is making Asia a more dangerous place. It is empowering kleptocrats and new configurations of the far right abroad, as at home. And as China faces "a choice between two visions: oligarchy or autocracy," U.S. choices are pushing the CCP firmly toward the latter.[86] There is no security in a future of great-power rivalry.

6

The Alternative to Great-Power Rivalry

To give America the best chance of learning to return from megalomania to rational foreign policy is the most immediate and urgent task of international politics.

—*Eric Hobsbawm,* On Empire

As it did during the Cold War, great-power rivalry today is embrittling democracy and exacerbating economic insecurity. It is also dimming hopes for a more peaceful future. Geopolitical confrontation, no matter how seemingly necessary, functions far too easily as a framework for circumscribing the rights of the people, redistributing society's wealth upward, stoking racial hate and mistrust, and justifying militarism—all while *increasing* the risks of great-power war.

Building on the insights from the previous chapters, we conclude the book by sketching out key elements of a pragmatic but innovative grand strategy. This entails a set of prescriptions that respond to the problems we have identified. We believe there are better alternatives to great-power rivalry. Here is our path forward.

An End to Primacy

Great-power competition sustains the U.S. pursuit of global primacy, which has led to disastrous foreign interventions that have expended unnecessary blood and treasure. Indeed, according to the political scientists Sidita Kushi and Monica Duffy Toft, the "U.S. has conducted 400 total military interventions in its history—50% in the past 70 years and 25% in the past 30 years. The rate of new interventions doubled after 1990."[1] The quest to outdo China only perpetuates interventionism and global violence. It is also preventing the international system from reaching balance, which is a prerequisite for peace.

Since World War II, the United States has pursued a grand strategy of primacy—global preeminence in military, economic, and political life. But the global conditions that spurred American primacy no longer exist.[2] In the early days of the post–Cold War era, global capitalism reigned. Washington controlled international financial institutions in ways both direct and indirect. And the U.S. military was not just second to none; its closest rival was North Korea, which nobody would mistake for either a great power or an existential threat, especially at a time when Pyongyang was without nuclear weapons and its society suffered from a prolonged famine.

But the unipolar moment of the 1990s proved fleeting, and it was neither as glorious nor as peaceful as many seem to remember. And while the violence of Pax Americana was mostly out of sight for Americans, its consequences were not. Blowback against U.S. hubris and adventurism came as a shock to Americans. "They hate us for our freedoms" became the kind of trope that substituted for serious reflection about how choices made "out there" are connected to choices made here and vice versa. If the War on Terror gave us Donald Trump, as Spencer Ackerman has argued, what might great-power competition birth?[3]

The United States must relinquish its ambitions for primacy and work toward a stable equilibrium with China and other regional actors. The world is increasingly multipolar; technological change is shaping societies and military balances beyond the control of Washington; and the gradual shift from U.S.-led globalization to geopoliticized economic ordering gives actors in the Global South—ones who control critical minerals, for instance—some leverage over the United States and European powers.

Pursuing primacy destabilizes the world system. We therefore propose three principles to guide a post-primacy alternative: prioritizing war prevention over war preparation, while refusing attempts to present the latter as the former; embracing associative balancing; and adopting new approaches for dealing with security dilemmas between the United States and China.

WAR PREVENTION OVER WAR PREPARATION

The Pentagon draws up contingency plans for every possible threat—from nuclear attacks to amphibious invasions of Taiwan. War preparation is never not happening. Military readiness is a priority of every defense budgetary submission to Congress.

But paranoid obsessions have overtaken reasonable precautions. U.S. policy now optimizes for war, which necessarily comes at the expense of trying to prevent it.

The United States must plan for war prevention instead of war preparation.

This means, first, revising the U.S. force posture in Asia

and the Pacific to avoid the appearance of encircling China. There is nothing wrong with securing access agreements that allow U.S. forces to use host-nation ports or airspace in a crisis. But exclusionary access agreements constrain smaller powers in ways that look like encirclement. More important, forward positioning of U.S. forces and weapons systems is not beneficial if it heightens Chinese paranoia or jingoism, or if it mistreats the local societies where America establishes outposts.

Second, U.S. war plans—which play a large role in determining U.S. force posture—should be based on more limited aims that account for the risks of nuclear escalation. That means, at a minimum, the United States should restrict itself to examining contingency scenarios that do not require striking the Chinese mainland—the most likely reason for nuclear escalation, should it occur.

Third, the United States should abandon the mindset that directs so much energy and resourcing of the national security state to ratcheting up "competitive" actions. Causing problems for our adversary only ensures that it will try to cause problems for us in kind; it is the logic of war strategy, not peace. Under Biden, the State Department's "China House"—the de facto office of great-power competition—generated a list of escalating competitive actions toward China. That list should not have even existed—let alone been implemented—without there also having been a list with equal and opposite valence. Say, a list of "cooperative actions." The American interest should reside in cataloging accommodative, bridge-building actions that escalate cooperation spirals rather than conflict spirals.

The United States and China are not at war, and cavalier assertions that they are, or will be, are simply unbridled jingoism. To prematurely adopt a posture of war will create a self-fulfilling prophecy that, at best, creates friction and animosity between both sides.

ASSOCIATIVE BALANCING

The concept of the balance of power is quite popular in Washington, but it is thoroughly misunderstood. Policymakers routinely justify military spending and war preparations to preserve a balance of power, but not because they seek "balance" in the international system. Rather, it is a grammar that justifies militarism.[4]

Primacy, by definition, seeks a favorable *imbalance* of power—a constant state of disequilibrium where one country overshadows all. But if states tend to balance against amassing power, as most international-relations scholars believe, then strategies of primacy are, at best, Sisyphean. Arms buildups tend not to increase security but instead to heighten risks of conflict. When states wish to "get the better of the balance," the system tends toward war.[5] In World War I, the balance-of-power system yielded great-power war. In the Cold War, the system yielded countless "small" wars by proxy while also risking great-power war.

There was, and remains, an alternative.

An "associative" balance of power had its conceptual origins in Renaissance Italy, where the elites of city-states forged collective arrangements through mutual agreement. It was a flawed, trustless system, but it was based on intelligence gathering, diplomacy, and accommodation—not coercion, armsracing, or brinkmanship—to preserve stability. And for more than a generation, it did.

Washington's national security community is unschooled in this associative form of balance of power. Policymakers embrace only the competitive mode.[6] Yet if you believe concentrated military and economic power is bad for stability, you must apply that standard to the United States as well.[7] So doing would temper hyperbole about China's very real military buildup because its context is one of America's declining hegemony. In context, this is not cause for alarm. On the contrary, it moves world order toward equilibrium, away from excessive concentrations of power in one place.

Associative balancing would also encourage military restraint. For example, if the United States is going to invest effort in transferring advanced conventional weapons to its allies, it should also hand the responsibility for regional balancing to those powers in Asia. Primacy becomes superfluous—at best—if America's allies are adequately armed. And allies taking on a greater role in the military balance of power would allow the United States to gradually shrink its military presence in both East Asia and the Pacific. Moving toward associative balancing also suggests that the United States should keep out of Sino-Indian rivalry. It should not build up a military presence in Australia. It should thin—rather than build up—its uncontestable military dominance of the Pacific, relinquish its formal sphere of influence there, and encourage rather than impede self-determination for the non-sovereign territories it controls (Guam, the Commonwealth of the Northern Mariana Islands, and American Samoa).[8] A truly Independent Pacific region is the credible strategic buffer that Sino-U.S. rivalry needs.

The United States should begin exploring long-term alternatives to extended nuclear deterrence provisions to Japan and South Korea, whose security is better preserved by friendly relations, arms control, and recognition of mutual vulnerability than by the fear of nuclear war. It should preserve a posture of strategic ambiguity—that is, *not* embrace a policy of unqualified commitment—toward the Taiwan Strait, which will encourage the PLA to not rattle its sabers. And it should radically restrain its nuclear strategy given its extremely favorable position of nuclear superiority.[9]

By carefully undertaking an agenda grounded in the principle of associative balancing, the United States can build up smaller powers' capacity to resist aggression while using diplomacy to facilitate an environment where smaller powers pursue their preferred strategy of "friend to all, enemy to none"—the perfect complement to a declining hegemon willing to restrain itself. In the absolute worst case, China might meet a period of consistent policy restraint, muted rhetoric, and diplomatic outreach with transgression against its neighbors. If so, its conduct would create a moment of moral clarity that would favor collective balancing by local powers better than if the context were defined by a struggle between the great powers.

A SECURITY DILEMMA SENSIBILITY

The previous chapter established that America's confrontation with China has, in its most militarized aspects, attributes of a security dilemma—neither side wants war, but the United States and China antagonize each other, leaving the world less secure. Even if this were not true, or even if the situation changed because one side or the other became an outright aggressor, the situation would still benefit from policymakers cultivating a security dilemma *sensibility*—"the ability to understand the role that fear might play in their attitudes and behavior, including, crucially, the role that one's own actions may play in provoking that fear."[10]

Deterrence—the art of making threats to prevent others from engaging in unwanted actions—is often suggested as the answer to this problem. China must fear the full weight of the American military if it were to, for example, invade Taiwan. But if the goal is to prevent an invasion of Taiwan, U.S. deterrence is a provocation since it relies upon military supremacy and brinkmanship. This is a clear lesson from the Cuban Missile Crisis. By avoiding tit-for-tat aggression, or arms-racing and military buildups, a security dilemma sensibility eliminates one of the most likely pathways to a Chinese invasion of Taiwan. Deterrence is an approach that should be used sparingly. It is *not* the foundation of a sound foreign policy, as leading security scholars once understood.[11]

Abandoning primacy requires rediscovering deterrence's limited role in statecraft. In an era when policymakers and politicians confuse deterrence with a grand strategy, we must question whether the ends of deterrence (the preservation of U.S. hegemony in the Pacific) justify the means (bloated defense budgets, economic nationalism, and arms buildups). Deterrence in an age of great-power competition naturalizes trade-offs between "guns and butter," stymies social democracy in the United States, and heightens rather than resolves conflicts of interest in international politics.

The PLA and Xi Jinping have made clear that they are prepared to use force against Taiwan if they must, and because of this there is merit in thinking that deterrence might be necessary. But deterrence worked in the 1990s and is working today; it is hardly in jeopardy. We know this because China has not invaded Taiwan, nor has it mobilized for an invasion. That is either because it does not intend to—in which case we need not think in terms of deterrence—or because it recognizes how costly such an action would be and thinks the better of it.

Deterrence in the twenty-first century, in the context of U.S.-China relations, does not require more resources from the national security state—whether nuclear weapons, intercontinental ballistic missiles, military bases, or military exercises. To the contrary, adopting a security dilemma sensibility means that for every new basing access agreement announced, for every new tariff or economic restriction unveiled, for every new arms sale, Washington should be asking, "How does this make us more secure? How might this feed into China's distorted view of our intentions?" Similarly, when China makes moves that Washington opposes, it must ask, "To what extent is China responding to what we are doing? Would they make the same decision in a different relational context?" If these questions were approached honestly, the answers to them would lead to a policy of military restraint instead of military competition.

Constructing a Fairer Global Order

Restraint offers an opening to pursue a more just, stable world. Abandoning primacy in favor of a less militarized foreign policy—supported by associative balancing and a security dilemma sensibility—prevents an avoidable war with China. These policy choices would generate momentum for a different, better global order. But what should—and could—that global order look like?

We must start by reexamining the functions of the "rules-based international order." Insofar as the rules-based international order exists, it describes a world that disproportionately benefits the richest, most advanced nations while treating the rest of the world as either markets for disaster capitalists or zones for geopolitical rivalry—or both.[12] But shouldn't international order serve the interests of the global majority rather than the richest few? Would that not create a more just, and therefore more stable, world order?

A world system that offers a fairer deal for the global majority would make environmental degradation—the only existential threat facing humanity other than nuclear war—among its chief priorities. A more just global order would also need to be less prone to compulsions of domination and convulsions of violence, which means focusing on public policy, not militaristic diversions. This is surely in the American interest.

REFRAMING CHINA

Thinking differently about China unlocks solutions to many hard-to-crack problems standing in the way of a better international order. For the foreseeable future, China and the United States are unlikely to enjoy bonhomie. But even during the Cold War, the United States and the Soviet Union managed to cooperate in a number of areas of mutual concern.[13]

The key is to ensure that the momentum of rivalry does not overtake the pursuit of common interests.

On the U.S. side, an associative balancing posture alleviates mounting pressures toward war and reduces the logical and emotional space for initiatives favoring war optimization. Although the United States cannot determine China's response, there is plenty within America's ability to tilt conditions in favor of Chinese reciprocal restraint. Similarly, we can leverage Sino-U.S. relations in a manner that helps tackle problems of global insecurity.

LEVERAGING A GREEN LEVIATHAN

First, the United States could rapidly accelerate the world's transition to green energy production by using industrial policy not to compete with China for leadership of the green tech sector but rather to *work with* China to satisfy the developing world's energy needs. America's green transition should be designed in a manner that encourages China's own accelerated green transition.

China has been, and continues to be, the world leader in renewable energy production. Whether we consider the generation of actual electricity from renewable sources or the manufacturing of wind turbines and photovoltaic cells for green technologies, China has sustained high levels of investment that far outpace even America's recent large investments in a green economy. In 2022, China was already responsible for 49 percent of renewable energy capacity globally, and by 2024, it was projected to "record 55% of global annual renewable capacity [and] deliver almost 70% of all new offshore wind projects globally."[14] It had 52 percent of global market share in solar panel installations as of 2022.[15] And in 2023, it also became the world's leading car exporter overall—it was already the world leader in the electric vehicles market.[16]

Grasping China's superior position in the green tech market—and working within this reality, rather than against it—is crucial for three reasons. First, its lead is so dramatic as to be unsurpassable. America's investments in renewable energy production via subsidies for electric vehicles and greening homes are positive, but they are not remotely at the scale necessary to become a leading exporter of green tech—especially if the United States insists on preserving the status of the U.S. dollar as the world's reserve currency (which makes its exports much more expensive for developing economies).

Second, the only path to global net zero carbon emissions by 2050 is by harnessing—not undercutting—China's momentum in renewable energy expansion. The Global South now represents the largest proportion of carbon emissions—the same parts of the world that can least afford a green energy transition on their own. But by pairing green financing from the Global North with China's manufacturing speed and scale, the Global South can "go green" on a schedule that avoids or slows some of the worst projections for environmental calamity. More important, adaptive, green economies in the Global South will have a more productive labor pool and greater means to consume, offering a way to avert a future of global low/no growth (discussed below).

Third, the United States still accounted for 14 percent of

global carbon emissions as recently as 2021, making the fate of America's green energy transition a potential spoiler of the goal of net zero by 2050. But since China also exercises unique control over some of the critical minerals necessary to manufacture renewable energy technologies, U.S. efforts toward techno-containment of and gradual decoupling from China put America's green industrial policy itself at risk. If the United States persists with forming rival geoeconomic blocs globally, then China will have greater incentive to cut off the United States from the resources it needs to support a global green transition. Our ability to achieve climate goals, in short, is closely tied to the valence of Sino-U.S. relations.

COORDINATING DEBT RELIEF AND TARIFF ROLLBACKS

The Global South faces a future of not just economic stagnation but also political instability if the United States does not act to help resolve an alarming debt sustainability crisis. In the past decade, China has emerged as both the developing world's largest creditor and its largest trading partner, making Chinese cooperation crucial to any solution that would stave off a cascading global fiscal nightmare. Accordingly, the United States, the Paris Club, the IMF, and China have held recurring meetings since the Covid-19 pandemic to discuss how and whether to restructure and relieve debt burdens for developing nations.

These meetings have achieved almost nothing relative to the scale of the problem.

The IMF continues to impose versions of "structural adjustment" (fiscal austerity) on governments desperate enough to accept IMF support. Washington has not pressured private U.S. debt holders (banks and hedge funds) to restructure developing-world repayments, and it refuses to forgive U.S.

government loans to developing nations even when the terms of the loans qualify as legally "odious" debt incurred by earlier politically illegitimate regimes (for example, in Cambodia and the Philippines). And China, as discussed in Chapter 4, has refused to write down the massive losses that it is carrying.

The solution is for the United States to undertake a campaign of debt restructuring with Global South economies while also rolling back U.S. tariffs on Chinese exports. By showing that debt relief is a priority, the United States would also be showing China that it would not be the only actor to take losses. And by relieving tariffs on Chinese exports, the United States would be offsetting some of China's losses from debt forgiveness. As a gesture, too, reversing the U.S. tariff regime simultaneously signals a willingness to transform the valence of Sino-U.S. relations to something more stable and constructive than deep rivalry.

INCREASING CHINA'S DOMESTIC CONSUMPTION

The only long-term solution to the imbalances in China's economic situation is for it to radically increase domestic consumption. The CCP knows this. Increasing domestic consumption will improve the economic security of China's massive precariat, reduce the need for the CCP to rely on ethnonationalism for its legitimacy, and give Chinese workers the means to consume what they produce rather than produce in excess of domestic demand only to have the surplus pushed to overseas markets.

The problem is that Chinese households are in dire financial straits, lacking the means to spend more. Increasing domestic consumption thus requires more redistributive economic policies—either some version of permanent "stimulus" payments from the party-state or significant wage growth at points of production. The CCP has been loath to go down this path because doing so threatens the privileges of Chinese oligarchs. It would fuel the political demands of a burgeoning middle class, strengthen labor organizing (undermining the CCP's rationale for labor repression), and jeopardize the export base of China's economy.

Xi Jinping has instead turned increasingly to national consolidation, which increases reliance on exploiting its own peripheral territories (such as Xinjiang) to serve as frontier markets in a more autarkic economy.[17] So rather than reducing worker exploitation, Xi appears on track to heighten it. This is troubling in its own right, but it also aggravates the low-consumption problem. Worst of all, it aligns with Xi's concept of "comprehensive national security," which involves the potential securitization (and therefore state control) of everything.

This is where the United States comes in: ameliorating Sino-U.S. rivalry takes the momentum out of Xi's reactionary and nationalist policies. Xi's imperative to securitize life in China is the direct consequence of geopolitical rivalry. Great-power rivalry provides Xi with a basis for his authoritarianism: surveilling Chinese society, demanding unflinching loyalty from citizens, and suppressing liberties. It gives an insecure regime the opportunity to point to an enemy "other" as the reason why it must protect itself from internal threats. Indeed, rivalry provides Xi with a justification to maintain his autocratic rule, to assert control rather than expand rights and protections for Chinese citizens.

Rivalry compounds other domestic challenges in China too: record-breaking youth unemployment, growing labor militancy, the overproduction of college-educated elites, declining profitability and overinvestment in key sectors of the economy, and a massive real estate bubble.[18] Adding the dread of "comprehensive national security" to these troubles makes for an anxiety-ridden society.[19] It also distracts from the project of increasing domestic consumption—which even some Chinese economists think should be the priority.[20]

Great-power competition—as framed in the minds of American and Chinese policymakers—weaponizes nationalism to foment global instability and potential aggression. Washington must do what it can to create an international environment that offers the CCP fewer excuses and opportunities to be jingoistic, with an understanding that a more placid context makes it easier for the CCP to adopt redistributive policies. Associative balancing, curbing the excesses of American defense spending, debt-relief collaboration, and a partnership on a global green transition all do precisely that. Above all, though, the United States must abandon techno-containment and reverse the trend toward economic decoupling with China.

Measures to make the American economy "more resilient" or "more secure" from Chinese influence exacerbate the current era of global economic stagnation and accelerate the CCP's reactionary turn. China's already declining growth makes it hard enough to stimulate domestic demand, but that is made all the more challenging by a global outlook of low/no growth (which translates into lower demand for exports). The only way to attenuate the trajectory of both Sino-U.S. rivalry and the global economy is to activate new sources of demand. That means both accommodating China's economic centrality to Asia (as opposed to forcing a rupture of interdependence) and focusing on the Global South as something other than a chessboard in an era of competition.

America's regime of subsidies, sanctions, and export controls is pushing smaller nations into the dilemma of having to choose between deeply entrenched economic relations with China (which is often their largest creditor and trading partner) and the United States (which has a massive consumer market and controls the pipes of the global economy). This is not an abstraction.

Despite being an appendage of the CCP, Huawei is a low-price leading provider of telecommunications and internet for developing economies in need of cheap digital infrastructure. Yet America's diplomatic campaign to effectively destroy Huawei offered no real alternative to it. The Uyghur Forced Labor Prevention Act, which bans all products suspected of being traceable to labor exploitation in Xinjiang, directly pits one great-power economy against the other because it is becoming impossible to prove that Chinese suppliers across Asia do not have ties to firms in China that have ties to Xinjiang.[21] U.S. subsidies for semiconductor makers and green manufacturing also force economies to choose between metaphorically giving up a leg or giving up an arm, because the subsidies are only accessible to firms locating in the United States *and* not tied to Chinese supply chains.

New investment can generate new demand. The Global South is full of not just underemployed workers but untapped consumer markets—but it needs capital, to avoid being ravaged by climate change, and to prevent debt burdens from suffocating development prospects. Growth in the Global South means more demand for goods and services from both the United States and China—a win for American and Chinese workers. But that growth requires access to the resources that both the United States and China can offer, not just one or the other.

Finally, keeping China embedded in the global economy is a far more powerful check on its aggression than forcing its withdrawal from the world. Economic interdependence does not guarantee peace; nothing does. But an autonomous, chauvinistic China that can spurn foreign direct investment and

thinks itself free from the fetters of transnational trade and production networks will have the fewest incentives to restrain itself in foreign policy. The United States must therefore deceler-
ate, and ideally reverse, China's slide toward ethnonationalism.

ENDING MILITARISM, ADDRESSING INSECURITY

A complementary step toward a fairer, more peaceful global
order would involve America doing its part to arrest the trend
of growing militarization in favor of addressing shared threats
to global security. Realistically, that could involve many measures, including limiting arms sales and security assistance to
only democratically governed militaries. It would also need to
reform World Bank and IMF governance to distribute voting
power in ways that reflect new power realities—which inevitably means giving others, including China, a greater voting share.

But the United States also has a world-historic opportunity to be a champion of two concrete initiatives: the Global
Peace Dividend campaign and the People Over Pentagon Act.

The Global Peace Dividend campaign is an initiative sponsored by dozens of Nobel laureates calling for a freeze in the
growth of military modernization and the diversion of 2 percent of world military spending into a United Nations fund.[22]
That fund would capitalize policy responses to the world's principal security threats—climate adaptation, public health, and
economic precarity worldwide. Because the United States is
by far the world's biggest military spender, its adherence to the
2 percent plan has a much better chance of rallying others to do
so as well. The United States could, moreover, choose to make
the Global Peace Dividend a focal point for public diplomacy
efforts, instead of expending diplomatic capital on chasing away
Chinese companies and brokering new military arrangements.

But the United States could go one step further toward

enabling the Global Peace Dividend by passing the People Over Pentagon Act (POPA). Congresswoman Barbara Lee—the sole vote in the House of Representatives against the legislation that launched the disastrous War on Terror after 9/11—has sponsored the POPA bill for several years. It reduces U.S. defense spending by $100 billion while protecting the salaries and benefits of the military and defense workers. It then uses those savings to invest in domestic programs that in recent years have been cut in order to accommodate higher defense appropriations. Although the United States could still cling to a primacy strategy with a 10 percent reduction in spending, abandoning primacy in favor of some of the proposals discussed above would naturally free up resources in a strategic way. And because much of the U.S. defense budget goes to paying defense contractors, this spending cut simultaneously functions as a disciplining mechanism on defense-industrial lobbying and associated corruption.[23]

By passing the People Over Pentagon Act, promoting the Global Peace Dividend campaign, and curtailing the growth of defense companies, the United States can create inertia toward shifting the ways other nations spend monies on their militaries. It can counter the trajectory of the great-power rivalry in ways that tilt global conditions toward a more durable security. In orienting U.S. statecraft toward balance in the international system, adaptation to climate change, greater equality, and democracy, America has nothing to lose, but much to gain.

Conclusion

Inside the Beltway, policy elites take as a given that "from the Peloponnesian War to the Cold War, great-power rivalry has shaped world order." But for whom is world order shaped? On whose back must be carried "smoldering long-term rivalries punctuated by war"?[24] To what benefit for the nation do national security states gamble with our collective fates, often on dubious analytical grounds? And perhaps most important of all, why should we naturalize rivalry as if there is no alternative?

This book is our intervention. We have taken pains to demystify geopolitical rivalry by showing how its costs and risks overtake its purported benefits. If peace and democracy are your goals, then great-power competition will not lead to them. Great-power rivalry is violent and oppressive because it is predicated on an airbrushed, heroic interpretation of the Cold War and the decades that followed. That history precedes a misdiagnosis of the problems China poses to the United States and the world.

A less romantic view of international struggles—past and present—is the starting point for a saner foreign policy. A durable security does not let fear become fate; it does not let the illusion of security foreclose on the possibilities of political and economic democracy.

A better future awaits.

Acknowledgments

Van's Acknowledgments

I'm grateful to Matt Duss and Nancy Okail at the Center for International Policy, as well as Omar Dahi and Security in Context, for giving a home not just to me but to serious alternative thinking about international security. Mike and I both owe Dan Kurtz-Phelan a debt of gratitude for giving us the space in *Foreign Affairs* to think through the early version of what became this book, as well as Kate Brannen, who helped bring out our central points in that earlier piece. I don't know how I could have written this without first road-testing ideas and getting feedback from readers of the *Un-Diplomatic Newsletter*. Thanks too to Mike Brenes, my partner in crime, for sticking it out with this project amid so many difficult circumstances—we're like Mos Def and Talib Kweli (at our best when we combine forces). At Yale University Press, Jaya Chatterjee, our editor, gave this book project substantial momentum by betting on us. As always, Kristin's encouragement more than balances out Anders's distractions from my writing (love ya, bud).

Mike's Acknowledgments

I must first thank my co-author, Van Jackson. Van and I became Twitter friends during the Covid pandemic when we started exchanging direct messages. That led to conversations about working together on an essay, which led to us writing a piece for *Foreign Affairs* in July 2022. That essay became the genesis of this book. Van is smart, down-to-earth, collegial, and prolific. He was patient with me when I missed our deadlines for personal reasons and he prodded me at the right moments when I needed to fulfill my end of the writing bargain.

Thanks also to our editors at *Foreign Affairs,* Daniel Kurtz-Phelan and Kate Brannen. Dan accepted our essay without hesitation, which surprised us both. Dan also became a friend and co-teacher through his involvement in the Grand Strategy program. I can't thank him enough. Kate sharpened our ideas and made sure we said what we intended to say. That proved helpful in thinking about this book and what we wanted to accomplish with it.

Our editor at Yale University Press, Jaya Chatterjee, championed this book from the first stages of the proposal. Jaya protected and encouraged our vision for the book while shepherding it into its current form. Thanks also to the entire editorial and administrative staff at Yale University Press, particularly Amanda Gerstenfeld.

I also wish to thank colleagues and friends who offered their support and advice. They include Peter-Christian Aigner, Daniel Bessner, Vivien Chang, Derek Davison, Alex Debs, Michael Franczak, John Gaddis, Beverly Gage, William Hartung, Paul Kennedy, Tim Keogh, Samuel Moyn, Daniel Steinmetz-Jenkins, Jing Tsu, and Stephen Wertheim. Kaete O'Connell saved this book. I would not have written it without her coming aboard Grand Strategy in November 2022 to support the teaching and administrative work in the program. Thanks, Kaete. I've also learned from the many insights of practitioners in the Grand Strategy program: Emily Byrne, Andrea Kendall-Taylor, Dan Kurtz-Phelan, Bonny Lin, Kica Matos, Emma Sky, and Evan Wolfson. Thanks also to my fantastic colleagues at International Security Studies: Enit Colon, Bess Oliver, Leslie Powell, Liz Vastakis, and Ted Wittenstein.

I must also thank my students in the Grand Strategy program. I have learned so much from all of you. You have made me a better teacher and person.

Arne Westad became a close colleague and informal mentor over the months Van and I wrote this book. I would not have been able to write it without his support, both professional and personal.

Then there is my family. My mother-in-law, Karen Wereszynski, is a source of unending inspiration and sage advice. My brother-in-law and sister-in-law, Sean and Kathleen Murray, are fantastic people. Kathleen is one of the best listeners I know, and I have leaned on her knowledge of publishing and public writing. Sean is the brother I never had. My nephew Connor is a source of great humor and exercise—I hope he keeps asking me to play basketball and soccer with him until I can't. My wife, Michelle, and my son, Nathan, are my world. They mean everything to me. I'm sorry I had to take time away from them to write this book.

This book is dedicated to two people that I miss dearly, my father-in-law, Paul Wereszynski, and my mother, Karen Parsons. Both passed in 2023. Their deaths unmoored me—it was not easy to finish this book without them. Both wanted a better future for their grandchildren. Let's make one.

Notes

Introduction

1. Robert Kuttner, "Steve Bannon, Unrepentant," *American Prospect,* August 16, 2017, https://prospect.org/power/steve-bannon-unrepentant/; Robert Kuttner, "U.S. vs. North Korea: The Winner? China," *American Prospect,* August 15, 2017, https://prospect.org/power/u.s.-vs.-north-korea-winner -china/.

2. Tina Nguyen, "Steve Bannon Goes Full Mooch in Bizarre, Unplanned Interview," *Vanity Fair,* August 17, 2017, www.vanityfair.com/news/2017/08 /steve-bannon-american-prospect-interview.

3. Devin Stewart, "National Unity Is a Foreign Policy Virtue—Especially Given China's Challenge," *The Hill,* May 23, 2019, https://thehill.com /opinion/international/445239-national-unity-is-a-foreign-policy-virtue -especially-given-chinas/; Kiron Skinner at the New America Foundation Future Security Forum, Washington, D.C. (April 29, 2019), www.newamerica .org/conference/future-security-forum-2019/.

4. Joshua Chaffin, "Steve Bannon Turns Huawei Saga into Anti-China Movie," *Financial Times,* October 19, 2019, www.ft.com/content/a1c7d8ae -f1c3-11e9-ad1e-4367d8281195.

5. Marco Rubio, press release, "ICYMI: Senator Marco Rubio Speaks on the Threat of Communist China at the Heritage Foundation," March 29, 2022, www.rubio.senate.gov/public/index.cfm/2022/3/icymi-rubio-speaks-on -the-threat-of-communist-china-at-the-heritage-foundation.

6. Hillary Clinton, "America's Pacific Century," *Foreign Policy,* October 11, 2011, https://foreignpolicy.com/2011/10/11/americas-pacific-century/.

7. Adam Tooze, "Whose Century?" *London Review of Books* 52, no. 15 (2020), www.lrb.co.uk/the-paper/v42/n15/adam-tooze/whose-century; David H. Autor, David Dorn, and Gordon H. Hanson, "The China Shock: Learning

from Labor Market Adjustment to Large Changes in Trade," *Working Paper 20916* (Washington, D.C.: National Bureau of Economic Research, 2016), www.nber.org/papers/w21906.

8. Alex Isenstadt, "GOP Memo Urges Anti-China Assault over Coronavirus," Politico, April 24, 2020, www.politico.com/news/2020/04/24/gop-memo-anti-china-coronavirus-207244.

9. Katie Rogers, Lara Jakes, and Ana Swanson, "Trump Defends Using 'Chinese Virus' Label, Ignoring Growing Criticism," *New York Times,* March 18, 2020, www.nytimes.com/2020/03/18/us/politics/china-virus.html.

10. Natasha Bertrand, "Trump Blows Past the Intelligence to Accuse China of Backing Biden," Politico, September 1, 2020, www.politico.com/news/2020/09/01/trump-says-china-supporting-biden-407054.

11. *Riding the Dragon: The Bidens' Chinese Secrets,* www.youtube.com/watch?v=JRmlcEBAiIs. The claims made in the "documentary" have been thoroughly debunked. See www.politifact.com/article/2020/oct/19/fact-checking-claims-about-hunter-biden-joe-biden-/.

12. Tim Ryan for Ohio, "One Word," March 29, 2022, www.youtube.com/watch?v=2AtaGf-SWKY.

13. Inu Manak, Gabriel Cabanas, and Natalia Feinberg, "The Cost of Trump's Trade War Is Still Adding Up," *Council on Foreign Relations,* April 18, 2023, www.cfr.org/blog/cost-trumps-trade-war-china-still-adding.

14. Some estimates put the U.S. defense budget as high as $1.537 trillion. See Gisela Cernadas and John Bellamy Foster, "Actual U.S. Military Spending Reached $1.537 Trillion in 2022—More than Twice Acknowledged Level: New Estimates Based on U.S. National Accounts," *Monthly Review,* November 1, 2023, https://monthlyreview.org/2023/11/01/actual-u-s-military-spending-reached-1-53-trillion-in-2022-more-than-twice-acknowledged-level-new-estimates-based-on-u-s-national-accounts/?mc_cid=494b2250c2&mc_eid=819a8e6349.

15. Nomaan Merchant, "One Year After Afghanistan, Spy Agencies Pivot Toward China," AP News, August 8, 2022, https://apnews.com/article/afghanistan-russia-ukraine-al-qaida-biden-ayman-zawahri-15e3f9282d6eac7b9c793394fff5497c; Michael German and Alex Liang, "Amid New Trial, End of Chinese Espionage 'Initiative' Brings Little Relief to US Academics Caught in Net of Fear," *Just Security,* March 22, 2022, www.justsecurity.org/80780/amid-new-trial-end-of-chinese-espionage-initiative-brings-little-relief-to-us-academics-caught-in-net-of-fear/.

16. Bill Burns, "Spycraft and Statecraft," *Foreign Affairs,* January 30, 2024, www.foreignaffairs.com/united-states/cia-spycraft-and-statecraft-william-burns.

17. John Ruwitch, "Security Comes First in U.S.-China Economic Rela-

tions, Says Treasury Secretary Yellen," NPR, April 20, 2023, www.npr.org /2023/04/20/1171048585/janet-yellen-speech-china-us-economic-relations.

18. V. R. Berghahn, *Militarism: The History of An International Debate, 1861–1979* (Cambridge: Cambridge University Press, 1984), pp. 105–106. See also C. Wright Mills, who called militarism "the doctrine of violence, and the inept opportunism based upon it" because it "substitutes for political and economic programs." C. Wright Mills, *The Causes of World War Three* (New York: Ballantine, 1960), p. 20.

19. Hal Brands, "The Art of the Arms Race," *Foreign Policy,* July 1, 2022, https://foreignpolicy.com/2022/07/01/arms-control-race-cold-war-geo political-rivalry/; Hal Brands and Evan Braden Montgomery, "One War Is Not Enough: Strategy and Force Planning for Great-Power Competition," *Texas National Security Review* 3, no. 2 (2020), pp. 80–92; Hal Brands, *The Twilight Struggle: What the Cold War Teaches Us About Great-Power Rivalry Today* (New Haven: Yale University Press, 2022).

20. Michael Beckley and Hal Brands, *Danger Zone: The Coming Conflict with China* (New York: W.W. Norton, 2022).

21. Robert Kaplan, "A New Cold War Has Begun," *Foreign Policy,* January 7, 2019, https://foreignpolicy.com/2019/01/07/a-new-cold-war-has-begun/.

22. For a representative critique, see especially Todd Hall, "The Long Game: China's Grand Strategy to Displace American Order," *International Affairs* 97, no. 6 (2021), pp. 2023–2025. The source work is Rush Doshi, *The Long Game: China's Grand Strategy to Displace American Order* (New York: Oxford University Press, 2021).

23. Elbridge Colby, *The Strategy of Denial: American Defense in an Age of Great-Power Conflict* (New Haven: Yale University Press, 2021). For a more even-handed yet still favorable approach to the subject of great-power competition, see Ali Wynne, *America's Great-Power Opportunity: Revitalizing U.S. Foreign Policy to Meet the Challenges of Strategic Competition* (Medford, Mass.: Polity, 2022).

1

The Cold War and the Origins
of "Great-Power Competition"

1. Antony J. Blinken, "Secretary of State Antony J. Blinken's Press Availability," June 19, 2023, www.state.gov/secretary-of-state-antony-j-blinkens -press-availability/.

2. Eric Hobsbawm, *The Age of Revolution: 1780–1848* (New York: Vintage, 1996).

3. Stella Ghervas, *Conquering Peace: From the Enlightenment to the European Union* (Cambridge: Harvard University Press, 2021), p. 86.

4. For more, see Christopher Clark, *Revolutionary Spring: Europe Aflame and the Fight for a New World, 1848–1849* (New York: Crown, 2023).

5. Richard Overy, *Blood and Ruins: The Last Imperial War, 1931–1945* (New York: Viking, 2022).

6. On historical analogies and their uses, see Ernest May and Richard Neustadt, *Thinking in Time: The Uses of History for Decision Makers* (New York: Free Press, 1986).

7. Judith Stein, *Pivotal Decade: How the United States Traded Factories for Finance in the Seventies* (New Haven: Yale University Press, 2010), pp. 7–8.

8. George F. Kennan, "The Sources of Soviet Conduct," *Foreign Affairs*, July 1947, www.foreignaffairs.com/russian-federation/george-kennan-sources -soviet-conduct.

9. Jeremi Suri, "Nuclear Weapons and the Escalation of Global Conflict Since 1945," *International Journal* 63, no. 4, *Nuclear Strategy in the Age of Weapons of Mass Destruction* (Autumn 2008), pp. 1013–1029.

10. Quoted in Alexandre Debs and Nuno Monteiro, *Nuclear Politics: The Strategic Causes of Proliferation* (New York: Cambridge University Press, 2017), p. 202.

11. C. Wright Mills, *The Power Elite* (New York: Oxford University Press, 1956). On the military-intellectual complex, see Daniel Bessner, "The Making of the Military-Intellectual Complex," *New Republic*, May 29, 2019, https://newrepublic.com/article/153997/making-military-intellectual -complex.

12. Fred Kaplan, *The Wizards of Armageddon* (Stanford: Stanford University Press, 1991).

13. John F. Kennedy, "Special Message to Congress on the Defense Budget," March 28, 1961, *Public Papers of the Presidents, John F. Kennedy,* www .presidency.ucsb.edu/documents/special-message-the-congress-the-de fense-budget.

14. Daniel Bessner, *Democracy in Exile: Hans Spier and the Rise of the Defense Intellectual* (Ithaca: Cornell University Press, 2018), pp. 223–224; John Dumbrell, "The Action Intellectuals," in *A Companion to John F. Kennedy,* ed. Marc J. Selverstone (Sussex: John Wiley and Sons, 2014), pp. 139– 141; "At the Brink; Interview with Thomas Schelling," March 4, 1986, https:// openvault.wgbh.org/catalog/V_5293F77426B84C68A360BD6283ACF4FC.

15. John F. Kennedy Tapes, Presidential Records, JFK Meeting Tape 31.2, October 19, 1962, UVA Miller Center, https://millercenter.org/listening-to -the-presidency/bad-appeasement-munich; John F. Kennedy Tapes, Presi-

dential Records, JFK Meeting Tape 31.2, October 19, 1962, UVA Miller Center, https://millercenter.org/listening-to-the-presidency/pretty-bad-fix.

16. Joy Rohde, *Armed with Expertise: The Militarization of American Social Research During the Cold War* (Ithaca: Cornell University Press, 2018), p. 21.

17. Reid Pauly, "The Pioneering Role of CIS in American War Gaming," MIT Center for International Studies (Fall 2015), https://cis.mit.edu/publications/magazine/pioneering-role-cis-american-war-gaming.

18. Nuclear Energy Matters: Inter-Agency Panel and The Schelling Study Group Report, 12 October 1962, John F. Kennedy Digital Library, www.jfklibrary.org/asset-viewer/archives/JFKNSF/376/JFKNSF-376-027.

19. Aleksandr Fursenko and Timothy Naftali, *Khrushchev's Cold War: The Inside Story of an American Adversary* (New York: W.W. Norton, 2006), p. 466.

20. Fursenko and Naftali, *Khrushchev's Cold War,* p. 491.

21. Paul Thomas Chamberlin, *The Cold War's Killing Fields: Rethinking the Long Peace* (New York: HarperCollins, 2018), p. 19.

22. Dwight D. Eisenhower, "The President's News Conference," April 7, 1954, *Public Papers of the Presidents, Dwight D. Eisenhower,* www.presidency.ucsb.edu/documents/the-presidents-news-conference-361.

23. Gregory Brew, "The Collapse Narrative: The United States, Mohammed Mossadegh, and the Coup Decision of 1953," *Texas National Security Review* 2, no. 4 (November 2019), pp. 38–59, http://dx.doi.org/10.26153/tsw/6666.

24. Suzanne Maloney, "1979: Iran and America," *Brookings,* January 24, 2019, www.brookings.edu/articles/1979-iran-and-america/. See also David S. Painter and Gregory Brew, *The Struggle for Iran: Oil, Autocracy, and the Cold War, 1951–1954* (Chapel Hill: University of North Carolina Press, 2023).

25. Greg Grandin, *The Last Colonial Massacre: Latin America in the Cold War* (Chicago: University of Chicago Press, 2005), pp. 65–68; Nick Cullather, *Secret History: The CIA's Classified Account of Its Operations in Guatemala, 1952–1954* (Stanford: Stanford University Press, 1999), p. xix.

26. Robert Buzzanco, *Masters of War: Military Dissent and Politics in the Vietnam War Era* (New York: Cambridge University Press, 1996), p. 98.

27. "Lyndon Johnson and the Dominican Intervention of 1965," National Security Archive Electronic Briefing Book No. 513, https://nsarchive2.gwu.edu/NSAEBB/NSAEBB513/docs/Tape%2004%20transcript.pdf.

28. Chamberlin, *The Cold War's Killing Fields,* p. 227.

29. Lindsay A. O'Rourke, *Covert Regime Change: America's Secret Cold War* (Ithaca: Cornell University Press, 2018), p. 73.

30. Jon Mitchell, *Poisoning the Pacific: The US Military's Secret Dumping*

of Plutonium, Chemical Weapons, and Agent Orange (New York: Rowan and Littlefield, 2020); Lauren Hirshberg, *Suburban Empire: Cold War Militarization of the US Pacific* (Berkeley: University of California Press, 2022).

31. O'Rourke, *Covert Regime Change.*

32. John Delury, "Spy Balloons Evoke Bad Cold War Memories for China," *Foreign Policy,* February 13, 2023, https://foreignpolicy.com/2023/02/13/spy-balloon-cold-war-china-us/.

33. Kurt M. Campbell and Rush Doshi, "The China Challenge Can Help America Avert Decline," *Foreign Affairs,* December 3, 2020, www.foreignaffairs.com/articles/china/2020-12-03/china-challenge-can-help-america-avert-decline.

34. Hal Brands, "The Upside of a New Cold War with China," *Bloomberg,* July 7, 2020, www.bloomberg.com/view/articles/2020-07-07/new-cold-war-with-china-can-make-u-s-democracy-stronger?sref=nmVx3tQ5&in_source=embedded-checkout-banner#xj4y7vzkg.

35. Stein, *Pivotal Decade,* p. 2.

36. Gretchen Heefner, *The Missile Next Door: The Minuteman in the American Heartland* (Cambridge: Harvard University Press, 2012); Kari Fredrickson, *Cold War Dixie: Militarization and Modernization in the American South* (Athens: University of Georgia Press, 2014).

37. See Fredrickson, *Cold War Dixie;* Josh Sides, *L.A. City Limits: African American Los Angeles from the Great Depression to the Present* (Berkeley: University of California Press, 2003).

38. Tim Keogh, *In Levittown's Shadow: Poverty in America's Wealthiest Suburb* (Chicago: University of Chicago Press, 2023), chapter 4, especially p. 115.

39. Martin Luther King, Jr., "The Montgomery Bus Boycott," 1955, www.blackpast.org/african-american-history/1955-martin-luther-king-jr-montgomery-bus-boycott/.

40. This history is deftly explored in Beverly Gage, *G-Man: J. Edgar Hoover and the Making of the American Century* (New York: Viking, 2022), p. 604; chapters 45 and 50.

41. Charles J. Shields, *Lorraine Hansberry: The Life Behind* A Raisin in the Sun (New York: Henry Holt, 2022), p. 255.

42. W. E. B. Du Bois, *In Battle for Peace* (New York: Oxford University Press, 2007), pp. 32–110.

43. Gage, *G-Man,* p. 600.

44. Radio and Television Report to the American People on Civil Rights, June 11, 1963, www.jfklibrary.org/archives/other-resources/john-f-kennedy-speeches/civil-rights-radio-and-television-report-19630611.

45. Nelson Lichtenstein, *State of the Union: A Century of American Labor* (Princeton: Princeton University Press, 2002), pp. 78–79.

46. On Blacks as members of the New Deal coalition, see Eric Schickler, *Racial Realignment: The Transformation of American Liberalism, 1932–1968* (Princeton: Princeton University Press, 2016).

47. Doug Rossinow, *Visions of Progress: The Left-Liberal Tradition in America* (Philadelphia: University of Pennsylvania Press, 2008), pp. 160–161.

48. See Manfred Berg, *Ticket to Freedom: The NAACP and the Struggle for Black Political Integration* (Gainesville: University of Florida Press, 2005), chapter 5; Jennifer A. Delton, *Making Minnesota Liberal: Civil Rights and the Transformation of the Democratic Party* (Minneapolis: University of Minnesota Press, 2002).

49. On how the Cold War and Supreme Court controlled the evolution of the civil rights movement, see Michael Klarman, *From Jim Crow to Civil Rights: The Supreme Court and the Struggle for Racial Equality* (New York: Oxford University Press, 2004), conclusion, especially pp. 450–455.

50. Mae Ngai, *Impossible Subjects: Illegal Aliens and the Making of Modern America* (Princeton: Princeton University Press, 2004), pp. 218 and 223.

51. Elaine Tyler May, *Homeward Bound: American Families in the Cold War Era* (New York: Basic, 2017).

52. Ruth Rosen, *The World Split Open: How the Modern Women's Movement Changed America* (New York: Penguin, 2000), p. 11. On gender and the Cold War, see especially May, *Homeward Bound*.

53. Betty Friedan, *The Feminine Mystique* ([1963] New York: W.W. Norton, 2001), p. 512.

54. Students for a Democratic Society, *The Port Huron Statement*, 1964, www.progressivefox.com/misc_documents/PortHuronStatement.pdf, pp. 32–33.

55. Rosen, *World Split Open*, pp. 95–99 and 201–203.

56. Interview with Ruthann Miller, "How the Strike for Equality Relaunched the Struggle for Women's Liberation in the US," *Jacobin,* November 1, 2020, https://jacobin.com/2020/11/womens-strike-equality-liberation-betty-friedan.

57. Campbell and Doshi, "The China Challenge Can Help America Avert Decline."

58. Benjy Sarlin and Sahil Kapur, "Why China May Be the Last Bipartisan Issue Left in Washington," NBC News, March 21, 2021, www.nbcnews.com/politics/congress/why-china-may-be-last-bipartisan-issue-left-washington-n1261407.

59. Robert Kuttner, "The China Challenge," *American Prospect,* October 5, 2021, https://prospect.org/world/china-challenge/.

60. Edward Wong and Amy Qin, "Asian American Officials Cite Unfair Scrutiny and Lost Jobs in China Spy Tensions," *New York Times,* December

31, 2023, www.nytimes.com/2023/12/31/us/politics/china-spy-asian-americans
.html.

61. See Jessica Chen Weiss, "The China Trap: U.S. Foreign Policy and the Perilous Logic of Zero-Sum Competition," *Foreign Affairs,* August 18, 2022, www.foreignaffairs.com/china/china-trap-us-foreign-policy-zero-sum -competition.

62. Nick Corasaniti and Maggie Haberman, "'Geriatric,' 'China's Puppet': Trump Campaign Unleashes Ads Attacking Biden," *New York Times,* May 15, 2020, www.nytimes.com/2020/05/15/us/politics/trump-ads-joe-biden .html.

2
The Fall and Return of Rivalry

1. "Address Before a Joint Session of the Congress on the State of the Union," January 28, 1992, *Public Papers of the Presidents, 41st President of the United States: 1989–1993,* www.presidency.ucsb.edu/documents/address -before-joint-session-the-congress-the-state-the-union-0.

2. For a summary of these points, see Daniel Deudney and G. John Ikenberry, "Who Won the Cold War?" *Foreign Policy,* no. 87 (Summer, 1992), pp. 123–128, 130–138.

3. Francis Fukuyama, "The End of History?" *National Interest,* no. 16 (Summer 1989), pp. 3–18, www.jstor.org/stable/24027184; John Mueller, *Retreat from Doomsday: The Obsolescence of Major War* (New York: Basic, 1989); Charles Krauthammer, "The Unipolar Moment," *Foreign Affairs,* January 1, 1990, www.foreignaffairs.com/articles/1990-01-01/unipolar-moment; John J. Mearsheimer, "Why We Will Soon Miss the Cold War," *The Atlantic,* August 1990.

4. Penny Von Eschen, *Paradoxes of Nostalgia: Cold War Triumphalism and Global Disorder Since 1989* (Durham: Duke University Press, 2022).

5. "Congressional Black Caucus Introduces Bill Based on Main Street Marshall Plan," *Dallas Examiner,* May 21, 2018; "Humphrey Urges New Aid to Poor," *New York Times,* August 3, 1967.

6. "Costs of the 20-Year War on Terror: $8 Trillion and 900,000 Deaths," *Costs of War Project,* September 1, 2021, www.brown.edu/news/2021-09-01 /costsofwar.

7. Hillary Clinton, "America's Pacific Century."

8. Wu Xinbo, "Understanding the Geopolitical Implications of the Global Financial Crisis," *Washington Quarterly* 33, no. 4 (2010), pp. 155–163.

9. See Nuno Monteiro, *Theory of Unipolar Politics* (New York: Cambridge University Press, 2014).

10. Merchant, "One Year After Afghanistan, Spy Agencies Pivot Toward China."

11. Nina Silove, "The Pivot Before the Pivot: U.S. Strategy to Preserve the Balance of Power in Asia," *International Security* 40, no. 4 (2016), pp. 45–88.

12. Bush quoted in Jeffrey A. Engel, *When the World Seemed New: George H. W. Bush and the End of the Cold War* (New York: Mariner, 2017), p. 313.

13. "Cheney Gives Plan to Reduce Forces by 25% in 5 Years," *New York Times,* June 20, 1990.

14. Interview with Fred Ikle, November 24, 1987, https://openvault.wgbh.org/catalog/V_C1A9B20A0E8841C8A2F0B2B14DC89790.

15. "Global Change and Budget Cuts Test Pentagon," *New York Times,* May 20, 1990.

16. George H. W. Bush, "Address Before a Joint Session of the Congress on the State of the Union," January 28, 1992.

17. R. W. Apple, Jr., "Bush Is Reported Ready to Retreat on Military Money," *New York Times,* March 18, 1990; Clifford Krauss, "House Easily Kills Bush Budget Plan," *New York Times,* March 5, 1992.

18. Greg Bischak, *US Conversion After the Cold War, 1990–1997: Lessons for Forging a New Conversion Policy* (Washington, D.C.: National Commission for Economic Conversion and Disarmament, 1997).

19. Hal Brands, *Making the Unipolar Moment: U.S. Foreign Policy and the Rise of the Post–Cold War Order* (Ithaca: Cornell University Press, 2016), p. 327.

20. Brands, *Making the Unipolar Moment,* p. 328.

21. Brands, *Making the Unipolar Moment,* p. 327. Some in the Clinton administration dismissed the DPG as anachronistic. See Michael Brenes, "Abandoning the Peace Dividend: Bill Clinton and the Political Economy of Defense Conversion, 1989–2000," in *Rethinking U.S. Power: Domestic Histories of U.S. Foreign Relations,* ed. Daniel Bessner and Michael Brenes (London: Palgrave MacMillan, 2024).

22. Andrew Krepinevich, Jr., "Measures of Power," *Foreign Affairs,* April 19, 2019, www.foreignaffairs.com/articles/china/2019-04-19/measures-power?check_logged_in=1.

23. Ken Silverstein, "The Man from ONA," *The Nation,* October 7, 1999, www.thenation.com/article/archive/man-ona/.

24. For a biography of Marshall that verges on hagiography, see Andrew Krepinevich, Jr., and Barry Watts, *The Last Warrior: Andrew Marshall and the Shaping of Modern American Defense Strategy* (New York: Basic, 2015).

25. Krepinevich, "Measures of Power."

26. Julian B. Gewirtz, "Only One Way Forward: The Chinese Communist Party and the Rupture of 1989," in *Before and After the Fall: World Politics*

and the End of the Cold War, ed. Nuno P. Monteiro and Fritz Bartel (New York: Cambridge University Press, 2021), p. 97.

27. Krepinevich and Watts, *The Last Warrior,* p. 193.

28. Derek Chollet and James Goldgeier, *America Between the Wars: The Misunderstood Years Between the Fall of the Berlin Wall and the Start of the War on Terror* (New York: Public Affairs, 2008), pp. 135–137.

29. Douglas Brinkley, "Democratic Enlargement: The Clinton Doctrine," *Foreign Policy* 106 (Spring, 1997), pp. 110–127. See also Clinton, "A National Security Strategy of Enlargement and Engagement" (1994), https://history .defense.gov/Portals/70/Documents/nss/nss1994.pdf.

30. Chollet and Goldgeier, *America Between the Wars,* pp. 135–137.

31. Ibid., p. 259.

32. Ibid.

33. John E. Yang, "House Backs Clinton on China Trade," *Washington Post,* June 28, 1996.

34. "Proposal Cuts Back on Some Weapons to Spend More on Personnel," *New York Times,* February 8, 1994.

35. "Defense Industry Layoffs Report," July 13, 1995, C-SPAN, www.c-span .org/video/?66157-1/defense-industry-layoff-report.

36. Nelson Lichtenstein and Judith Stein, *A Fabulous Failure: The Clinton Presidency and the Transformation of American Capitalism* (Princeton: Princeton University Press, 2023).

37. "WMD Domestic Preparedness—Related Testimony," Donald Rumsfeld papers, Part II, Box 88, folder 3, Library of Congress, Washington, D.C.

38. For more, see Spencer Ackerman, *Reign of Terror: How the 9/11 Era Destabilized America and Produced Trump* (New York: Viking, 2021).

39. Stephen Biddle, *Military Power: Explaining Victory and Defeat in Modern Battle* (Princeton: Princeton University Press, 2004), p. 4.

40. Jeanne Morefield, *Empires Without Imperialism: Anglo-American Decline and the Politics of Deflection* (Oxford: Oxford University Press, 2014).

41. "President Outlines War Effort, Remarks by the President to the George C. Marshall ROTC Award Seminar on National Security," April 17, 2002, https://georgewbush-whitehouse.archives.gov/news/releases/2002/04 /20020417-1.html/.

42. Richard Baum, "From 'Strategic Partners' to 'Strategic Competitors': George W. Bush and the Politics of U.S. China Policy," *Journal of East Asian Studies* 1, no. 2 (August 2001), pp. 191–220; David E. Sanger, "U.S. Would Defend Taiwan, Bush Says," *New York Times,* April 26, 2001.

43. Carter Malkasian, *The American War in Afghanistan: A History* (New York: Oxford University Press, 2022), pp. 78–83.

44. "President Bush Delivers Graduation Speech at West Point, United States Military Academy, West Point, New York," June 1, 2002, https://georgewbush-whitehouse.archives.gov/news/releases/2002/06/20020601-3.html.

45. Robert Draper, *To Start a War: How the Bush Administration Took America into Iraq* (New York: Penguin, 2020), pp. 41 and 422.

46. Lloyd C. Gardner, *The Long Road to Baghdad: A History of U.S. Foreign Policy from the 1970s to the Present* (New York: New Press, 2008), 128.

47. "Top Bush Officials Push Case Against Saddam," CNN, September 8, 2002, www.cnn.com/2002/ALLPOLITICS/09/08/iraq.debate/index.html.

48. Ackerman, *Reign of Terror,* pp. 98–99.

49. Friedman as quoted in Noreen Malone, "Why So Many Liberals Supported Invading Iraq," *Slate,* May 14, 2021, https://slate.com/news-and-politics/2021/05/iraq-war-liberal-media-support-humanitarian-intervention.html.

50. "Iraq Body Count, 2003–2005," Oxford Research Group, www.iraqbodycount.org/analysis/reference/pdf/a_dossier_of_civilian_casualties_2003-2005.pdf.

51. "Iraqi Civilians," Costs of War Project, Brown University, March 2023, https://watson.brown.edu/costsofwar/costs/human/civilians/iraqi.

52. "Chirac Says War in Iraq Spreads Terrorism," *New York Times,* November 18, 2004; "Interview with Jacques Chirac," *New York Times,* September 8, 2002.

53. John Lewis Gaddis, *Surprise, Security, and the American Experience* (Cambridge: Harvard University Press, 2005).

54. Melvyn P. Leffler, *Confronting Saddam Hussein: George W. Bush and the Invasion of Iraq* (New York: Oxford University Press, 2023), p. 213.

55. "President Bush Addresses United Nations General Assembly," September 23, 2003, https://georgewbush-whitehouse.archives.gov/news/releases/2003/09/20030923-4.html#:~:text=I%20proposed%20to%20Congress%20that,kind%20since%20the%20Marshall%20Plan.

56. "Coalition Provisional Authority Order Number 39," https://govinfo.library.unt.edu/cpa-iraq/regulations/20031220_CPAORD_39_Foreign_Investment_.pdf; "So, Mr Bremer, Where Did All the Money Go?" *The Guardian,* July 6, 2005, www.theguardian.com/world/2005/jul/07/iraq.features11; Doug Smith and Borzou Daragahi, "'Marshall Plan' for Iraq Fades," *Los Angeles Times,* January 15, 2006.

57. On the outcome of the Iraq War, and whether it was due to "hubris" or delusion, see Joseph Stieb, "Confronting the Iraq War: Melvyn Leffler, George Bush and the Problem of Trusting Your Sources," *War on the Rocks,*

January 30, 2023, https://warontherocks.com/2023/01/confronting-the-iraq
-war-melvyn-leffler-george-bush-and-the-problem-of-trusting-your
-sources/.

58. On the surge, see Timothy Andrews Sayle, Jeffrey A. Engel, Hal Brands, and William Inboden, eds., *The Last Card: Inside George W. Bush's Decision to Surge in Iraq* (Ithaca: Cornell University Press, 2019).

59. "Remarks by President Bush and President Jiang Zemin in Press Availability Western Suburb Guest House," October 19, 2001, https://georgew bush-whitehouse.archives.gov/news/releases/2001/10/20011019-4.html.

60. See Dennis Wilders's memo on China dated November 19, 2008, in *Hand-Off: The Foreign Policy George W. Bush Passed to Barack Obama,* ed. Stephen J. Hadley et al. (Washington, D.C.: Brookings Institution, 2023), p. 420.

61. Paul Blustein, "The Untold Story of How George W. Bush Lost China," *Foreign Policy,* October 2, 2019, https://foreignpolicy.com/2019/10/04/the -untold-story-of-how-george-w-bush-lost-china/.

62. Peter Van Ness, "China's Response to the Bush Doctrine," *World Policy Journal* 21, no. 4 (Winter 2004/05), pp. 38–47.

63. Van Jackson, *Pacific Power Paradox: American Statecraft and the Fate of the Asian Peace* (New Haven: Yale University Press, 2023), pp. 114–120.

64. "Remarks by the President in Address to the Nation on the Way Forward in Afghanistan and Pakistan," December 1, 2009, https://obamawhite house.archives.gov/the-press-office/remarks-president-address-nation-way -forward-afghanistan-and-pakistan.

65. Adam Tooze, *Crashed: How a Decade of Financial Crises Changed the World* (New York: Viking, 2018), p. 5.

66. Léonce Ndikumana, Theresa Mannah-Blankson, and Angelica Espiritu Njuguna, "Looming Debt Crisis in Sub-Saharan Africa: Drivers, Implications and Policy Options," Political Economy Research Institute, University of Massachusetts, Amherst, November 2020, https://scholarworks.umass.edu /cgi/viewcontent.cgi?article=1255&context=peri_workingpapers.

67. This history is derived from Tooze, *Crashed,* pp. 243–246.

68. Xinbo, "Understanding the Global Implications of the Asian Financial Crisis," p. 158.

69. Tooze, *Crashed,* pp. 266–268; Xinbo, "Understanding the Global Implications of the Asian Financial Crisis."

70. Quadrennial Defense Review Report, February 2010, https://dod .defense.gov/Portals/1/features/defenseReviews/QDR/QDR_as_of_29 JAN10_1600.pdf.

71. The name "Indo-Pacific" itself was a rhetorical marker of great-power competition. See Van Jackson, "America's Indo-Pacific Folly," *Foreign Affairs,*

March 12, 2021, www.foreignaffairs.com/articles/asia/2021-03-12/americas
-indo-pacific-folly.

72. *Sustaining U.S. Global Leadership: Priorities for 21st Century Defense*
(Washington, D.C.: Department of Defense, 2012), https://ntrl.ntis.gov
/NTRL/dashboard/searchResults/titleDetail/PB2012103890.xhtml.

73. U.S. Department of Defense, "Military and Security Developments
Involving the People's Republic of China, Annual Report to Congress, 2023,"
https://media.defense.gov/2023/Oct/19/2003323409/-1/-1/1/2023-military
-and-security-developments-involving-the-peoples-republic-of-china.pdf.

74. Josh Rogin, "Ash Carter Talks Tough on China, But It's Just Talk,"
Bloomberg, May 30, 2015, www.bloomberg.com/view/articles/2015-05-30/ash
-carter-talks-tough-on-china-but-it-s-just-talk?embedded-checkout=true.

75. "Remarks by Secretary Carter on the Budget at the Economic Club
of Washington, D.C., Feb. 2, 2016," www.defense.gov/News/Transcripts
/Transcript/Article/648901/remarks-by-secretary-carter-on-the-budget-at
-the-economic-club-of-washington-dc/.

3

How Rivalry Poisons American Politics

1. Jim Banks, as quoted in Gaby Orr and Nahal Toosi, "CPAC Puts a
Bulls-Eye on China," Politico, February 27, 2021, www.politico.com/news
/2021/02/27/cpac-china-trump-471825.

2. "Full Transcript of 'Face the Nation' on February 7, 2021," CBS, www
.cbsnews.com/news/full-transcript-of-face-the-nation-on-february-7-2021/.

3. Nick Gass, "Trump: 'We Can't Continue to Allow China to Rape Our
Country,'" Politico, May 2, 2016, www.politico.com/blogs/2016-gop-primary
-live-updates-and-results/2016/05/trump-china-rape-america-222689.

4. Robert Kaplan, "A New Cold War Has Begun," *Foreign Policy,* January
7, 2019, https://foreignpolicy.com/2019/01/07/a-new-cold-war-has-begun/.
Kaplan later became one of the few Iraq War boosters to recant his support, but he has been enthusiastic in his view of the necessity of Sino-U.S.
rivalry.

5. *National Security Strategy of the United States of America,* December
2017, https://trumpwhitehouse.archives.gov/wp-content/uploads/2017/12/NSS
-Final-12-18-2017-0905.pdf; Hal Brands, "How to Make Biden's Free World
Strategy Work," *Foreign Affairs,* May 24, 2022, www.foreignaffairs.com/ar
ticles/united-states/2022-05-24/how-make-bidens-free-world-strategy
-work.

6. As quoted in "Pompeo: Chinese Threat May Be Worse Than a 'Cold
War 2.0,'" Politico, August 12, 2020, www.politico.com/news/2020/08/12

/pompeo-chinese-threat-may-be-worse-than-cold-war-communism
-394350.

7. Office of Policy Planning, *Elements of the China Challenge* (Washington, D.C.: U.S. Department of State, 2020), p. 46.

8. Rubio, "Senator Marco Rubio Speaks on the Threat of Communist China at the Heritage Foundation."

9. As quoted in Greg Myre, "CIA Nominee William Burns Talks Tough on China," NPR, February 24, 2021, www.npr.org/2021/02/24/971013669/cia-nominee-william-burns-talks-tough-on-china.

10. As quoted in Quint Forgey and Phelim Kine, "Blinken Calls China 'Most Serious Long-Term' Threat to World Order," Politico, May 26, 2022, www.politico.com/news/2022/05/26/blinken-biden-china-policy-speech-00035385.

11. As quoted in Brook Singman, "China Poses 'Biggest Long-Term Threat to Economic and National Security,' FBI Director Wray Warns," Fox News, July 6, 2022, www.foxnews.com/politics/china-poses-biggest-long-term-threat-economic-national-security-fb-director-wray-warns.

12. Robert C. O'Brien and Arthur Herman, "The President Can't Counter China on His Own," *Foreign Affairs*, May 5, 2023, www.foreignaffairs.com/china/president-biden-counter-china-congress-american-bipartisan.

13. "Fact Sheet: Historic Bipartisan Infrastructure Deal," White House, July 28, 2021, www.whitehouse.gov/briefing-room/statements-releases/2021/07/28/fact-sheet-historic-bipartisan-infrastructure-deal/; Jim Tankersley, "Biden Signs Infrastructure Bill, Promoting Benefits for Americans," *New York Times*, November 15, 2021.

14. "Remarks of President Joe Biden—State of the Union Address, as Prepared for Delivery," White House, Washington, D.C., February 7, 2023, www.whitehouse.gov/briefing-room/speeches-remarks/2023/02/07/remarks-of-president-joe-biden-state-of-the-union-address-as-prepared-for-delivery/.

15. Campbell and Doshi, "The China Challenge Can Help America Avert Decline."

16. David Sanger, "'As Long as It Takes': Biden Adds to Talk of a New Cold War," *New York Times*, July 14, 2023.

17. Biden's National Security Strategy in 2022 also stated baldly that "the *post–Cold War era* is definitively over" (emphasis added). *National Security Strategy, October 2022* (Washington, D.C.: White House, 2022), www.whitehouse.gov/wp-content/uploads/2022/10/Biden-Harris-Administrations-National-Security-Strategy-10.2022.pdf.

18. Mike Gallagher, as quoted in Phelim Kline, "New House Select Committee Seeks 'Cold War' Victory over China," Politico *China Watcher*, Janu-

ary 5, 2023, www.politico.com/newsletters/politico-china-watcher/2023/01/05/new-house-select-committee-seeks-cold-war-victory-over-china-00076465.

19. Andrew Desiderio and Marianne Levine, "Bipartisanship in a Divided Senate? On China, Perhaps," Politico, March 17, 2021, www.politico.com/news/2021/03/17/senate-bipartisanship-china-schumer-476406.

20. Ibid.

21. As quoted in Gavin Bade, "'A Sea Change': Biden Reverses Decades of Chinese Trade Policy," Politico, December 26, 2022, www.politico.com/news/2022/12/26/china-trade-tech-00072232.

22. Dan Sullivan and Daniel Twining, "Only Bipartisanship Can Defeat Authoritarian Aggression," Foreign Affairs, August 25, 2022, www.foreignaffairs.com/united-states/only-bipartisanship-can-defeat-authoritarian-aggression.

23. Rachel Myrick, "Do External Threats Unite or Divide? Security Crises, Rivalries, and Polarization in American Foreign Policy," International Organization 75, no. 4 (Fall, 2021), pp. 921–958.

24. Beverley Silver, The Forces of Labor: Workers' Movements and Globalization Since 1870 (New York: Cambridge University Press, 2012).

25. Isenstadt, "GOP Memo Urges Anti-China Assault over Coronavirus."

26. Two-way trade with China during the Clinton presidency alone nearly quadrupled. See U.S. Census Bureau, "Trade in Goods with China," 1992–2000, www.census.gov/foreign-trade/balance/c5700.html. See also Brent Cebul, Illusions of Progress: Business, Poverty, and Liberalism in the American Century (Philadelphia: University of Pennsylvania Press, 2023).

27. Alec Macgillis, "Tim Ryan: The Working-Class Jobs Candidate in the Era of Resentment," Ohio Capital Journal, October 27, 2022, https://ohiocapitaljournal.com/2022/10/27/tim-ryan-the-working-class-jobs-candidate-in-the-era-of-resentment/.

28. Van Jackson, "Election Takeaways MSNBC Won't Tell You," Un-Diplomatic Newsletter, November 11, 2022, www.un-diplomatic.com/p/election-takeaways-msnbc-wont-tell-you.

29. Makena Kelly, "Facebook Funded Anti-TikTok Campaign Through GOP Firm," The Verge, March 31, 2022, www.theverge.com/2022/3/30/23003168/facebook-tiktok-targeted-victory-news-column-campaign-gop.

30. National Security Strategy, October 2022, p. 9.

31. Neta Crawford, The Pentagon, Climate Change, and War: Charting the Rise and Fall of U.S. Military Emissions (Cambridge, Mass.: MIT Press, 2022), pp. 7–8. Crawford notes that while direct Department of Defense emissions are a tiny portion of greenhouse gas emissions, defense-industrial enterprises make up some 17 percent of total emissions.

32. Maxine Joselow, "Biden Pushes to Require Big Federal Contractors to Cut Climate Pollution," *Washington Post,* November 10, 2022, www.washingtonpost.com/climate-solutions/2022/11/10/biden-climate-federal-suppliers -cop27/; press release, "Lankford, Hoeven, Colleagues Lead Efforts to Stop Defense Department's Costly Green New Deal Mandates," January 4, 2023, www.lankford.senate.gov/news/press-releases/lankford-hoeven-colleagues -lead-efforts-to-stop-defense-departments-costly-green-new-deal -mandates.

33. Brendan Cole, "Marjorie Taylor Greene Says Green New Deal Helps China but Shows Symbol of Soviet Union," *Newsweek,* September 23, 2021, www.newsweek.com/marjorie-taylor-greene-soviet-symbol-green-new -deal-helps-china-1631819.

34. See, for example, Senator Joe Manchin pointing to "geopolitical uncertainty as tensions rise with both Russia and China" as the reason to oppose Biden's more ambitious legislative efforts for public spending on climate and the economy. Press release, "Manchin Statement on Build Back Better Act," December 19, 2021, www.manchin.senate.gov/newsroom/press -releases/manchin-statement-on-build-back-better-act.

35. In a poll taken in April 2023, 53 percent of Republicans identified China as an "enemy" versus only 27 percent of Democrats. Laura Silver, Christine Huang, Laura Clancy, and Moira Fagan, "Americans Are Critical of China's Global Role—As Well as Its Relationship with Russia," *Pew Research Center,* April 12, 2023, www.pewresearch.org/global/2023/04/12/amer icans-are-critical-of-chinas-global-role-as-well-as-its-relationship-with -russia/.

36. David Weigel and Shelby Talcott, "Mike Pompeo: 'The Most Dangerous Person in the World Is Randi Weingarten,'" *Semafor,* November 22, 2022, www.semafor.com/article/11/21/2022/mike-pompeo-2024-trump.

37. Navarro's report was considered polemical enough that the Mercatus Center published a rebuttal calling many of its conclusions exaggerated and dangerous. Daniel Griswold, "White House Report Exaggerates the Threat of Chinese Central Planning," *International Freedom and Trade Blog,* June 20, 2018, www.mercatus.org/economic-insights/expert-commentary/white-house -report-exaggerates-threat-chinese-central-planning.

38. *How China's Economic Aggression Threatens the Technologies and Intellectual Property of the United States and the World* (Washington, D.C.: White House Office of Trade and Manufacturing Policy, 2018), pp. 14–16.

39. "CPAC Agenda Featuring More Focus on Threats from China," Newsmax, February 27, 2021, www.newsmax.com/us/cpac-policy-republicans-trade -war/2021/02/27/id/1011775/.

40. Tucker Carlson, "Tucker Carlson: U.S. Government Officials Helped

China Cover Up Covid Origins," Fox News, June 3, 2021, www.foxnews
.com/opinion/tucker-carlson-us-government-officials-helped-china
-cover-up-covid-origins; Tucker Carlson, "Tucker Carlson Reacts to Hunter
Biden's Business Dealings: Whatever Helps China, Joe Biden Has Dutifully
Done," Fox News, July 11, 2022, www.foxnews.com/opinion/tucker-carlson
-us-government-officials-helped-china-cover-up-covid-origins; Tucker Carlson, "Tucker Carlson: Apple Is Covering for the Chinese Government," Fox
News, November 30, 2022, www.youtube.com/watch?v=aHJ_tzgTZno.

41. Ethan Paul, "China Says It Wants to Stay Out of the U.S. Election. Fox
News Has Other Ideas," *South China Morning Post,* October 11, 2020, www
.scmp.com/news/china/politics/article/3104715/china-says-it-wants-stay
-out-us-election-fox-news-has-other.

42. Tucker Carlson, as quoted in Paul, "China Says It Wants to Stay Out
of the U.S. Election."

43. Gideon Lewis-Kraus, "Have Chinese Spies Infiltrated American Cam-
puses?" *New Yorker,* March 14, 2022, www.newyorker.com/magazine/2022/03
/21/have-chinese-spies-infiltrated-american-campuses.

44. See, for instance, Elsa Kania, a China hand who was personally tar-
geted by such labeling. @EBKania, February 27, 2021, https://twitter.com
/EBKania/status/1365357366015844358. For context, see also Ian Johnson,
"A Professor Who Challenges the Washington Consensus on China," *New
Yorker,* December 13, 2022, www.newyorker.com/news/persons-of-interest
/a-professor-who-challenges-the-washington-consensus-on-china.

45. Kristen Altus, "Ted Cruz Warns Biden Foreign Policy Agenda Is 'Great
for Enemies of America,'" Fox Business, March 30, 2023, www.foxbusiness
.com/politics/ted-cruz-torches-joe-bidens-foreign-policy-agenda-great
-enemies-america.

46. Azi Paybarah, "Democrats Defend Rep. Chu Against 'Xenophobic'
Accusations of Disloyalty to U.S.," *Washington Post,* February 24, 2023, www
.washingtonpost.com/politics/2023/02/24/asian-americans-judy-chu
-china-gooden/.

47. As quoted in Harris Mylonas and Scott Radnitz, "The Disturbing Return of the Fifth Column," *Foreign Affairs,* August 22, 2022, www.foreignaffairs
.com/russian-federation/disturbing-return-fifth-column.

48. As quoted by the Office of Trade and Manufacturing Policy in *How
China's Economic Aggression Threatens the Technologies and Intellectual Property of the United States and the World,* p. 14.

49. Tobita Chow, "What America's Fear of China Really Says About
Us," *New America,* October 5, 2021, www.newamerica.org/the-thread/what
-americas-fear-of-china-really-says-about-us/.

50. *Stop AAPI Hate National Report* (San Francisco: Stop AAPI Hate

Coalition, 2021); *Two Years and Thousands of Voices: What Community-Generated Data Tells Us About Anti-AAPI Hate* (San Francisco: Stop AAPI Hate Coalition, 2022).

51. Annabelle Timsit, "San Francisco Police Mark 567% Increase in Anti-Asian Hate Crime Reports in 2021," *Washington Post*, January 26, 2022, www.washingtonpost.com/nation/2022/01/26/anti-asian-hate-crime-san -francisco-covid/.

52. Russell Contreras, "Nearly 75% of Chinese Americans Report Discrimination in Past Year," Axios, May 1, 2023, www.axios.com/2023/05/01 /chinese-americans-report-racial-discrimination-asian-hate.

53. Daniel De Vise, "As Hate Crimes Surge, Most Are Going Uncounted," *The Hill*, January 20, 2023, https://thehill.com/policy/national-security/3819963 -as-hate-crimes-surge-most-are-going-uncounted/.

54. Hua Hsu, "The Muddled History of Anti-Asian Violence," *New Yorker*, February 28, 2021, www.newyorker.com/culture/cultural-comment/the-mud dled-history-of-anti-asian-violence.

55. Stop AAPI Hate Coalition, *Two Years and Thousands of Voices*, p. 13.

56. "U.S. Cancels over 1,000 Visas for Chinese Nationals Deemed Security Risks," CNBC, September 9, 2020, www.cnbc.com/2020/09/10/us-cancels -over-1000-visas-for-chinese-nationals-deemed-security-risks.html. In May 2020, Tom Cotton and Marsha Blackburn introduced the "Secure Campus Act" that would "prohibit Chinese nationals from receiving visas to the United States for graduate or post-graduate studies in STEM fields." "Cotton, Blackburn, Kustoff Unveil Bill to Restrict Chinese Stem Graduate Student Visas and Thousand Talents Participants," May 27, 2020, www.cotton.senate.gov /news/press-releases/cotton-blackburn-kustoff-unveil-bill-to-restrict -chinese-stem-graduate-student-visas-and-thousand-talents-participants.

57. "Biden Keeps Costly Trump Visa Policy Denying Chinese Grad Students," *Forbes*, August 10, 2021, www.forbes.com/sites/stuartanderson/2021 /08/10/biden-keeps-costly-trump-visa-policy-denying-chinese-grad -students/?sh=6d4161953641; Legislature of the State of Texas, H.B. No. 4736, https://capitol.texas.gov/tlodocs/88R/billtext/html/HB04736I.htm.

58. Eileen Guo, Jesse Aloe, and Karen Hao, "The U.S. Crackdown on Chinese Economic Espionage Is a Mess. We Have the Data to Show It," *MIT Technology Review*, December 2, 2021, www.technologyreview.com/2021/12 /02/1040656/china-initative-us-justice-department/.

59. Margaret Lewis, "Criminalizing China," *Journal of Criminal Law and Criminology* 111, no. 1 (2021), p. 146; Nathan Greenfield, "Professor Acquittal—Is China Initiative Out of Control?" *University World News*, September 25, 2021, www.universityworldnews.com/post.php?story=20210924 083109792.

60. Guo, Aloe, and Hao, "The U.S. Crackdown on Chinese Economic Espionage Is a Mess."

61. Ellen Nakashima, "More Than 1,000 Visiting Researchers Affiliated with the Chinese Military Fled the United States This Summer, Justice Department Says," *Washington Post,* December 2, 2020, www.washingtonpost .com/national-security/more-than-1000-visiting-researchers-affiliated -with-the-chinese-military-fled-the-united-states-this-summer-justice -department-says/2020/12/02/9c564dee-34e1-11eb-b59c-adb7153d10c2 _story.html.

62. *Racial Profiling Among Scientists of Chinese Descent and Consequences for the U.S. Scientific Community* (Tucson: University of Arizona and Committee of 100, 2021), p. 32. The final survey sample included 658 Chinese scientists, 782 non-Chinese scientists, and 509 scientists who did not report their ethnic background. The survey method is explained on page 29.

63. In New York, for example, an ethnically Tibetan police officer and former U.S. Marine was jailed for six months and later released without trial. In a separate incident, an FBI agent admitted to profiling a Chinese American professor in Tennessee and falsely accusing him of being a spy. Joseph Choi, "Federal Agents Admit to Falsely Accusing Chinese Professor of Being a Spy," *The Hill,* June 14, 2021, https://thehill.com/regulation/court-battles /558345-federal-agents-admit-to-falsely-accusing-chinese-professor-of -being/; Ed Shanahan, "U.S. Asks to Drop Case Accusing N.Y.P.D. Officer of Spying for China," *New York Times,* January 16, 2023, www.nytimes.com /2023/01/16/nyregion/nypd-officer-china-spy-angwang.html.

64. Richard Hofstadter, *Anti-Intellectualism in American Life* (New York: Knopf, 1963).

65. David Goldman, "Bannon Tells Asia Times: U.S. Election Is All About China," *Asia Times,* June 12, 2020, https://asiatimes.com/2020/06/bannon -tells-at-us-election-is-all-about-china/.

66. "Chinese Fentanyl Was in George Floyd Explains Everything," Episode 1013, Real Coffee With Scott Adams, June 1, 2020, www.youtube.com /watch?v=BzZ1lHOpo64; "Fact-Check—No Evidence Drug Overdose Was Main Cause of Death for George Floyd in 2020," Reuters, November 9, 2022, www.reuters.com/article/factcheck-george-floyd-overdose-death/fact -check-no-evidence-drug-overdose-was-main-cause-of-death-for-george -floyd-in-2020-idU.S.L1N3241XJ.

67. Bethany Allen-Ibrahimian, "Right-Wing Media Falsely Ties Black Lives Matter Movement to Beijing," Axios, October 21, 2020, www.axios.com /2020/10/20/right-wing-media-falsely-ties-black-lives-matter-movement -to-beijing.

68. Phelim Kine, "A Heartland GOP Primary Battle Goes All-In on

Bashing China," Politico, February 16, 2022, www.politico.com/news/2022
/02/16/a-heartland-gop-primary-battle-china-00009095.

69. Goldman, "Bannon Tells Asia Times"; Dave Davies, "Journalist Traces
the Peculiar Story of Steve Bannon's Enigmatic Chinese Benefactor," NPR,
October 20, 2022, www.npr.org/2022/10/20/1130184401/the-inscrutable-aims
-of-steve-bannons-enigmatic-chinese-benefactor.

70. At one point Kwok asserted specifically that "the CCP wants to gain
control of all aspects of the world, and the Jews are in their way." As quoted
in Dan Friedman, "Exclusive: Leaked Messages Reveal the Origins of the
Most Vile Hunter Biden Smear," *Mother Jones,* April 7, 2022, www.mother
jones.com/politics/2022/04/hunter-biden-laptop-guo-wengui-bannon
-giuliani/.

71. Benjamin Weiser and Michel Forsythe, "Exiled Billionaire Charged
in New York with Financial Conspiracy," *New York Times,* March 15, 2023,
www.nytimes.com/2023/03/15/nyregion/guo-wengui-billionaire-charged
.html.

72. As quoted in Dan Friedman, "Exclusive: Leaked Messages Reveal the
Origins of the Most Vile Hunter Biden Smear."

73. Dan Friedman, "More Leaked Audio: Bannon Bragged That He Used
Porn to Smear Hunter Biden," *Mother Jones,* July 26, 2022, www.mother
jones.com/politics/2022/07/bannon-leaked-audio-porn-hunter-biden
-laptop-guo/.

74. *2021 State Export Report: Goods and Services Exports by U.S. States to
China over the Past Decade* (Washington, D.C.: U.S.-China Business Council, 2021), p. 45.

75. Tea Party Patriots, "Stop Helping the Chinese Buy Our Farms," You-
Tube, July 23, 2016, www.youtube.com/watch?v=czJkER7BZXw.

76. Bess Levin, "Josh Hawley Proudly Declares Himself Pro Hate Crimes,"
Vanity Fair, April 22, 2021, www.vanityfair.com/news/2021/04/josh-hawley
-hate-crime-bill.

77. Greitens placed a close third in the Republican primary, garnering a
little over 18 percent of the vote.

78. Herb Scribner, "Eric Greitens' 'RINO Hunting' Video Removed from
Facebook," Axios, June 21, 2022, www.axios.com/2022/06/20/eric-greitens
-rino-hunting-video.

79. Madeline Peltz, "Disgraced Former Missouri Gov. Eric Greitens Is
Launching a Comeback on the Back of Steve Bannon," *Media Matters for
America,* March 22, 2021, www.mediamatters.org/january-6-insurrection/dis
graced-former-missouri-gov-eric-greitens-launching-comeback-back
-steve.

80. Kine, "A Heartland GOP Primary Battle Goes All-In on Bashing China."

81. Trudy Busch Valentine, @BuschValentine, October 22, 2022, https://twitter.com/buschvalentine/status/1583477343661662211.

82. Samantha Aschieris, "Why China Owning U.S. Land Is a Bigger Deal Than You Might Think," Daily Signal, August 12, 2022, www.dailysignal.com/2022/08/12/why-china-owning-us-land-is-bigger-deal-than-you-might-think/.

83. Dan Newhouse, @RepNewhouse, July 1, 2021, https://twitter.com/repnewhouse/status/1410336888981004292.

84. Press release, "Governor Ron DeSantis Counteracts Malign Influence by China and Other Hostile Nations in Florida Through New Action," September 22, 2022, www.flgov.com/2022/09/22/governor-ron-desantis-counteracts-malign-influence-by-china-and-other-hostile-nations-in-florida-through-new-action/.

85. Bethany Blankley, "New Bill Would Ban Certain Foreign Entities from Purchasing Land in Texas," Center Square, January 15, 2023, https://www.thecentersquare.com/texas/new-bill-would-ban-certain-foreign-entities-from-purchasing-land-in-texas/article_d1604e42-94eb-11ed-a16d-57b52d89086c.html?utm_medium=social&utm_source=twitter&utm_campaign=user-share.

86. Tom Cotton, 117th Congress, 2nd Session, ROS22A43, "Securing America's Land from Foreign Interference Act," www.cotton.senate.gov/imo/media/doc/securing_american_farmland.pdf.

87. See the collection of unhinged quotes in Phelim Kine, "Biden's 'Supercharged' African Diplomacy," Politico *China Watcher Newsletter,* January 26, 2023, www.politico.com/newsletters/politico-china-watcher/2023/01/26/bidens-supercharged-african-diplomacy-00079578.

4
How Rivalry Worsens Economic Inequality

1. The New Deal aimed to realize economic democracy, the civil rights movement had economic democracy high on its list of demands, and progressives from Henry Wallace to Tom Hayden campaigned on the slogan and substance of economic democracy. See especially Michael Dennis, *The Full Employment Horizon in 20th Century America: The Movement for Economic Democracy* (New York: Bloomsbury, 2022); Ronald Lee, "The New Populist Campaign for Economic Democracy: A Rhetorical Exploration," *Quarterly Journal of Speech* 72, no. 3 (1986), pp. 274–289. On Humphrey, see

Carl Solberg, *Hubert Humphrey: A Biography* (St. Paul: Borealis, 2003), 309–310.

2. Michael Kalecki, "Political Aspects of Full Employment," *Political Quarterly* 14, no. 4 (1943), pp. 322–330. See also Michael Brenes, *For Might and Right: Cold War Defense Spending and the Making of American Democracy* (Amherst: University of Massachusetts Press, 2020).

3. As the economist Paul Sweezy wrote to his co-author Paul Baran, "Either you see that this is a question of the class structure of society and the location of political power, or you don't." Nicholas Baran and John Bellamy Foster, eds., *Age of Monopoly Capital: Selected Correspondence of Paul A. Baran and Paul M. Sweezy, 1949–1964* (New York: Monthly Review, 2017), p. 107.

4. We generally describe this brutalist, notionally post-neoliberal political economy as "national security Keynesianism," but others describe it simply as "political capitalism." See Dylan Riley and Robert Brenner, "Seven Theses on American Politics," *New Left Review,* no. 138 (2022), https:// newleftreview.org/issues/ii138/articles/dylan-riley-robert-brenner-seven -theses-on-american-politics.

5. On the history of neoliberalism, see Quinn Slobodian, *Globalists: The End of Empire and the Birth of Neoliberalism* (Cambridge: Harvard University Press, 2018).

6. The new American right, in fact, has positioned itself as responding to the inequities of neoliberalism—it is just that their solutions involve policies of racial hierarchy, exclusion, and greater wealth hoarding. John Feffer, *Right Across the World: The Global Networking of the Far-Right and the Left Response* (London: Pluto, 2021).

7. The history of this era is still being written, but for a brilliant capsule of how these trends shaped our historical conjuncture, see Tim Sahay and Ted Fertik, "Bidenomics and Climate Action: The Case of the Inflation Reduction Act," Presentation at the Watson Institute of International and Public Affairs, Brown University, Rhode Island, February 4, 2023, www.youtube .com/live/WQ-K2PTsN2I?feature=share.

8. See especially Jennifer Harris and Jake Sullivan, "America Needs a New Economic Philosophy. Foreign Policy Experts Can Help," *Foreign Policy,* February 7, 2020, https://foreignpolicy.com/2020/02/07/america-needs -a-new-economic-philosophy-foreign-policy-experts-can-help/.

9. "Remarks by National Security Advisor Jake Sullivan on Renewing American Economic Leadership at the Brookings Institution," April 27, 2023, White House, www.whitehouse.gov/briefing-room/speeches-remarks/2023 /04/27/remarks-by-national-security-advisor-jake-sullivan-on-renewing -american-economic-leadership-at-the-brookings-institution/.

10. Harry S. Truman, "Letter to the Speaker Transmitting Supplemental

Appropriation Estimates for the National Military Establishment," May 13, 1948, www.trumanlibrary.gov/library/public-papers/98/letter-speaker-trans mitting-supplemental-appropriation-estimates-national.

11. See Quinn Slobodian, *Crack-Up Capitalism: Market Radicals and the Dream of a World Without Democracy* (New York: Henry Holt, 2023).

12. Matthew Specter, *The Atlantic Realists: Empire and International Political Thought Between Germany and the United States* (Palo Alto: Stanford University Press, 2022).

13. Dani Rodrik, "The New Productivism Paradigm?" *Project Syndicate*, July 5, 2022, www.project-syndicate.org/commentary/new-productivism-eco nomic-policy-paradigm-by-dani-rodrik-2022-07.

14. See especially the analysis of Biden's thinking about manufacturing as "the arsenal of democracy" rather than a New Deal in Kelsey Atherton, "CHIPS Fall," *Wars of Future Past Newsletter*, July 30, 2022, https://athertonkd .substack.com/p/chips-fall.

15. "Senator Baldwin Celebrates One Year of the Inflation Reduction Act Delivering Lower Costs to Wisconsin Families," August 16, 2023, www.baldwin .senate.gov/news/press-releases/senator-baldwin-celebrates-one-year -of-the-inflation-reduction-act-delivering-lower-costs-to-wisconsin-families; Matt Sheehan, "Biden's Unprecedented Semiconductor Bet," Carnegie Endowment for International Peace, October 27, 2022, https://carnegieendowment .org/2022/10/27/biden-s-unprecedented-semiconductor-bet-pub-88270.

16. William Rivers Pitt, "The Best Parts of the Inflation Reduction Act Came Out of Progressive Advocacy," *Truthout*, August 8, 2022, https://truth out.org/articles/the-best-parts-of-the-inflation-reduction-act-came-out-of -progressive-advocacy/.

17. Kelsey Atherton, "Should U.S. Pay Semiconductor Makers to Compete Vs. China?" *Breaking Defense*, July 28, 2020, https://breakingdefense .com/2020/07/should-us-pay-semiconductor-makers-to-compete-vs-china/.

18. Gregory Hooks, "The Rise of the Pentagon and U.S. State Building: The Defense Program as Industrial Policy," *American Journal of Sociology* 96, no. 2 (September, 1990), pp. 358–404.

19. Yakov Feygin, "SVB, Bailouts, and How to Regulate Capitalism," *Building on a Ruin Newsletter*, March 13, 2023, https://building-a-ruin.ghost.io/svb -regulation-bailouts-capitalism/?ref=building-a-ruin-newsletter.

20. Robert Kuttner, "Using Industrial Policy to Promote Social Justice," *American Prospect*, March 27, 2023, https://prospect.org/blogs-and-newsletters /tap/2023-03-27-industrial-policy-social-justice/.

21. *Guidelines for a Just Transition Towards Environmentally Sustainable Societies and Economies for All* (Geneva: International Labor Organization, 2015), p. 4.

22. On the United States as an oligarchy, see especially Jeffrey Winter, *Oligarchy* (New York: Cambridge University Press, 2011).

23. "Remarks by National Security Advisor Jake Sullivan at the Special Competitive Studies Project Global Emerging Technologies Summit," September 16, 2022, www.whitehouse.gov/briefing-room/speeches-remarks/2022 /09/16/remarks-by-national-security-advisor-jake-sullivan-at-the-special -competitive-studies-project-global-emerging-technologies-summit/. For Raimondo's quote, see Brad Glosserman, "High-Tech Tensions in the Japan-U.S. Relationship," *Japan Times,* November 8, 2022, www.japantimes.co.jp /opinion/2022/11/08/commentary/japan-commentary/u-s-japan-tech/.

24. "Remarks by National Security Advisor Jake Sullivan on Renewing American Economic Leadership at the Brookings Institution."

25. "Special—Biden's China Tech Controls," *American Prestige* podcast, August 21, 2023, www.americanprestigepod.com/p/special-bidens-china-tech -controls.

26. Goldman Sachs, "Why the CHIPS Act Is Unlikely to Reduce U.S. Reliance on Asia," October 22, 2022, www.goldmansachs.com/intelligence/pages /why-the-chips-act-is-unlikely-to-reduce-the-us-reliance-on-asia.html.

27. Ibid.

28. Derek Brower and Amanda Chu, "The U.S. Plan to Become the World's Cleantech Superpower," *Financial Times,* February 15, 2023, www.ft.com /content/e0b55820-3a16-4018-a417-0e7c91737ffd.

29. Ibid.

30. Noah Berman, "President Biden Has Banned Some U.S. Investment in China. Here's What to Know," *Council on Foreign Relations,* August 29, 2023, www.cfr.org/in-brief/president-biden-has-banned-some-us-investment -china-heres-what-know.

31. Jacob Fawcett, *The Global Green New Deal* (New York: People's Policy Project, 2019).

32. Lee Harris, "Congressional Authority over Trade Deals," *American Prospect,* March 3, 2023, https://americanprospect.bluelena.io/index.php ?action=social&chash=c164bbc9d6c72a52c599bbb43d8db8e1.1940&s =b3cb5fcee05c9eefd7a01e549cb03acc.

33. "Remarks by National Security Advisor Jake Sullivan on Renewing American Economic Leadership at the Brookings Institution."

34. Ibid.

35. Dean Baker, "Industrial Policy Is Not a Remedy for Income Inequality," *Center for Economic Policy Research Blog,* December 21, 2022, https:// cepr.net/industrial-policy-is-not-a-remedy-for-income-inequality/?utm _source=substack&utm_medium=email.

36. Bhashkar Mazumder, "Intergenerational Mobility in the United States:

What We Have Learned from the PSID," *Annals of the American Academy of Political and Social Science* 680, no. 1 (2018), pp. 213–234.

37. Kaitlyn Henderson, *The Crisis of Low Wages in the U.S.* (Boston: Oxfam America, 2022), www.oxfamamerica.org/explore/research-publications/the -crisis-of-low-wages-in-the-us/.

38. Martha Ross, Nicole Bateman, and Alec Friedhoff, "A Closer Look at Low-Wage Workers Across the Country," *Brookings Institution,* March 2020, www.brookings.edu/interactives/low-wage-workforce/.

39. Ibid.

40. Henderson, *The Crisis of Low Wages in the U.S.,* pp. 10–17.

41. From 2008 to 2019, some measures suggest that income inequality in the United States fell modestly before spiking again once the pandemic hit— an observation that implies economic life was getting slightly better in the pre-pandemic status quo. But that observation includes income from capital gains and real estate appreciation—assets that low-skilled workers and work- ers under the age of forty disproportionately cannot afford. And in addition to bracketing off the larger history of accelerating income inequality dating back to the 1970s, the measure of modest inequality reduction starting in 2009 also includes government transfers to households from benefits like the Affordable Care Act, suggesting the necessary role of government pro- grams in closing the gap between reality and economic democracy. See Aus- tin Clemens, "U.S. Income and Wealth Inequality Are No Longer Increasing, But a Return to the Equitable Levels of the Mid-20th Century Isn't Likely Anytime Soon," *Washington Center for Equitable Growth,* January 17, 2023, https://equitablegrowth.org/u-s-income-and-wealth-inequality-are-no -longer-increasing-but-a-return-to-the-equitable-levels-of-the-mid-20th -century-isnt-likely-anytime-soon/.

42. Shannon Pettypiece, "Evictions Are Piling Up Across the U.S. as Covid-Era Protections End and Rents Climb," NBC News, November 6, 2022, www.nbcnews.com/politics/politics-news/evictions-are-piling-us-covid -era-protections-end-rents-climb-rcna54798.

43. Heather Gautney, *The New Power Elite* (New York: Oxford University Press, 2022), p. 151.

44. Stephen Semler, "Budget Battle on Capitol Hill: Forecasting the Win- ners and Losers," *Speaking Security,* May 18, 2023, https://stephensemler .substack.com/p/budget-battle-on-capitol-hill-forecasting?utm _source=post-email-title&publication_id=37298&post_id=122304023&is Freemail=true&utm_medium=email.

45. As of 2019, the wage share was only lower in the aftermath of the global financial crisis of 2008. See "Share of Labor Compensation in GDP at Current National Prices for United States," May 11, 2023 (St. Louis: Federal

Reserve Bank of St. Louis), https://fred.stlouisfed.org/series/LABSHPUSA 156NRUG.

46. Isabella Weber and Evan Wasner, "Sellers' Inflation, Profits and Conflict: Why Can Large Firms Hike Prices in an Emergency?" *Economics Department Working Paper Series* (Amherst: University of Massachusetts, 2023), p. 25.

47. Tara Copp, "Defense Budget Speeds Toward $1 Trillion, with China in Mind," AP News, March 13, 2023, https://apnews.com/article/pentagon -trillion-defense-china-budget-d5ae4061b047291ef124257e24c7ec0b.

48. Cernadas and Bellamy Foster, "Actual U.S. Military Spending Reached $1.537 Trillion in 2022."

49. Heidi Garrett-Peltier, "Job Opportunity Cost of War," May 24, 2017, *Costs of War Project,* Brown University, https://watson.brown.edu/costsof war/files/cow/imce/papers/2017/Job%20Opportunity%20Cost%20of%20 War%20-%20HGP%20-%20FINAL.pdf.

50. Branko Milanovic, "What Happened to Social Mobility in America?" *Foreign Affairs,* January 8, 2021, www.foreignaffairs.com/articles/americas /2021-01-08/what-happened-social-mobility-america.

51. Richard Reeves, *Dream Hoarding: How the American Upper Middle Class Is Leaving Everyone Else in the Dust, Why That Is a Problem, and What to Do About It* (Washington, D.C.: Brookings Institution, 2017).

52. "Incomes Are Rising in America, Especially for the Poorest," *Economist,* January 15, 2023, www.economist.com/united-states/2023/01/15/incomes -are-rising-in-america-especially-for-the-poorest#.

53. The childcare provisions and "diversity, equity, and inclusion" plans were among such progressive instructions, not laws or rights; Kuttner, "Using Industrial Policy to Promote Social Justice." It is important to note that Republicans have been opposed to all the investment provisions of the so-called New Washington Consensus; they only support the anti-China restrictions.

54. The Taft-Hartley Act, in effect since 1947, outlaws some of the most powerful tactics of organized labor, including solidarity/secondary strikes and boycotts.

55. Tim Barker, "Cold War Capitalism: The Political Economy of American Military Spending, 1947–1990" (Ph.D. diss., Harvard University, 2022), p. 201.

56. Rosella Capella-Zielinski, *How States Pay for Wars* (Ithaca: Cornell University Press, 2016), p. 29.

57. "Build Back Better Cost Would Double with Extensions," Committee for a Responsible Federal Budget, November 15, 2021, www.crfb.org/blogs /build-back-better-cost-would-double-extensions.

58. The labor-friendly aspects of the IRA took the form of corporate in-

centives rather than restrictions or requirements. The most attractive "pro-worker" aspect of the IRA is a provision offering tax credits for paying workers the "prevailing local wage" standard. In principle, that tax credit incentivizes better worker pay. In practice, it depends on (1) where manufacturing is located and (2) whether firms value the tax credit more than cheap or controllable labor.

59. Amanda Chu and Oliver Roeder, "'Transformational Change': Biden's Industrial Policy Begins to Bear Fruit," *Financial Times,* April 17, 2023, www.ft.com/content/b6cd46de-52d6-4641-860b-5f2c1b0c5622.

60. Oliver Milman, "Republicans in the U.S. 'Battery Belt' Embrace Biden's Climate Spending," *The Guardian,* February 22, 2023, www.theguardian.com/environment/2023/feb/22/climate-spending-republican-states-clean-energy-funding.

61. Elizabeth Tandy Shermer, *Sunbelt Capitalism: Phoenix and the Transformation of American Politics* (Philadelphia: University of Pennsylvania Press, 2015).

62. Erik Baker, "The People, It Depends," *N+1* (Summer 2021), www.nplusonemag.com/issue-40/reviews/the-people-it-depends-2/. On the unique politics that made the New Deal possible, see especially Jefferson Cowie, *The Great Exception: The New Deal and the Limits of American Politics* (Princeton: Princeton University Press, 2017).

63. Saijel Kishan, "This Conservative Group Is Advocating for Renewable Energy," *Bloomberg,* March 16, 2023, www.bloomberg.com/news/articles/2023-03-15/the-conservative-group-that-loves-renewables-green-insight.

64. As quoted in Gregory Schneider, "Youngkin Says He Blocked Ford Battery Plant on China Concerns," *Washington Post,* January 13, 2023, www.washingtonpost.com/dc-md-va/2023/01/13/youngkin-virginia-ford-battery-china/.

65. Ibid.

66. Jeff Schuhrke and Sarah Lazare, "Republicans Are Using Anti-China Rhetoric to Undercut Striking UAW Workers' Demands," *In These Times,* October 12, 2023, https://inthesetimes.com/article/uaw-auto-workers-strike-gop-republicans-china-electric-vehicles.

67. UAW president Walter Reuther famously supported U.S. Cold War militarism and promoted anti-communist paranoia within the Congress of Industrial Organizations (CIO). In so doing, eleven unions were expelled from the CIO. Gary Chaison, "Federal Expulsions and Union Mergers in the United States," *Industrial Relations* 28, no. 2 (1973), pp. 345–346.

68. Heidi Garrett-Peltier, *The Cost of Debt-Financed War: Public Debt and Rising Interest for Post-9/11 War Spending* (Providence, R.I.: Brown University Costs of War Project, 2020), p. 1.

69. Ibid.

70. Corey Payne, "Financialization Feeds Endless War," *Convergence,* June 2, 2022, https://convergencemag.com/articles/financialization-feeds-endless -war/.

71. Norman Augustine, "Law XVI" in *Augustine's Laws* (Reston, Va.: American Institute of Aeronautics and Astronautics, 1997), p. 107.

72. Timothy Barker, "'Don't Discuss Jobs Outside This Room': Reconsidering Military Keynesianism in the 1970s," in *The Military and the Market,* ed. Jennifer Mittelstadt and Mark Wilson (Philadelphia: University of Pennsylvania Press, 2022), pp. 135–149.

73. Chu and Roeder, "'Transformational Change.'"

74. Ibid.

75. On how the Pentagon uses the Taiwan war scenario to justify military primacy, see Jackson, *Pacific Power Paradox,* pp. 166–168. On the uniquely insurmountable imbalance of forces in the Taiwan Strait, see Van Jackson, "On Washington's China Fetish," *Un-Diplomatic Newsletter,* January 2, 2023, www.un-diplomatic.com/p/on-washingtons-china-fetish.

76. Michael Mastanduno, "System Maker and Privilege Taker: U.S. Power and the International Political Economy," *World Politics* 61, no. 1 (2009), pp. 121–154.

77. Thomas Oatley, *A Political Economy of American Hegemony: Buildups, Booms, and Busts* (New York: Cambridge University Press, 2015), pp. 129–132.

78. Oatley, *A Political Economy of American Hegemony,* pp. 127–149.

5

How Rivalry Threatens Peace

1. David Kang, "Thought Games About China," *Journal of East Asian Studies* 20, no. 2 (2020), pp. 135–150.

2. The Obama administration saw AIIB as a threat and attempted to combat it. See Jackson, *Pacific Power Paradox,* p. 152. On the general threat perception of Chinese global governance, see Liza Tobin, "Xi's Vision for Transforming Global Governance: A Strategic Challenge for Washington and Its Allies," *Texas National Security Review* 2, no. 1 (2018), pp. 154–166.

3. Jackson, *Pacific Power Paradox,* p. 150.

4. Xi Jinping, as quoted in Oscar Almen, "Beijing's Extraterritorial Authoritarian Rule," *Indo-Pacific Defense Forum,* May 17, 2021, https://ip defenseforum.com/2021/05/the-ccp-and-the-diaspora/.

5. Randall Schweller and Xiaoyu Pu, "After Unipolarity: China's Visions of International Order in an Era of U.S. Decline," *International Security* 36, no. 1 (2011), pp. 41–72; Andrew Chubb, "PRC Assertiveness in the South

China Sea: Measuring Continuity and Change, 1970–2015," *International Security* 45, no. 3 (2021), pp. 79–121.

6. See Jackson, *Pacific Power Paradox,* pp. 150–151.

7. For Blackburn quote, see @MarshaBlackburn, December 4, 2020, https://twitter.com/MarshaBlackburn/status/1334510812552163328?lang=en.

8. For the best example of this ideological claim, see Policy Planning Staff, *The Elements of the China Challenge* (Washington, D.C.: U.S. Department of State, 2020).

9. Yuen Yuen Ang, *China's Gilded Age: The Paradox of Economic Boom and Vast Corruption* (New York: Cambridge University Press, 2020).

10. For a historical account of how this happened and what it means for stability, see Jackson, *Pacific Power Paradox.* See also Kanishka Jayasuriya, "The Age of Political Disincorporation: Geo-Capitalist Conflict and the Politics of Authoritarian Statism," *Journal of Contemporary Asia* 53, no. 1 (2023), pp. 165–178.

11. China has leveraged its economic ties to secure dozens of "strategic comprehensive partnerships" throughout the region that require political commitments as part of enjoying economic relations. See Feng Zhongping and Huang Jing, "China's Strategic Partnership Diplomacy," *ESPO Working Paper* No. 8 (2014), https://papers.ssrn.com/sol3/papers.cfm?abstract_id=2459948.

12. Ho-fung Hung, *The China Boom: Why China Will Not Rule the World* (New York: Columbia University Press, 2014), pp. 153–154.

13. Matthew Klein and Michael Pettis, *Trade Wars Are Class Wars: How Rising Inequality Distorts the Global Economy and Threatens International Peace* (New Haven: Yale University Press, 2020), p. 111.

14. "Premier Li Keqiang Meets the Press: Full Transcript of Questions and Answers," Ministry of Foreign Affairs of the People's Republic of China, May 28, 2020, www.fmprc.gov.cn/eng/wjdt_665385/zyjh_665391/202005/t20200529_678861.html.

15. Leo Panitch and Sam Gindin, *The Making of Global Capitalism: The Political Economy of American Empire* (New York: Verso, 2013).

16. Klein and Pettis, *Trade Wars Are Class Wars,* p. 3.

17. Ang, *China's Gilded Age,* pp. 13–14.

18. Thomas Rawski, "Will Investment Behavior Constrain China's Growth?" *China Economic Review* 13, no. 4 (2002), pp. 361–372.

19. Hung, *The China Boom,* pp. 157–163.

20. See especially Michael Pettis, "Will China's Common Prosperity Upgrade Dual Circulation?" *Carnegie Endowment for International Peace: China Financial Markets,* October 15, 2021, https://carnegieendowment.org/chinafinancialmarkets/85571.

21. Wu Xinbo, "Understanding the Global Implications of the Asian Financial Crisis."

22. Jeremy Wallace, "Why Does China Remain Locked on Growth Targets?" *Noema Magazine,* May 16, 2023, www.noemamag.com/why-does-china-remain-locked-on-growth-targets/.

23. Yueran Zhang, "The Chongqing Model One Decade On," *Made in China Journal,* January 11, 2021, https://madeinchinajournal.com/2021/01/11/the-chongqing-model-one-decade-on/.

24. Ibid.

25. Branko Milanovic, "China's Inequality Will Lead It to a Stark Choice," *Foreign Affairs,* February 11, 2021, www.foreignaffairs.com/articles/china/2021-02-11/chinas-inequality-will-lead-it-stark-choice.

26. The mechanisms discussed here are elaborated in greater detail in Hung, *The China Boom,* pp. 148–157; Klein and Pettis, *Trade Wars Are Class Wars,* pp. 108–114; Ho-fung Hung, "Repressing Labor, Empowering China," *Phenomenal World,* July 2, 2021, www.phenomenalworld.org/analysis/repressing-labor-empowering-china/.

27. On the way China prevents worker power formally, through control of the All-China Federation of Trade Unions, see Eli Friedman, *Insurgency Trap: Labor Politics in Postsocialist China* (Ithaca: Cornell University Press, 2014).

28. On the role of the *hukou* system in China's economic development, see Jeremy Wallace, *Cities and Stability: Urbanization, Redistribution, and Regime Survival in China* (New York: Oxford University Press, 2014), pp. 159–186.

29. Klein and Pettis, *Trade Wars Are Class Wars,* p. 112.

30. See especially Kanishka Jayasuriya, "The Age of Political Disincorporation," pp. 165–178.

31. Jayasuriya, "The Age of Political Disincorporation," p. 166.

32. Prabhat Patnaik, "Why Neoliberals Need Neofascists," *Boston Review,* July 19, 2021, www.bostonreview.net/articles/why-neoliberalism-needs-neofascists/.

33. Kaiser Kuo interview with Yuen Yuen Ang, *Sinica* podcast, September 8, 2022, https://thechinaproject.com/2022/09/08/is-chinas-bureaucracy-holding-steady-under-xi/.

34. Suisheng Zhao, "A State-Led Nationalism: The Patriotic Education Campaign in Post-Tiananmen China," *Communist and Post-Communist Studies* 31, no. 3 (1998), pp. 287–302; Peter Hays Gries, *China's New Nationalism: Pride, Politics, and Diplomacy* (Berkeley: University of California Press, 2004); Bruce Dickinson, *The Dictator's Dilemma: The Chinese Communist Party's Strategy for Survival* (New York: Oxford University Press, 2016), pp. 232–237;

Jessica Chen Weiss, *Powerful Patriots: Nationalist Protest in China's Foreign Relations* (New York: Oxford University Press, 2014).

35. Ethnonationalism is particularly toxic, but some scholars argue that not all nationalisms are equal and some can be productive—a point we return to in the final chapter. See Aram Hur, *Narratives of Civic Duty: How National Stories Shape Democracy in Asia* (Ithaca: Cornell University Press, 2022).

36. Repression has been a tool to manage anti-Japan populism for decades. See James Reilly, *Strong Society, Smart State: The Rise of Public Opinion in China's Japan Policy* (New York: Columbia University Press, 2012).

37. Yuen Yuen Ang, "How Resilient Is the CCP?" *Journal of Democracy* 33, no. 3 (2022), pp. 84–88.

38. Cheng Li, "How Washington's Hawkish China Policy Alienates Young Chinese," *Brookings Institution Commentary,* November 4, 2021, www.brookings.edu/articles/how-washingtons-hawkish-china-policy-alienates-young-chinese/.

39. The surge in popularity of the term *Baizuo* ("white left") as an epithet in China coincides with Trump's election. See Frankie Huang, "'Baizuo' Is a Chinese Word Conservatives Love," *Foreign Policy,* March 27, 2021, https://foreignpolicy.com/2021/03/27/baizuo-chinese-conservatives-liberals-decoder-tucker-carlson/. As a gesture toward global far-right sympathies, in 2021, Tucker Carlson even did a segment praising Chinese conservatives for being "antiwoke." Tucker Carlson, "Tucker: Even the Chinese Know America Won't Survive with 'Woke' Liberals in Charge," Fox News, March 20, 2021, www.foxnews.com/opinion/tucker-china-america-white-liberalism-biden.

40. Chenchen Zhang, "Right-Wing Populism with Chinese Characteristics? Identity, Otherness, and Global Imaginaries in Debating World Politics Online," *European Journal of International Relations* 26, no. 1 (2020), p. 100.

41. Huang, "'Baizuo' Is a Chinese Word Conservatives Love."

42. Darren Byler, *Terror Capitalism: Uyghur Dispossession and Masculinity in a Chinese City* (Durham: Duke University Press, 2022), p. 34.

43. Adrian Zenz, "Measuring Non-Internment State-Imposed Forced Labor in Xinjiang and Central Asia: An Assessment of ILO Measurement Guidelines," *Journal of Human Trafficking* (2023), https://doi.org/10.1080/23322705.2023.2270366.

44. Richard Bernstein, "When China Convinced the U.S. That Uighurs Were Waging Jihad," *The Atlantic,* March 19, 2019, www.theatlantic.com/international/archive/2019/03/us-uighurs-guantanamo-china-terror/584107/.

45. Byler, *Terror Capitalism,* p. 45.

46. Darren Byler, *In the Camps: China's High-Tech Penal Colony* (New York: Columbia Global Reports, 2021), pp. 123–135.

47. Evan Feigenbaum, *China's Techno-Warriors: National Security and Strategic Competition from the Nuclear to the Information Age* (Palo Alto: Stanford University Press, 2003).

48. See especially Susan Shirk, *Overreach: How China Derailed Its Peaceful Rise* (New York: Oxford University Press, 2022).

49. Ed White and Sun Yu, "Xi Jinping's Dream of a Chinese Military-Industrial Complex," *Financial Times,* June 19, 2023, www.ft.com/content /6f388e4b-9c4e-4ca3-8040-49962f1e155d.

50. "China's Share of Global GDP," *World Economics,* www.worldeco nomics.com/Share-of-Global-GDP/China.aspx.

51. Adam Behsudi, "The 'Rift is There': China vs. the World on Global Debt," Politico, April 11, 2023, www.politico.com/news/2023/04/11/china -lending-imf-world-bank-00090588.

52. "East Asia and Pacific Economic Update," *World Bank,* April 2023, https://thedocs.worldbank.org/en/doc/ec4c157d173d52b330c122aa27 fd34a5-0070012022/related/EAP-Economic-Update-April-2023-Key-Findings .pdf.

53. David Oks and Henry Williams, "The Long, Slow Death of Global Development," *American Affairs* 6, no. 4 (2022), https://americanaffairsjournal .org/2022/11/the-long-slow-death-of-global-development/.

54. Tim Barker, "The End of Development," *Dissent* (Spring 2021), www .dissentmagazine.org/article/the-end-of-development/.

55. Rebeca Grynspan, "The World Lacks an Effective Global System to Deal with Debt," *Financial Times,* February 2, 2023, www.ft.com/content /d767580d-2db3-43f2-a509-2b29eb81003a.

56. *Crisis Upon Crisis: IMF Annual Report 2022* (Washington, D.C.: International Monetary Fund, 2022), www.imf.org/external/pubs/ft/ar/2022 /downloads/imf-annual-report-2022-english.pdf.

57. Development Committee, "Evolution of the World Bank Group: A Report to Governors," March 30, 2023, p. iv, www.devcommittee.org/sites /dc/files/download/Documents/2023-03/Final_DC2023-0002%20evolution %20paper%20for%20DC%20website.pdf.

58. "For every $1 the IMF encouraged a set of poor countries to spend on public goods, it has told them to cut four times more through austerity measures," Oxfam International press release, April 13, 2023, www.oxfam.org/en/ press-releases/every-1-imf-encouraged-set-poor-countries-spend-public -goods-it-has-told-them-cut.

59. Anne Krueger, "Breaking the Debt-Relief Paralysis," *Project Syndicate,*

April 17, 2023, www.project-syndicate.org/commentary/imf-china-international
-debt-restructuring-process-is-broken-by-anne-o-krueger-2023-04?barrier
=accesspaylog.

60. Stephen Semler, "Biden Is Selling Weapons to the Majority of the
World's Autocracies," *The Intercept,* May 11, 2023, https://theintercept.com
/2023/05/11/united-states-foreign-weapons-sales/.

61. Mike Pompeo, "The Middle East and North Africa: Dimensions and
Challenges," *Newsweek,* April 1, 2022, www.newsweek.com/middle-east-north
-africa-dimensions-challenges-opinion-1693576.

62. Olafimihan Oshin, "Top Democrat Warns Saudi Arms Freeze Could
Benefit Russia and China," *The Hill,* October 11, 2022, https://thehill.com
/policy/3683461-top-democrat-warns-saudi-arms-freeze-could-benefit
-russia-and-china/.

63. David Sanger and Peter Baker, "As Biden Reaches Out to Middle East
Dictators, His Eyes Are on China and Russia," *New York Times,* July 16, 2022,
www.nytimes.com/2022/07/16/world/middleeast/biden-saudi-arabia-china
-russia.html.

64. Jackson, *Pacific Power Paradox,* p. 170.

65. Basav Sen, "Why Did a U.S. Envoy Meet with the Head of a Fascist
Militia in India?" *Foreign Policy in Focus,* September 29, 2021, https://fpif
.org/why-did-a-u-s-envoy-meet-with-the-head-of-a-fascist-militia-in-india/.

66. Mahika Khosla, "Securitization of Punjab's Political Economy Crisis,"
The Diplomat, June 20, 2023, https://thediplomat.com/2023/06/the-securiti
zation-of-punjabs-political-economy-crisis/.

67. Murtaza Hussein and Ryan Grim, "Secret Indian Memo Ordered
'Concrete Measures' Against Hardeep Singh Nijjar Two Months Before His Assassination in Canada," *The Intercept,* December 10, 2023, https://theintercept
.com/2023/12/10/india-sikhs-leaked-memo-us-canada/.

68. Sehar Iqbal, "The Myth of Underdevelopment," *Phenomenal World,*
July 5, 2023, www.phenomenalworld.org/analysis/myth-of-underdevelop
ment/.

69. James Baldwin, *The Fire Next Time* ([1962] New York: Vintage, 1993),
p. 89.

70. On the false-certainty driven security dilemma, see Alastair Iain
Johnston, "Identity, Race, and U.S.-China Conflict," Sir Howard Kippenberger
Lecture, Victoria University of Wellington, June 6, 2023, www.youtube.com
/watch?v=LnUT13zi2zg.

71. Jackson, *Pacific Power Paradox,* p. 162.

72. Dan Murtaugh, "China Mulls Solar Export Ban As Trade Tensions
Grow," *Australian Financial Review,* January 27, 2023, www.afr.com/policy

/energy-and-climate/china-mulls-solar-export-ban-as-trade-tensions-soar
-20230127-p5cfy8.

73. "China Adviser Warns Chipmaking Export Curbs Are 'Just a Start,' as Yellen Visit Looms," *Channel News Asia,* July 5, 2023, www.channelnewsasia .com/business/china-chipmaking-export-curbs-just-start-yellen-visit -3607016.

74. Seth Jones, *The U.S. Defense-Industrial Base Is Not Prepared for a Conflict with China* (Washington, D.C.: CSIS, 2022), https://features.csis.org /preparing-the-U.S.-industrial-base-to-deter-conflict-with-China/.

75. Barry Naughton, Siwen Xiao, and Yaosheng Xu, "The Trajectory of China's Industrial Policies," *UC IGCC Working Paper,* June 2, 2023, https:// ucigcc.org/publication/working-papers/the-trajectory-of-chinas-indus trial-policies/.

76. For a summary of PLA expansion that explores why it is overdeter-mined, see Timothy Heath, "Why Is China Strengthening Its Military? It's Not All About War," *Defense News,* March 24, 2023, www.rand.org/blog/2023 /03/why-is-china-strengthening-its-military-its-not-all.html.

77. Jackson, *Pacific Power Paradox,* pp. 139–140.

78. M. Taylor Fravel and Christopher Twomey, "Projecting Strategy: The Myth of Chinese Counter-Intervention," *Washington Quarterly* 37, no. 4 (2015), pp. 171–187.

79. Jeffrey Lewis, *The Minimum Means of Reprisal: China's Search for Se-curity in the Nuclear Age* (Cambridge, Mass.: MIT Press, 2007).

80. *Military and Security Developments Involving the People's Republic of China 2021* (Washington, D.C.: Office of the Secretary of Defense, 2021), p. viii.

81. Van Jackson, "Who's Afraid of China's Nukes?" *Duck of Minerva,* No-vember 22, 2021, www.duckofminerva.com/2021/11/whos-afraid-of-chinas -nukes.html.

82. Henrik Stålhane Hiim, M. Taylor Fravel, Magnus Langset Trøan, "The Dynamics of an Entangled Security Dilemma: China's Changing Nuclear Posture," *International Security* 47, no. 4 (2023), pp. 147–187.

83. *Annual Threat Assessment of the U.S. Intelligence Community* (Wash-ington, D.C.: Office of the Director of National Intelligence, 2023), pp. 7–8.

84. Joe McDonald, "Xi Accuses U.S. of Trying to Hold Back China's De-velopment," AP, March 9, 2023, https://apnews.com/article/china-us-relations -sabotage-development-taiwan-cb60a10bc988243af53c98f2c9e92104.

85. Ho-fung Hung, *Clash of Empires: From "Chimerica" to "New Cold War"* (New York: Cambridge University Press, 2022), p. 34.

86. Milanovic, "China's Inequality Will Lead It to a Stark Choice."

6
The Alternative to Great-Power Rivalry

Epigraph: Eric Hobsbawm, *On Empire: America, War, and Global Supremacy* (New York: Pantheon, 2008), p. 59.

1. Sidita Kushi and Monica Duffy Toft, "Introducing the Military Intervention Project: A New Dataset on U.S. Military Interventions, 1776–2019," *Journal of Conflict Resolution* 67, no. 4 (2023), p. 752.

2. See Stephen Wertheim, *Tomorrow, the World: The Birth of U.S. Global Supremacy* (Cambridge: Harvard University Press, 2020); Stephen Wertheim, "The Price of Primacy: Why America Shouldn't Dominate the World," *Foreign Affairs*, February 10, 2020, www.foreignaffairs.com/articles/afghanistan/2020-02-10/price-primacy.

3. Ackerman, *Reign of Terror*.

4. Daniel Nexon, "The Balance of Power in the Balance," *World Politics* 61, no. 2 (2009), p. 355.

5. G. Lowes Dickinson, *The International Anarchy, 1904–1914* ([1926] Honolulu: University Press of the Pacific, 2003), pp. 5–6.

6. Richard Little, "Deconstructing the Balance of Power: Two Schools of Thought," *Review of International Studies* 15, no. 2 (1989), pp. 87–100.

7. Monteiro, *Theory of Unipolar Politics*.

8. Van Jackson, "Trapped by Empire," *Dissent*, February 8, 2023, www.dissentmagazine.org/online_articles/trapped-by-empire/; Van Jackson, "The Blue Pacific Has a Sphere of Influence Problem," *Duck of Minerva*, November 10, 2023, www.duckofminerva.com/2023/11/the-blue-pacific-has-a-sphere-of-influence-problem.html.

9. For specific nuclear restraint proposals, see Van Jackson, "Time for U.S. Nuclear Strategy to Embrace No First Use," *East Asia Forum*, July 4, 2021, www.eastasiaforum.org/2021/07/04/time-for-us-nuclear-strategy-to-embrace-no-first-use/.

10. Ken Booth and Nicholas Wheeler, *The Security Dilemma: Fear, Cooperation, and Trust in World Politics* (Basingstoke: Palgrave, 2007), p. 7.

11. Alexander George and Richard Smoke, *Deterrence in American Foreign Policy: Theory and Practice* (New York: Columbia University Press, 1974), p. 5.

12. For more, see Slobodian, *Crack-Up Capitalism*.

13. Alexander George, Philip Farley, and Alexander Dallin, eds., *U.S.-Soviet Security Cooperation: Achievements, Failures, Lessons* (New York: Oxford University Press, 1988).

14. *Renewable Energy Market Update: Outlook for 2023 and 2024* (Paris:

International Energy Agency, 2023), p. 10, https://iea.blob.core.windows
.net/assets/63c14514-6833-4cd8-ac53-f9918c2e4cd9/RenewableEnergy
MarketUpdate_June2023.pdf.

15. David Waterworth, "Solar Is King 2023—50% Global Growth Predicted," *CleanTechnica*, August 11, 2023, https://cleantechnica.com/2023/08/11/solar-is-king-2023-50-global-growth-predicted/.

16. From 2022 to 2023, total car exports from China grew at 76.9 percent, while electric vehicle exports grew by 113 percent. Xiao Yisi, "China Overtakes Japan as World's Top Car Exporter in First Half," *Yicai Global*, August 9, 2023, www.yicaiglobal.com/news/china-overtakes-japan-as-worlds-top-car-exporter-in-first-half.

17. Aaron Glasserman, "Chinese Sanctions Enforcement Just Got Even Harder," *Foreign Policy*, August 15, 2023, https://foreignpolicy.com/2023/08/15/china-sanctions-enforcement-uyghur-xinjiang-forced-labor-trade-export-import/?utm_source=Sailthru&utm_medium=email&utm_campaign=Editors%20Picks%20-%2008152023&utm_term=editors_picks.

18. Charlie Campbell, "China's Aging Population Is a Concern. But Its Youth May Be An Even Bigger Problem," *Time*, June 6, 2023, https://time.com/6284994/china-youth-unemployment-aging-demographics/; Ho-fung Hung, "Zombie Economy," *New Left Review*, August 4, 2023, https://newleftreview.org/sidecar/posts/zombie-economy.

19. See, for example, James Kynge, "China Has Fallen into a Psycho-Political Funk," *Financial Times*, August 12, 2023, www.ft.com/content/c1670ac4-5eaf-453a-b5fe-497d0a5368fe?trk=feed_main-feed-card_feed-article-content; Campbell, "China's Aging Population Is a Concern. But Its Youth May Be An Even Bigger Problem."

20. See, for example, Jiaoyu Liu, Yixiu We, and Zichen Wang, "Zheng Yongnian on What China Needs to Do for a Domestic Demand-Driven Society," *Pekingnology*, January 8, 2023, www.pekingnology.com/p/zheng-yongnian-on-what-china-needs?

21. Glasserman, "Chinese Sanctions Enforcement Just Got Even Harder."

22. Dan Sabbagh, "'Colossal Waste': Nobel Laureates Call for 2% Cut to Military Spending Worldwide," *The Guardian*, December 14, 2021, www.theguardian.com/world/2021/dec/14/nobel-laureates-cut-military-spending-worldwide-un-peace-dividend.

23. Stephen Semler, "The New U.S. Military Budget Enriches Private Contractors at the Cost of Human Well-Being," *Jacobin*, December 3, 2022, https://jacobin.com/2022/12/fiscal-year-2023-biden-defense-budget-stimulus-checks.

24. Brands, *The Twilight Struggle*, p. 1.

Index